Brooklands Books

LOTUS ELAN
OWNERS WORKSHOP MANUAL

By the Autobooks Team
of Writers and Illustrators

Lotus *Elan 1600 1962-64*

Lotus *Elan Series 2 Convertible, Sports Convertible, Special Equipment 1964-66*

Lotus *Elan Series 3 FH Coupé, FH Coupé Special Equipment, DH Coupé, DH Coupé Special Equipment 1965-68*

Lotus *Elan Series 4 FH Coupé, FH Coupé Special Equipment, DH Coupé, DH Coupé Special Equipment, FH Coupé Sprint, DH Coupé Sprint 1968-73*

Lotus *Elan Plus 2 FH Coupé 1967-69*

Lotus *Elan Plus 2S FH Coupé, FH Coupé 130, FH Coupé 130/5 1969-74*

Brooklands Books

BROOKLANDS BOOKS LTD.
P.O. BOX 146, COBHAM,
SURREY, KT11 1LG. UK
sales@brooklands-books.com

D1279096

B-LT10WH

www.brooklands-books.com

Printed in China

The following Autobook Workshop Manuals are currently available from Brooklands Books Ltd.

Alfa Romeo Giulia-Spider 1962-1978   OWM 724
Citroen 19-20-21-23 1955-1975   OWM 742 and 954
Fiat X1/9 1974-1982   OWM 928
Land Rover Series 2 • 2A • 3 1959-1983   OWM 895
Lotus Elan 1962-1974   OWM 600
Morgan Four 1936-1981   OWM 796
MGA & MGB 1955-1968   OWM 955*
MGB 1968-1981   OWM 935*
Sprite & Midget 1958-1980 OWM 745*
Opel GT   OWM 727
Porsche 356 1957-1965   OWM 827
Reliant Scimitar 1968-1979   OWM 896
Toyota Celica 1600 1971-1977 OWM 804
Triumph Spitfire Mk.III, Mk.IV, 1500 1969-1980   OWM 711*
Triumph TR5 • 250 • TR6 1967-1975   OWM 826*
Volvo 1800 & 120 1960-1973   OWM 759 & 776
Volvo 164 1968-1975   OWM 782
VW Transporter 1954-1967   OWM 834

* Glovebox edition

ISBN 185520 0228

OWM 600

CONTENTS

Brooklands Books

MOTORING
B.B. ROAD TEST SERIES
Abarth Gold Portfolio 1950-1971
AC Ace & Aceca 1953-1983
Alfa Romeo Giulietta Gold Portfolio 1954-1965
Alfa Romeo Giulia Coupés 1963-1976
Alfa Romeo Giulia Coupés Gold Port. 1963-1976
Alfa Romeo Spider 1966-1990
Alfa Romeo Alfasud 1972-1984
Alfa Romeo Alfetta Gold Portfolio 1972-1987
Alfa Romeo Alfetta GTV6 1980-1986
Alvis Gold Portfolio 1919-1967
AMX & Javelin Muscle Portfolio 1968-1974
Armstrong Siddeley Gold Portfolio 1945-1960
Aston Martin Gold Portfolio 1948-1971
Aston Martin Gold Portfolio 1972-1985
Aston Martin Gold Portfolio 1985-1995
Audi Quattro Gold Portfolio 1980-1991
Audi Quattro Takes On The Competition
Austin-Healey 100 & 100/6 Gold Port. 1952-1959
Austin-Healey 3000 Ultimate Portfolio 1959-1967
Austin-Healey Sprite Gold Portfolio 1958-1971
Berkeley Sportscars Limited Edition
BMW 6 & 8 Cyl. Cars Limited Edition 1935-1960
BMW 1600 Collection No. 1 1966-1981
BMW 2002 Gold Portfolio 1968-1976
BMW 6 Cylinder Coupés & Saloons Gold P. 1969-1976
BMW 316, 318, 320 (4 cyl.) Gold Port. 1975-1990
BMW 320, 323, 325 (6 cyl.) Gold Port. 1977-1990
BMW 3 Series Gold Portfolio 1991-1997
BMW 5 Series Gold Portfolio 1981-1987
BMW 5 Series Gold Portfolio 1988-1995
BMW 6 Series Gold Portfolio 1976-1989
BMW 7 Series Performance Portfolio 1977-1986
BMW 7 Series Performance Portfolio 1986-1993
BMW 8 Series Limited Edition
BMW Alpina Performance Portfolio 1967-1987
BMW Alpina Performance Portfolio 1988-1998
BMW Z3 & Z3M Limited Edition
Borgward Isabella Limited Edition
Bricklin Gold Portfolio 1974-1975
Bristol Cars Portfolio
Buick Performance Portfolio 1947-1962
Buick Muscle Portfolio 1963-1973
Buick Riviera Performance Portfolio 1963-1978
Cadillac Automobiles 1949-1959
Cadillac Automobiles 1960-1969
Cadillac Eldorado Performance Portfolio 1967-1978
Checker Limited Edition
Chevrolet 1955-1957
Impala & SS Muscle Portfolio 1958-1972
Corvair Performance Portfolio 1959-1969
El Camino & SS Muscle Portfolio 1959-1987
Chevy II & Nova SS Muscle Portfolio 1962-1974
Chevelle & SS Muscle Portfolio 1964-1972
Caprice Limited Edition 1965-1976
Chevy Blazer 1969-1981
Camaro Muscle Portfolio 1967-1973
Camaro Performance Portfolio 1993-2000
Chevrolet Corvette Gold Portfolio 1953-1962
Chevrolet Corvette Sting Ray Gold Port. 1963-1967
Chevrolet Corvette Gold Portfolio 1968-1977
High Performance Corvettes 1983-1989
Chrysler 300 Gold Portfolio 1955-1970
Valiant 1960-1962
Citroen Traction Avant Gold Portfolio 1934-1957
Citroen 2CV Ultimate Portfolio 1948-1990
Citroen DS & ID 1955-1975
Citroen DS & ID Gold Portfolio 1955-1975
Citroen SM Limited Edition Extra 1970-1975
Shelby Cobra Gold Portfolio 1962-1969
Cobras & Cobra Replicas Gold Portfolio 1962-1989
Crosley & Crosley Specials Limited Edition
Cunningham Automobiles 1951-1955
Datsun Roadsters Performance Portfolio 1960-71
Datsun 240Z & 260Z Gold Portfolio 1970-1978
Datsun 280Z & ZX 1975-1983
DeLorean Gold Portfolio 1977-1995
De Soto Limited Edition 1952-1960
Dodge Limited Edition 1949-1959
Dodge Dart Limited Edition Extra 1960-1976
Dodge Muscle Portfolio 1965-1971
Charger Muscle Portfolio 1966-1974
Dodge Viper Performance Portfolio 1990-1998
ERA Gold Portfolio 1934-1994
Facel Vega Limited Edition Extra 1954-1964
Ferrari Limited Edition 1947-1957
Ferrari Limited Edition 1958-1963
Ferrari Dino Limited Edition Extra 1965-1974
Ferrari Dino 308 & Mondial Gold Portfolio 1974-1985
Ferrari 328 348 Mondial Ultimate Portfolio 1986-94
Fiat 600 & 850 Gold Portfolio 1955-1972
Fiat Dino Limited Edition
Fiat Pininfarina 124 & 2000 Spider 1968-1985
Fiat X1/9 Gold Portfolio 1973-1989
Fiat Abarth Performance Portfolio 1972-1987
Ford Consul, Zephyr, Zodiac Mk. I & II 1950-1962
Ford Zephyr, Zodiac, Executive Mk. III & IV 1962-1971
Ford Cortina 1600E & GT 1967-1970
High Performance Capris Gold Portfolio 1969-1987
Capri Muscle Portfolio 1974-1987
High Performance Fiestas 1979-1991
Ford Escort RS & Mexico Limited Edition 1970-1979
High Performance Escorts Mk. I 1968-1974
High Performance Escorts Mk. II 1975-1980
High Performance Escorts 1980-1985
High Performance Escorts 1985-1990
High Perf. Sierras & Merkurs Gold Port. 1983-1990
Ford Thunderbird Performance Portfolio 1955-1957
Ford Thunderbird Performance Portfolio 1958-1963
Ford Thunderbird Performance Portfolio 1964-1976
Ford Automobiles 1949-1959
Ford Fairlane Performance Portfolio 1955-1970
Ford Ranchero Muscle Portfolio 1957-1979
Edsel Limited Edition 1957-1960
Ford Galaxie & LTD Gold Portfolio 1960-1976
Falcon Performance Portfolio 1960-1970
Ford GT40 Gold Portfolio 1964-1987
Ford Bronco 4x4 Performance Portfolio 1966-1977
Ford Bronco 1978-1988
Goggomobil Limited Edition
Holden 1948-1962
Honda S500 • S600 • S800 Limited Edition 1962-1970
Honda CRX 1983-1987
International Scout Gold Portfolio 1961-1980
Isetta Gold Portfolio 1953-1964
ISO & Bizzarrini Gold Portfolio 1962-1974
Jaguar and SS Gold Portfolio 1931-1951
Jaguar C-Type & D-Type Gold Portfolio 1951-1960
Jaguar XK120, 140, 150 Gold Portfolio 1948-1960
Jaguar Mk. VII, VIII, IX, X, 420 Gold Port. 1950-1970
Jaguar Mk. 1 & Mk. 2 Gold Portfolio 1955-1969
Jaguar E-Type Gold Portfolio 1961-1971
Jaguar E-Type V-12 1971-1975
Jaguar S-Type & 420 Limited Edition 1963-1968
Jaguar XJ12, XJ5.3, V12 Gold Portfolio 1972-1990
Jaguar XJ6 Series I & II Gold Portfolio 1968-1979
Jaguar XJ6 Series III Perf. Portfolio 1979-1986
Jaguar XJ6 Gold Portfolio 1986-1994
Jaguar XJS Gold Portfolio 1975-1988
Jaguar XJ-S V12 Ultimate Portfolio 1988-1996
Jaguar XK8 Limited Edition
Jeep CJ-5 & CJ-6 1960-1976
Jeep CJ-5 & CJ-7 4x4 Perf. Portfolio 1976-1986
Jeep Wagoneer Performance Portfolio 1963-1991
Jeep J-Series Pickups 1970-1982
Jeepster & Commando Limited Edition 1967-1973
Jeep Cherokee & Comanche Pickups P. P. 1984-91
Jeep Wrangler 4x4 Performance Portfolio 1987-99
Jeep Cherokee & Grand Cherokee 4x4 P. P. 1992-98
Jensen - Healey Limited Edition 1972-1976
Kaiser - Frazer Limited Edition 1946-1955
Lagonda Gold Portfolio 1919-1964
Lancia Aurelia & Flaminia Gold Portfolio 1950-1970
Lancia Fulvia Gold Portfolio 1963-1976
Lancia Beta Gold Portfolio 1972-1984
Lancia Stratos 1972-1985
Lancia Delta & integrale Ultimate Portfolio
Land Rover Series I 1948-1958
Land Rover Series II & IIa 1958-1971
Land Rover Series III 4x4 Perf. Portfolio 1971-1985
Land Rover 90 110 Defender Gold Portfolio 1983-1994
Land Rover Discovery Perf. Port. 1989-2000
Land Rover Story Part One 1948-1971
Fifty Years of Selling Land Rover
Lincoln Gold Portfolio 1949-1960
Lincoln Continental Performance Portfolio 1961-1969
Lincoln Continental 1969-1976
Lotus Sports Racers Portfolio - covering 1951-1965
Lotus Seven Gold Portfolio 1957-1973
Lotus Elite Limited Edition 1957-1964
Lotus Elan Ultimate Portfolio 1962-1974
Lotus Elan & SE 1989-1992
Lotus Europa Gold Portfolio 1966-1975
Lotus Elite & Eclat 1974-1982
Lotus Elise Limited Edition
Marcos Coupés & Spyders Gold Portfolio 1960-1997
Maserati Cars Performance Portfolio 1957-1970
Maserati Cars Performance Portfolio 1971-1982
Maserati Cars Performance Portfolio 1982-1998
Matra Limited Edition 1965-1983
Mazda Miata MX-5 Performance Portfolio 1989-1997
Mazda Miata MX-5 Takes On The Competition
Mazda RX-7 Gold Portfolio 1978-1991
Mercedes 190 & 300 SL 1954-1963
Mercedes G-Wagen 1981-1994
Mercedes S & 600 1965-1972
Mercedes S Class 1972-1979
Mercedes S Class Limited Edition Extra 1980-1991
Mercedes 230 • 250 • 280SL Gold Portfolio 1963-1971
Mercedes SLs & SLCs Gold Portfolio 1971-1989
Mercedes SLs Performance Portfolio 1989-1994
Mercedes 190 Limited Edition Extra 1983-1993
Mercedes CLK & SLK Limited Edition
Mercury Comet & Cyclone Limited Edition 1960-1970
Cougar Muscle Portfolio 1967-1973
Messerschmitt Gold Portfolio 1954-1964
MG Gold Portfolio 1929-1939
MG TA & TC Gold Portfolio 1936-1949
MG TD & TF Gold Portfolio 1949-1955
MGA & Twin Cam Gold Portfolio 1955-1962
MG Midget Gold Portfolio 1961-1979
MGB Roadsters 1962-1980
MGB MGC & V8 Gold Portfolio 1962-1980
MGB GT 1965-1980
MGC & MGB GT V8 Limited Edition
MG Y-Type & Magnette ZA/ZB Limited Edition
MGF Limited Edition
Mini Gold Portfolio 1959-1969
Mini Gold Portfolio 1969-1980
Mini Gold Portfolio 1981-1997
High Performance Minis Gold Portfolio 1960-1973
Mini Cooper Gold Portfolio 1961-1971
Mini Moke Gold Portfolio 1964-1994
Morgan Three-Wheeler Gold Portfolio 1910-1952
Morgan Plus 4 & Four 4 Gold Portfolio 1936-1967
Morgan Cars Portfolio 1968-2001
Morris Minor Collection No. 1 1948-1980
Shelby Mustang Muscle Portfolio 1965-1970
Mustang Muscle Portfolio 1967-1973
High Performance Mustang IIs 1974-1978
Mustang 5.0L Muscle Portfolio 1982-1993
Mustang 5.0L Takes On The Competition
Nash & Nash-Healey Limited Edition 1949-1957
Nash-Austin Metropolitan Gold Portfolio 1954-1962
NSU Ro80 Limited Edition
NSX Performance Portfolio 1989-1999
Oldsmobile Automobiles 1955-1963
Oldsmobile Muscle Portfolio 1964-1971
Cutlass & 4-4-2 Muscle Portfolio 1964-1974
Oldsmobile Toronado 1966-1978
Opel GT Gold Portfolio 1968-1973
Opel Manta Limited Edition 1970-1975
Packard Gold Portfolio 1946-1958
Pantera Ultimate Portfolio 1970-1995
Panther Gold Portfolio 1972-1990
Plymouth Limited Edition 1950-1960
Plymouth Fury Limited Edition Extra 1956-1976
Barracuda Muscle Portfolio 1964-1974
Plymouth Muscle Portfolio 1965-1971
Pontiac Limited Edition 1949-1960
Pontiac Tempest & GTO 1961-1965
GTO Muscle Portfolio 1964-1974
Firebird & Trans-Am Muscle Portfolio 1967-1972
Firebird & Trans-Am Muscle Portfolio 1973-1981
High Performance Firebirds 1982-1988
Firebird & Trans Am Performance Portfolio 1993-2000
Pontiac Fiero Performance Portfolio 1984-1988
Porsche 356 Gold Portfolio 1953-1965
Porsche 912 Limited Edition
Porsche 911 1965-1969
Porsche 911 1970-1972
Porsche 911 1973-1977
Porsche 911 SC & Turbo Gold Portfolio 1978-1983
Porsche 911 Carrera & Turbo Gold Port. 1984-1989
Porsche 911 Gold Portfolio 1990-1997
Porsche 911 Takes On The Competition 1990-1997
Porsche 914 Ultimate Portfolio
Porsche 924 Gold Portfolio 1975-1988
Porsche 928 Performance Portfolio 1977-1994
Porsche 928 Takes On The Competition
Porsche 944 Ultimate Portfolio
Porsche 968 Limited Edition Extra
Railton & Brough Superior Gold Portfolio 1933-1950
Range Rover Gold Portfolio 1970-1985
Range Rover Gold Portfolio 1985-1995
Range Rover Takes on the Competition
Renault Alpine Gold Portfolio 1958-1994
Riley Gold Portfolio 1924-1939
Rolls Royce Silver Shadow Ultimate Portfolio 1965-80
Rolls Royce & Bentley Gold Portfolio 1980-1989
Rover P4 1949-1959
Rover 2000 & 2200 1963-1977
Studebaker Gold Portfolio 1947-1966
Studebaker Hawks & Larks 1956-1963
Avanti Limited Edition Extra 1962-1991
Starion & Conquest Performance Portfolio 1982-90
Subaru Impreza Turbo Limited Edition Extra 1994-2001
Suzuki SJ Gold Portfolio 1971-1997
Vitara, Sidekick & Geo Tracker Perf. Port. 1988-1997
Sunbeam Tiger & Alpine Gold Portfolio 1959-1967
Toyota Land Cruiser Gold Portfolio 1956-1987
Toyota Land Cruiser 1988-1997
Toyota MR2 Gold Portfolio 1984-1997
Toyota MR2 Takes On The Competition
Triumph TR2 & TR3 Gold Portfolio 1952-1961
Triumph TR4, TR5, TR250 1961-1968
Triumph TR6 Gold Portfolio 1969-1976
Triumph Herald 1959-1971
Triumph Vitesse 1962-1971
Triumph Spitfire Gold Portfolio 1962-1980
Triumph 2000, 2.5, 2500 1963-1977
Triumph GT6 Gold Portfolio 1966-1974
Triumph Stag Gold Portfolio 1970-1977
Triumph Dolomite Sprint Limited Edition
TVR Gold Portfolio 1959-1986
TVR Performance Portfolio 1986-1994
TVR Performance Portfolio 1995-2000
VW Beetle Gold Portfolio 1935-1967
VW Beetle Gold Portfolio 1968-1991
VW Karmann Ghia 1955-1982
VW Bus, Camper, Van Perf. Portfolio 1954-1967
VW Bus, Camper, Van Perf. Portfolio 1968-1979
VW Bus, Camper, Van Perf. Portfolio 1979-1989
VW Scirocco 1974-1981
Volvo PV444 & PV544 Perf. Portfolio 1945-1965
Volvo 120 Amazon Ultimate Portfolio
Volvo 1800 Gold Portfolio 1960-1973
Volvo 140 & 160 Series Gold Portfolio 1966-1975
Forty Years of Selling Volvo

B.B. ROAD & TRACK SERIES
Road & Track on Aston Martin 1962-1990
Road & Track on Audi & Auto Union 1952-1980
Road & Track on Audi & Auto Union 1980-1986
Road & Track on Austin Healey 1953-1970
Road & Track on BMW Cars 1966-1974
Road & Track on BMW Cars 1975-1978
Road & Track on BMW Cars 1979-1983
R & T Camaro & Firebird Portfolio 1993-2002
R & T on Cobra, Shelby & Ford GT40 1962-1992
Road & Track on Corvette 1953-1967
Road & Track on Corvette 1968-1982
Road & Track on Corvette 1982-1986
Road & Track on Corvette 1986-1990
Road & Track Corvette Portfolio 1997-2002
Road & Track Dodge Viper Portfolio 1992-2002
Road & Track on Ferrari 1975-1981
Road & Track on Ferrari 1981-1984
Road & Track on Ferrari 1984-1988
Road & Track Ferrari F355 & 360 Portfolio 1995-02
Road & Track on Fiat Sports Cars 1968-1987
Road & Track on Jaguar 1950-1960
Road & Track on Jaguar 1961-1968
Road & Track on Jaguar 1968-1974
Road & Track on Jaguar 1974-1982
Road & Track on Jaguar 1983-1989
Road & Track on Lamborghini 1964-1985
Road & Track MX-5 Miata Portfolio 1989-2002
Road & Track on Mercedes 1952-1962
Road & Track on Mercedes 1963-1970
Road & Track on Mercedes 1971-1979
Road & Track on MG Sports Cars 1949-1961
Road & Track on MG Sports Cars 1962-1980
Road & Track Mustang Portfolio 1994-2002
R & T on Nissan 300-ZX & Turbo 1984-1989
Road & Track on Pontiac 1960-1983
Road & Track on Porsche 1951-1967
Road & Track on Porsche 1968-1971
Road & Track on Porsche 1972-1975
Road & Track on Porsche 1975-1978
Road & Track on Porsche 1979-1982
Road & Track on Porsche 1985-1988
Road & Track Porsche 928 Portfolio 1977-1994
Road & Track Porsche 911 Portfolio 1990-1997
R & T on Rolls Royce & Bentley 1950-1965
R & T on Rolls Royce & Bentley 1966-1984
Road & Track on Saab 1972-1992
R & T on Toyota Sports & GT Cars 1966-1984
R & T on Triumph Sports Cars 1967-1974
R & T on Triumph Sports Cars 1974-1982
Road & Track on Volkswagen 1951-1968
Road & Track on Volkswagen 1968-1978
Road & Track on Volkswagen 1978-1985
Road & Track on Volvo 1957-1974
Road & Track on Volvo 1977-1994
Road & Track - Henry Manney at Large & Abroad
Road & Track - Best of PS
Road & Track - Peter Egan "At Large"
Road & Track - Peter Egan Side Glances 1983-92
Road & Track - Peter Egan Side Glances 1992-97

B.B. CAR AND DRIVER SERIES
Car and Driver on BMW 1955-1977
Car and Driver on Corvette 1978-1982
Car and Driver on Corvette 1983-1988
C and D on Datsun Z 1600 & 2000 1966-1984
Car and Driver on Ferrari 1955-1962
Car and Driver on Ferrari 1963-1975
Car and Driver on Ferrari 1976-1983
Car and Driver on Mopar 1956-1967
Car and Driver on Mustang 1964-1973
Car and Driver on Pontiac 1961-1975
Car and Driver on Porsche 1955-1962
Car and Driver on Porsche 1963-1970
Car and Driver on Porsche 1970-1976
Car and Driver on Porsche 1977-1981
Car and Driver on Porsche 1982-1986

RACING & THE LAND SPEED RECORD
The Land Speed Record 1898-1919
The Land Speed Record 1920-1929
The Land Speed Record 1930-1939
The Land Speed Record 1940-1962
The Land Speed Record 1963-1999
The Land Speed Record 1898-1999 - Hard Bound
Can-Am Racing 1966-1969
Can-Am Racing 1970-1974
Can-Am Racing Cars 1966-1974
The Carrera Panamericana Mexico - 1950-1954
Le Mans - The Bentley & Alfa Years - 1923-1939
Le Mans - The Jaguar Years - 1949-1957
Le Mans - The Ferrari Years - 1958-1965
Le Mans - The Ford & Matra Years - 1966-1974
Le Mans - The Porsche Years - 1975-1982
Le Mans - The Porsche & Jaguar Years - 1983-91
Le Mans - The Porsche & Peugeot Years - 1992-99
Le Mans - 1923-1999 - Hard Bound
Mille Miglia - The Alfa & Ferrari Years - 1927-1951
Mille Miglia - The Ferrari & Mercedes Years - 1952-57
Targa Florio - The Post War Years - 1948-1973 - H.B.
Targa Florio - The Porsche & Ferrari Years - 1955-1964
Targa Florio - The Porsche Years - 1965-1973

B.B. PRACTICAL CLASSICS SERIES
PC on Land Rover Restoration
PC on Midget/Sprite Restoration
PC on MGB Restoration
PC on Sunbeam Rapier Restoration
PC on Triumph Herald/Vitesse

B.B. HOT ROD 'ENGINE' SERIES
Chevy 265 & 283
Chevy 302 & 327
Chevy 348 & 409
Chevy 396 & 427
Chevy 454 thru 512
Chrysler Hemi
Chrysler 273, 318, 340 & 360
Chrysler 361, 383, 400, 413, 426 & 440
Ford 289, 302, Boss 302 & 351W
Ford 351C & Boss 351

B.B. RESTORATION & GUIDE SERIES
BMW 2002 - A Comprehensive Guide
BMW '02 Restoration Guide
Classic Camaro Restoration
Chevrolet High Performance Tips & Techniques
Chevy-GMC Pickup Repair
Engine Swapping Tips & Techniques
Land Rover Restoration Portfolio
Combat Land Rover Portfolio No. 1
Lotus Elan Restoration Guide
MG 'T' Series Restoration Guide
MGA Restoration Guide
Mustang Restoration Tips & Techniques
Practical Gas Flow
Restoring Sprites & Midgets an Enthusiast's Guide
SU Carburetters Tuning Tips & Techniques
The Great Classic Muscle Cars Compared

MOTORCYCLING
B.B. ROAD TEST SERIES
AJS & Matchless Gold Portfolio 1945-1966
BMW Motorcycles Gold Portfolio 1950-1971
BMW Motorcycles Gold Portfolio 1971-1976
BMW K100 Series Performance Portfolio 1983-1993
BSA Singles Gold Portfolio 1945-1963
BSA Singles Gold Portfolio 1964-1974
BSA Twins A7 & A10 Gold Portfolio 1946-1962
BSA Twins A50 & A65 Gold Portfolio 1962-1973
BSA & Triumph Triples Gold Portfolio 1968-1976
Ducati Gold Portfolio 1974-1978
Ducati Gold Portfolio 1978-1982
Ducati 851 & 888 Performance Portfolio 1987-1994
Harley-Davidson Sportsters Perf. 1965-1976
Harley-Davidson Super Glide Perf. Port. 1971-1981
Harley-Davidson FXR Series Perf. Port. 1982-1992
Hesketh Limited Edition Extra 1980-1991
Honda CB750 Gold Portfolio 1969-1978
Honda CB500 & 550 Fours Perf. Port. 1971-1977
Honda CB350 & 400 Fours Perf. Port. 1972-1978
Honda Gold Wing Gold Portfolio 1975-1995
Honda CBX 1000 Gold Portfolio 1978-1982
Honda RC30 Performance Portfolio 1988-1992
Kawasaki Z1 900 Performance Portfolio 1972-1977
Kawasaki 500 & 750 Triples Perf. Port. 1969-1976
Kawasaki GPZ 900R Ninja Perf. Port. 1984-1996
Laverda Gold Portfolio 1967-1977
Laverda Performance Portfolio 1978-1988
Laverda Jota Performance Portfolio 1976-1985
Moto Guzzi Gold Portfolio 1949-1973
Moto Guzzi Le Mans Performance Portfolio 1976-89
Moto Morini 3½ & 500 Performance Port. 1974-84
Norton Dominators Performance Portfolio 1949-70
Norton Commando Ultimate Portfolio 1968-1977
Norton Rotaries Limited Edition Extra 1984-1992
Suzuki GT750 Performance Portfolio 1971-1977
Suzuki GS1000 Performance Portfolio 1978-1981
Suzuki GSX-R750 Performance Portfolio 1985-1996
Vincent Gold Portfolio 1945-1980
Yamaha RD350/400 Performance Portfolio 1972-79
Yamaha XS650 Performance Portfolio 1969-1985

B.B. CYCLE WORLD SERIES
Cycle World on BMW 1974-1980
Cycle World on BMW 1981-1986
Cycle World on Ducati 1982-1991
Cycle World on Honda 1962-1967
Cycle World on Honda 1968-1971
Cycle World on Honda 1971-1974
Cycle World on Husqvarna 1966-1976
Cycle World on Husqvarna 1977-1984
Cycle World on Kawasaki 1966-1971
Cycle World on Kawasaki Off-Road Bikes 1972-1979
Cycle World on Kawasaki Street Bikes 1972-1976
Cycle World on Suzuki 1962-1970
Cycle World on Suzuki Off-Road Bikes 1971-1976
Cycle World on Suzuki Street Bikes 1971-1976
Cycle World on Triumph 1967-1972
Cycle World on Yamaha 1962-1969
Cycle World on Yamaha Off-Road Bikes 1970-1974
Cycle World on Yamaha Street Bikes 1970-1974

MILITARY
VEHICLES & AEROPLANES
Complete WW2 Military Jeep Manual
Dodge WW2 Military Portfolio 1940-1945
German Military Equipment WW2
Hail To The Jeep
Land Rover Military Portfolio
Military & Civilian Amphibians 1940-1990
Off Road Jeeps Civilian & Military 1944-1971
Silhouette Handbook of US Army Air Forces Aeroplanes
US Military Vehicles 1941-1945
US Army Military Vehicles WW2-TM9-2800
VW Kubelwagen Military Portfolio 1940-1990
WW2 Allied Vehicles Military Portfolio 1939-1945
WW2 Jeep Military Portfolio 1941-1945

10/10Z2

LOTUS ELAN

Elan +2 introduced in 1967

Introduction :

The Lotus Elan was first shown to the public at the Earls Court Motor Show in 1962. The first cars became available in January 1963. Following on after the original Elite, the Elan was aimed at the kit car market. At that time a number of companies offered kits that could be assembled at home. A lot of the cars either made excessive demands on the home builder or, when built, offered rather spartan and unexciting cars. The Elan was one car that changed that image in the most effective way possible.

Largely assembled at the factory, most buyers found the work to be done at home was well within their scope. Aided by a good set of instructions and a well produced kit, they were soon producing a very sound motor car.

The amount of thought involved at the design stage, under the direct guidance of Lotus Chief, Colin Chapman, was reflected in the end product. Much work was done to help reduce weight and, of course, Lotus success on the race track influenced the design and construction of the car.

The result of all this was the birth of an outstanding sports car. In the Elan, Lotus had combined a lightweight attractive car with new standards of performance and roadholding.

The basic method of construction was common throughout the series. The glass fibre body covered a strong steel backbone chassis. Front and rear Y-shaped extensions carried the suspension mountings and the engine was attached directly onto the chassis. A substantial rear crossmember carried the final drive and unsprung weight was reduced by the fitting of inboard rear disc brakes.

At the beginning a $1498cm^3$ engine was supplied, but this was quickly superseded by a $1558cm^3$ unit. All early cars were then recalled to the factory and the later engine fitted. Although more powerful engines appeared from time to time this twin cam four-cylinder engine was the basic power plant throughout the life of the car.

Based on a Ford 1500 unit, the engine was extensively re-worked by Lotus engineers and, after replacing the pushrod and rocker-type cylinder head with twin overhead camshafts, the engine bore little resemblance to the original. Bore and stroke were altered to allow for higher revs and different carburation was introduced. The $1558cm^3$ engine then produced 105bph.

Elan Special Equipment coupé

Front suspension employed conventional unequal length wishbones and combined damper spring units. Body roll was controlled by a single trailing anti-roll bar at the front. The precise steering was achieved by using rack and pinion steering gear. The cars weight distribution that put 53% of the weight over the rear wheels greatly contributed to the accurate and light steering.

For the first time MacPherson-type struts were used on the rear suspension. These were combined with coil springs and wide based A brackets. Inboard rear disc brakes kept unsprung weight to the minimum and provided very positive stopping power. Stops of 195 feet from 70mph (0.85g) were recorded. Here again the weight distribution was a major factor in allowing each wheel to do its fair share of the work.

The rear wheels were driven by substantial shafts with Rotoflex couplings at each end. These couplings cushioned the drive line and prevented undue strain on the various components. People unused to their 'winding up' would often find difficulty in achieving smooth take offs until they became familiar with the car.

The clean lined body incorporated fully retractable headlights and frameless side windows. The hand-laid glass fibre gave a good finish and has proved very durable. Naturally, rust is not a problem on the Elans bodywork. In this respect the steel chassis has also proved to be exceptionally resistant to corrosion.

The Series 2 Elan was introduced in November 1964. Among the extra refinements included were a full width veneer dashboard and larger diameter front disc brakes. Small pedals made driving easier and a quick release petrol cap with optional centre-lock wheels enhanced the sporty image of the car.

For the first time a hard top version was made available in November 1965 in the form of the Series 3 fixed-head coupé. Apart from the hard top the styling was the same as the convertibles with just a few detail changes. The boot lid was extended to the rear of the car and the battery repositioned in the boot. A luxury touch was added with the provision of electrically operated side windows as standard. A final drive of 3.5 : 1 was offered as an optional extra and countered any criticisms of the standard 3.77 : 1 car being under-geared. The convertible continued in Series 2 form, but in January 1966 a Special Equipment version was announced.

A number of desirable features were standard on this model. Power output was increased to 115bhp and a close ratio gearbox fitted. To cope with the increased power servo-assisted brakes were fitted, and equipment included centre-lock wheels and side repeater flashers. In June 1966 the convertible was brought up to Series 3 specifications and framed side windows fitted.

In June 1967 the Elan took a further step up market with the introduction of the Elan +2. Although basically similar to the Elan, the +2 offered a larger body with two occasional seats behind the driver. This 2+2 configuration widened the appeal of the original Elan and gave the family man a chance to enjoy the delights of

Series 4 Elan convertible

High performance Elan Sprint

driving a real sports car. In keeping with the image, the Elan +2 sported throughflow ventilation and a much improved interior. Servo-assisted brakes were standard and engine output increased to 118bhp. Whilst retaining many of the virtues of the Elan the new model offered more in the way of comfort equipment and space.

March 1968 saw the arrival of the Series 4 convertible and coupé. Flared wheel arches were fitted to accommodate the new low profile tyres. +2 rear light units replaced the Elan type and the new facia incorporated rocker switches. Seat trim was improved and a bulge on the bonnet made identification easy.

A de luxe version of the +2 was introduced in October 1968 and was designated the Elan +2S. This was the first Elan not to be available in kit form and perhaps provided a pointer to later development of the company. The interior was lavishly equipped with much more comfort and more comprehensive instrumentation. Fog lights were standard.

About this time most models in the range were supplied with Stromberg carburetters in place of the Webers usually fitted. Later in 1969, however, all models reverted to Webers.

The Elan Series 4 and Elan +2S continued in production for a few years. The next major change came in February 1971 when the 'Sprint' version of the Elan S4 was introduced. Like the SE version before it, the 'Sprint' came with many improvements as standard. The most obvious difference was the engine. Although still based on the original unit the new engine had larger inlet valves, revised porting and different camshaft characteristics. With Weber carburetters the engine produced a healthy 126bhp. To match this extra power the differential and drive shafts were strengthened. The flexible couplings were also improved to reduce 'surge'. Trim and equipment were to the old SE specification and two-tone paintwork, often in Lotus racing colours, gave the car a distinctive look.

Also in 1971 the Elan +2 was given the new big-valve engine and became known as the Elan +2S/130. To identify this change all cars were supplied with a silver coloured roof. In October 1972 a 5-speed gearbox was made available as an extra on the Elan +2S/130 which became known as the Elan +2S/130/5. The Elan ceased production in 1973 and the Elan +2 in 1974.

Throughout it's lifespan the Elan was known all over the world as one of the best small sports cars produced. Whilst it required the regular attention that every thoroughbred demands, its tremendous performance and outstanding handling characteristics gave it an edge over most of its competitors. The motoring press then hailed it as 'the ideal sports car' and even as 'the ultimate sports car'. No mean achievement for a car that had its origins firmly rooted in the kit car market. Even now, long after it's demise, the Elan still provokes praise from all quarters.

The strong and reliable engine contributed a lot to the car's appeal. The glass fibre body and steel chassis combined to give the ideal compromise between the need for adequate strength and the desire to reduce overall weight. This type of construction also had the advantage of concentrating the weight close to the road to give a a low centre of gravity. All this with the ideal weight distribution and tuned suspension gave the car its legendary roadholding.

In all the Elan was a car that introduced many people to the world of the sophisticated sports car. Using the latest technology gleaned from the race track it was available to the public at a reasonable price. The Elan can justifiably claim to be one of the modern classics.

The last Elan, a Series 4 coupé

The Autobook, having been written and published in England, is produced using all English phrases, terms, spellings and component descriptions. Some of these do, of course, differ from those in general use in America and, therefore, in order to simplify the identification of components, the following glossary is provided.

Glossary

English	American	English	American
Aerial	Antenna	Layshaft (of gearbox)	Countershaft
Accelerator	Gas pedal	Leading shoe (of brake)	Primary shoe
Alternator	Generator (AC)	Locks	Latches
Anti-roll bar	Stabiliser or sway bar	Motorway	Freeway, turnpike, etc
Battery	Energizer	Number plate	License plate
Bodywork	Sheet metal	Paraffin	Kerosene
Bonnet (engine cover)	Hood	Petrol	Gasoline
Boot lid	Trunk lid	Petrol tank	Gas tank
Boot (luggage compartment)	Trunk	'Pinking'	'Pinging'
Bottom gear	1st gear	Propeller shaft	Driveshaft
Bulkhead	Firewall	Quarter light	Quarter window
Cam follower or tappet	Valve lifter or tappet	Retread	Recap
Carburetter	Carburetor	Reverse	Back-up
Catch	Latch	Rocker cover	Valve cover
Choke/venturi	Barrel	Roof rack	Car-top carrier
Circlip	Snap-ring	Saloon	Sedan
Clearance	Lash	Seized	Frozen
Crownwheel	Ring gear (of differential)	Side indicator lights	Side marker lights
Disc (brake)	Rotor/disk	Side light	Parking light
Drop arm	Pitman arm	Silencer	Muffler
Drop head coupe	Convertible	Spanner	Wrench
Dynamo	Generator (DC)	Sill panel (beneath doors)	Rocker panel
Earth (electrical)	Ground	Split cotter (for valve spring cap)	Lock (for valve spring retainer)
Engineer's blue	Prussian blue	Split pin	Cotter pin
Estate car	Station wagon	Steering arm	Spindle arm
Exhaust manifold	Header	Sump	Oil pan
Fast back (Coupe)	Hard top	Tab washer	Tang; lock
Fault finding/diagnosis	Trouble shooting	Tailgate	Liftgate
Float chamber	Float bowl	Tappet	Valve lifter
Free-play	Lash	Thrust bearing	Throw-out bearing
Freewheel	Coast	Top gear	High
Gudgeon pin	Piston pin or wrist pin	Trackrod (of steering)	Tie-rod (or connecting rod)
Gearchange	Shift	Trailing shoe (of brake)	Secondary shoe
Gearbox	Transmission	Transmission	Whole drive line
Halfshaft	Axleshaft	Tyre	Tire
Handbrake	Parking brake	Van	Panel wagon/van
Hood	Soft top	Vice	Vise
Hot spot	Heat riser	Wheel nut	Lug nut
Indicator	Turn signal	Windscreen	Windshield
Interior light	Dome lamp	Wing/mudguard	Fender

CHAPTER 1

THE ENGINE

1 : 1 Description

Each of the models covered by this manual is fitted with an engine of 1558cc capacity. The bore is 82.550mm and the stroke 72.746mm. Refer to the **Technical Data** section of the **Appendix** for further dimensional and other details.

A partial cut-away view of the engine is shown in **FIG 1 : 1**. It is a four-cylinder in-line four-stroke type and is provided with twin overhead camshafts which are chain driven from a sprocket at the forward end of the crankshaft. The single roller-type chain is spring tensioned by an adjustable sprocket arrangement. One camshaft operates the inlet valves and the other the exhaust valves. The valves are inclined at an angle of 27° to the vertical and are operated via piston-type cam followers (tappets). Each valve is fitted with two concentric valve springs. Valve seat inserts and valve guides are renewable. Inlet and exhaust valve heads are of differing diameters and their stems are of differing lengths. Axial location of the camshafts is controlled at the forward end of each shaft.

A jackshaft, which is situated in the righthand side of the engine, is driven at camshaft speed (half crankshaft speed) by the camshaft drive chain. A skew gear which

is integral with the jackshaft drives the distributor and the externally mounted oil pump. An eccentric on the jackshaft operates the lever and diaphragm-type fuel pump. The distributor, oil pump and fuel pump are all mounted on the righthand side of the engine.

The counterbalanced crankshaft which is of cast iron construction is dynamically balanced during manufacture. It runs in five steel-backed lead/bronze lined shell bearings. End float is controlled by split thrust washers at the centre bearing. The H-section forged steel connecting rods have steel-backed bronze small-end bushes and steel-backed copper/lead shell big-end bearings. The big-end bearing caps are doweled and retained by two bolts. The solid skirt aluminium alloy pistons are fitted with two compression and one oil control rings. The gudgeon pins are a finger push-fit in the pistons and are retained by circlips.

The cylinder block is of cast iron. The cylinder head is of aluminium with fully machined hemispherical combustion chambers. The clutch is mounted on and operates directly against the rear face of the cast iron flywheel which is provided with a renewable ring gear for starter motor pinion engagement.

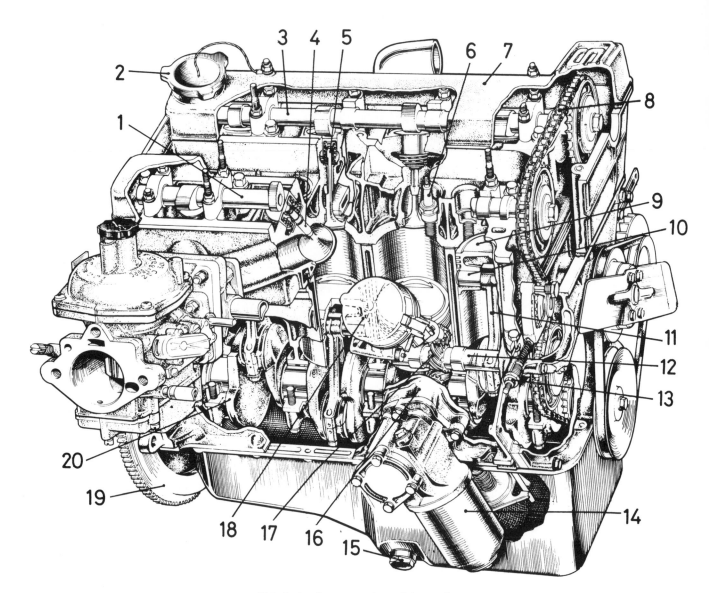

FIG 1 : 1   Cut-away view of the engine

Key to Fig 1 : 1   1 Camshaft (inlet)   2 Oil filler cap   3 Camshaft (exhaust)   4 Inlet valve   5 Exhaust valve
6 Sparking plug   7 Camshaft cover   8 Camshaft drive chain   9 Piston (No 1 cylinder)   10 Gudgeon pin   11 Connecting
rod   12 Jackshaft   13 Camshaft drive chain tensioner   14 Oil filter   15 Sump drain plug   16 Oil pump   17 Jackshaft
skew gear (distributor and oil pump drive)   18 Distributor   19 Flywheel   20 Crankshaft

Lubrication is force fed. The oil pump is an eccentric dual rotor type. It incorporates a non-adjustable plunger-type relief valve and draws oil from the sump via a gauze strainer. To prevent aeration, relief oil is returned to the bottom of the sump. Pressure oil passes to the engine via a fullflow filter which is integral with the oil pump. Pressure oil is fed to the big-end bearings via the crankshaft main journals. Lubrication of the small-end bushes, the gudgeon pins and the non-thrust side of the cylinder bores is by oil mist and forced feed oil jets from drillings in the connecting rod webs. The jackshaft bearings are fed from the main bearings and a metered jet of oil lubricates the camshaft drive chain and sprockets. Camshaft lubrication is controlled by a flat machined on the jackshaft front journal. Spilled oil from the camshaft bearings drains back to the sump.

Depending upon the model, the engine may be fitted with Weber, Zenith-Stromberg or Dellorto carburetters. Where relevant, the carburetters incorporate emission control features. Ignition timing varies with the model and type of carburetters fitted.

A coolant pump is incorporated in the engine front cover. This, and on earlier models, the cooling fan are belt driven from a pulley on the forward end of the crankshaft. The cooling fan on later models is electrically operated.

1 : 2 *Servicing*

Oil level :

Maintain the oil level in the sump between the FILL and the FULL marks on the dipstick. Preferably use the same grade and brand of oil as that already in use.

Oil changes:

At the mileage intervals stated in **Chapter 13**, drain the sump and refill with new oil. The drain plug is shown at 15 in **FIG 1 : 1** and the' draining should preferably be carried out after a run when the oil is warm. Use an SAE 20W/50 oil of reputable brand or, if the ambient temperature is consistently below 0°C (32°F), use an SAE 10W/40 oil.

The use of a flushing oil after draining is not recommended.

Oil filter:

The filter renewal procedure is described in **Section 1 : 3**. Renew the filter at the mileage intervals stated in **Chapter 13**.

Camshaft drive chain tension:

Adjust the chain tension at the mileage intervals stated in **Chapter 13**. The procedure is described in **Section 1 : 5**.

Valve clearances and cylinder head bolts:

At the mileage intervals stated in **Chapter 13**, check and, if necessary, adjust the valve clearances as described in **Section 1 : 4**. While the camshaft cover is removed, torque tighten the cylinder head bolts as described in **Section 1 : 7**.

1 : 3 The oil filter and pump

Oil filter renewal (before engine No G23607):

Refer to **FIG 1 : 2**. Remove the retaining bolt and aluminium washer. Discard the washer. Dismount the filter bowl and element downwards, discard the element and clean the bowl thoroughly. Locate a new sealing ring in the groove and fit the new element and the bowl to the pump. Fit a new aluminium washer to the retaining bolt and torque tighten it to 1.63 to 2.03daNm (12 to 15lbf ft).

Oil filter renewal (from engine No G23607):

From engine No G23607 a disposable canister-type filter is fitted to a modified pump. The canister-type filter cannot be fitted to earlier engines. If necessary, use a strap wrench to remove the old canister. Clean the mating surfaces and apply a film of oil to the sealing ring. Screw on the new canister and, after it seats, tighten by about a further three-quarters of a turn. Run the engine and check for leakage. If necessary, tighten further but do not overtighten.

Pump removal:

Refer to **FIG 1 : 2**. Remove the three retaining bolts and withdraw the pump and filter as an assembly. Discard the joint washer.

Dismantling the pump:

Depending upon the engine No, remove the filter bowl and element or unscrew the disposable canister filter. Extract the sealing ring. Remove four bolts and separate the end plate from the pump body. Remove the 'O' ring. Refer to **FIGS 1 : 3** and **1 : 4**. The clearance between the lobes of the inner and outer rotors should not exceed 0.15mm (0.006in). The inner and outer rotor end float should not exceed 0.13mm (0.005in) and the outer rotor to housing clearance should not exceed 0.25mm (0.010in). The rotor to face clearance as shown in **FIG 1 : 4** may, if necessary, be corrected by careful lapping of the housing face. New rotors are supplied only in matched sets. If it is necessary to renew the rotors or the drive shaft, remove the outer rotor, drive out the retaining pin and pull off the skew gear. The inner rotor and drive shaft may now be withdrawn.

Reassembling and refitting the pump:

Fit the inner rotor and drive shaft assembly to the pump housing, press the skew gear onto the shaft and, with the shaft supported at the rotor end on a suitable spacer, fit a new retaining pin. Peen the pin ends to lock. Assemble with the internal parts and surfaces wetted with clean engine oil. Fit the outer rotor with its chamfered face inwards. Fit the 'O' ring to the body. Fit the end plate and tighten the four retaining bolts. Install a new filter element or canister as described earlier. Mount the pump and filter assembly on the engine with a new gasket and torque tighten the three retaining bolts to 1.63 to 2.03daNm (12 to 15lbf ft).

1 : 4 Valve clearance adjustment

As routine servicing, the valve clearances should be checked at the mileage intervals stated in **Chapter 13** and also whenever the camshafts have been disturbed or the cylinder head bolts have been check tightened. The measurement and adjustment procedures are as follows:

1 Remove the camshaft cover. Torque tighten the cylinder head bolts. Turn the crankshaft until the cam lobe is vertically away from the valve being measured as shown in **FIG 1 : 5**.
2 Using feeler gauges, measure and carefully note the clearance between the cam and the cam follower. Turn the crankshaft to bring each valve in turn to the measurement position. Measure and carefully note all the valve clearances.
3 The desired **cold inlet** clearance for all engines is 0.127 to 0.177mm (0.005 to 0.007in). The desired **cold exhaust** clearance for engines up to No 9951 is 0.152 to 0.203mm (0.006 to 0.008in) and for engine No 9952 and onwards is 0.228 to 0.279mm (0.009 to 0.011in).
4 To adjust incorrect clearances, remove the camshaft(s) as described in **Section 1 : 6**. Identify and remove the relevant cam follower(s). Remove, identify and carefully measure the thickness of each relevant adjusting shim and substitute a shim (**one only to each valve**) of revised thickness to achieve the correct clearance.

A thinner shim will increase the clearance; a thicker shim will reduce the clearance. The thickness of the new shim will be the thickness of the original shim plus the measured valve clearance less the desired clearance. Measure the thickness of each shim accurately with a micrometer even though a thickness is marked round its periphery or on its underside. Using

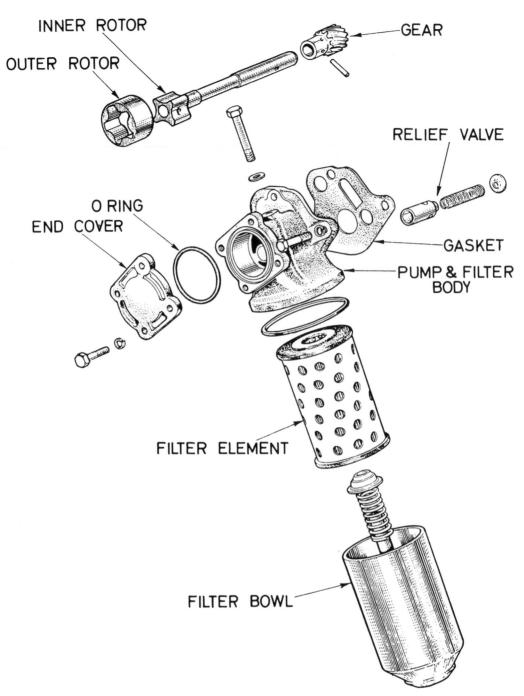

FIG 1 : 2   Components of the oil pump and filter

fine emery cloth, remove any roughness caused by the etching of the marks on the surface before fitting a shim.

When all clearances have been corrected, fit the cam followers to their identified positions, refit the camshaft as described in **Section 1 : 6** and recheck the clearances. Readjust if necessary. Finally, fit the camshaft cover, run the engine and check that the cover is oil tight.

1 : 5 *The camshaft drive sprockets and drive chain*

The camshaft sprockets and the drive chain are included in **FIG 1 : 6**.

It cannot be too strongly emphasised that, after disconnecting a camshaft sprocket, neither the crankshaft nor the camshaft must be moved. To do so may cause an open valve to hit a piston.

Removing the camshaft drive sprockets :

Remove the camshaft cover and its gasket. Set the engine in the camshaft timing position by aligning the timing mark on the crankshaft pulley with the lower mark (TDC) on the front cover and the timing marks on the camshaft sprockets adjacent to each other and level with the camshaft cover mounting face as shown in **FIG 1 : 7**.

Loosen the locknut and turn out (anticlockwise) the timing chain tensioner (19 in **FIG 1 : 6**) until the chain is loose enough to be slipped off one of the sprockets. Do not fail to maintain an upward pull on the chain, otherwise it will fall down inside the timing case or disengage from the crankshaft sprocket. If this happens it will require removal of the front cover.

Identify and dismount the sprockets by removing their retaining bolts and washers. To remove the drive chain completely, the front cover must be removed as described in **Section 1 : 10**.

Refitting the camshaft drive sprockets :

Fit the camshaft sprockets and engage the drive chain. Ensure that the exhaust sprocket is fitted to the exhaust camshaft and the inlet sprocket is fitted to the inlet camshaft. Align the timing marks as described earlier and as shown in **FIG 1 : 7**. Torque tighten the sprocket retaining bolts to 3.4 to 4.1daNm (25 to 30 lbf ft).

Tensioning the drive chain :

Release the locknut and adjust the chain tensioner until approximately 12.5mm (0.50in) total movement of the chain exists between the two camshaft sprockets as shown in **FIG 1 : 7**. Refit the camshaft cover. Fit a new gasket if the condition of the original is suspect. Run the engine and check for cover leakage.

1 : 6 *The camshafts and bearings*

The camshafts and their bearings are included in **FIG 1 : 6**. Be most careful to ensure that, if the crankshaft is moved from its timing position after a camshaft has been removed from the cylinder head, the crankshaft is returned to the timing position before refitting the camshaft. Before lifting out a camshaft, correctly mark its fitted position so that it can be refitted in the same position.

Removing the camshafts :

Remove the camshaft sprockets as described in **Section 1 : 5**. Identify the camshaft bearing caps to their positions, remove the retaining bolts and lift off the caps. Extract the bearing shells. Identify the shells if they are to be refitted.

Refitting the camshafts :

Fit the original bearing shells if they are serviceable or fit new. Ensure that the bearing location tags are correctly positioned in both the cylinder head and the bearing caps. Lubricate the shells with engine oil. Fit the camshafts and the caps. Tighten the cap retaining bolts progressively working from the centre bearing outwards, and finally torque tighten them to 1.2daNm (9lbf ft). Fit the camshaft sprockets and adjust the drive chain tension as described in **Section 1 : 5**. Check and, if necessary, adjust the valve clearances as described in **Section 1 : 4**.

1 : 7 *Removing and refitting the cylinder head*

Removal :

Drain the cooling system as described in **Chapter 4, Section 4 : 2**. Dismount the carburetter air box as described in **Chapter 2, Sections 2 : 6, 2 : 9** or **2 : 13** as relevant. Uncouple the radiator top hose and the heater hose from the cylinder head. Refer to the relevant section in **Chapter 2** and disconnect the throttle and choke cables and uncouple the fuel feed pipes from the carburetters. Refer to **Section 1 : 21** and uncouple the exhaust system. Remove the camshaft sprockets as described in **Section 1 : 5**. Disconnect the leads from the sparking plugs. Uncouple the vacuum pipe from the inlet manifold.

Refer to **FIG 1 : 8** and, working to the reverse of the tightening sequence, progressively and evenly (and not forgetting the head to front cover bolts) loosen and remove the head bolts. Lift off the cylinder head. Do not lay it face down while the camshafts are in position as valve damage may result. Remove and discard the cylinder head gasket and the front cover cork gasket.

Refitting :

Clean the joint faces of the cylinder block, head and front cover. Refer to **FIG 1 : 9** and, to position the gasket when fitting the head, use location studs which may be made from old head bolts from which the heads have been removed and screwdriver slot cut. Use a new head gasket. Fit a new front cover cork gasket

Check Clearance Where Shown by Arrows

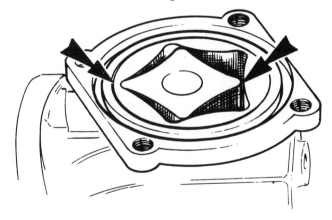

FIG 1 : 3   Checking the rotor lobe clearance

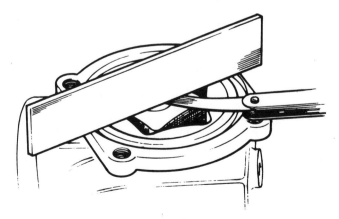

FIG 1 : 4   Checking the rotor face clearance

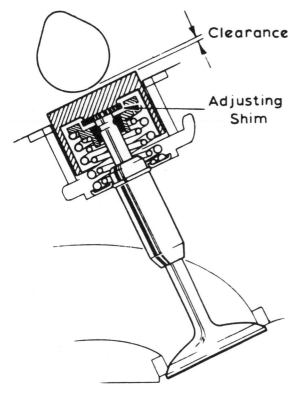

FIG 1 : 5   Valve clearance adjustment

which should have 3Ms EC776 jointing compound applied to the face which will be in contact with the front cover and Hylomar jointing compound on the face which will be in contact with the cylinder head.

Check that the crankshaft and the camshafts are all in the timing position, then refit the head assembly and ensure that the breather connections engage. Loosely refit the cylinder head bolts. Fit the head to front cover bolts. Tighten the head bolts part of a turn at a time in the sequence shown in **FIG 1 : 8**. Finally, torque tighten the head bolts to 8.14 to 8.81daNm (60 to 65lbf ft) and the head to front cover bolts to 1.36 to 2.03daNm (10 to 15lbf ft).

The remaining operations are the reverse of the removal sequence. Refer, as required, to **Sections 1 : 5** and **1 : 21** and to the relevant sections in **Chapter 2**. On completion, refill the cooling system as described in **Chapter 4, Section 4 : 2**, run the engine and check for oil and coolant leaks.

1 : 8   *Servicing the valves and cylinder head*

Remove the cylinder head and the camshafts as described in **Sections 1 : 6** and **1 : 7**. The valve gear components are shown in **FIG 1 : 6**. Identify and remove the cam followers. Identify and remove the adjustment shims. Refer to **FIG 1 : 10**. Using a suitable spring compressing tool, compress the valve springs, remove the split collets, the spring retainers, the springs and the valves. Keep the components in an identified order for refitting (if serviceable) to their original positions.

Cylinder heads :

Refer to **FIG 1 : 11** and note that there are two sizes of inlet valves. Cylinder heads are identified as follows.

Small valve 'S' (and Federal big valve); big valve 'N' or 'H' (and S/E Stromberg). Cylinder head depths are: small valve, 117.8 to 117.9mm (4.638 to 4.643in); big valve, 116.8 to 116.9mm (4.598 to 4.603in).

Decarbonising the head and lapping the valves :

Avoid the use of sharp tools which could damage the light alloy surfaces. Remove all carbon deposits from the combustion chambers, inlet and exhaust ports and joint faces. For decarbonising of the piston crowns, refer to **Section 1 : 13**.

Lap the valves to their seats. Start with course grade and finish with fine grade carborundum paste. If the seats and valve faces are in good condition, fine grade paste alone may be adequate. When the seat and valve faces show a smooth, matt finish, lapping is complete. Keep the valves identified to the positions to which they were lapped and clean all traces of lapping paste from the seats, valves and guides.

If seats and valve faces will not clean up by lapping, if valve guides and cam follower bores are excessively worn, work will be required on the head and valves. Note, however, that these salvage procedures are only suitable for an owner who has access to the necessary machine tools and ovens and has appropriate experience. Others should pass the head and valves to a fully equipped agent.

Valves :

Clean off carbon deposits and inspect the valves for serviceability. Discard valves with bent stems or badly burned heads. Valves that are too pitted to clean up by lapping them to their seats may be refaced but the maximum metal removal is limited to 1.14mm (0.045in) for small valves and 0.254mm (0.010in) for big valves. New valves will be required if this limited machining does not clean up the faces. Check the stems for wear and scoring and compare the stem diameters with those quoted in the **Technical Data** section of the **Appendix**. Renew valves with damaged or excessively worn stems.

Valve guides and seats :

If a valve guide is damaged or worn so that its valve is a loose fit, a new guide should be fitted. If a valve seat insert is too pitted to clean up by simply lapping in the valve, this also should be renewed. Either of these operations should be entrusted to a service station where the proper equipment will be available to ensure concentricity.

Cam followers :

The external diameter of a new cam follower is 34.904 to 34.912mm (1.3742 to 1.3745in) and the desired follower to sleeve bore clearance is 0.013 to 0.036mm (0.0005 to 0.0014in).

Valve springs :

Check valve springs by comparing their free lengths and dimensions under load with the information quoted in the **Technical Data** section of the **Appendix**. Discard cracked and weakened springs.

Reassembly and refitment of the cylinder head :

Refer to all relevant sections and follow the reverse of the dismantling sequence. Assemble with valve stems, guide bores, cam followers and camshaft

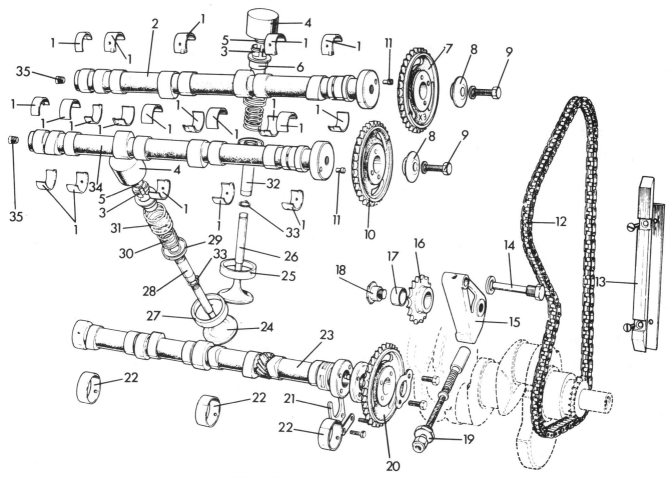

FIG 1 : 6   Components of the valve gear

Key to Fig 1 : 6   1 Bearing shell (camshaft)   2 Camshaft (exhaust valves)   3 Split collets   4 Cam follower (tappet)
5 Adjusting shim   6 Spring seat (upper)   7 Camshaft sprocket (exhaust)   8 Washer   9 Bolt   10 Camshaft sprocket
(inlet)   11 Dowel   12 Camshaft drive chain   13 Chain slipper assembly   14 Tensioner bracket pivot bolt   15 Tensioner
bracket   16 Tensioner sprocket   17 Bush   18 Sprocket retainer   19 Tensioner adjuster   20 Camshaft sprocket
21 Thrust plate   22 Jackshaft bearing   23 Jackshaft   24 Inlet valve   25 Valve seat (exhaust)   26 Exhaust valve
27 Valve seat (inlet)   28 Valve guide (inlet)   29 Spring seat (lower)   30 Valve spring (inner)   31 Valve spring (outer)
32 Valve guide (exhaust)   33 Circlip   34 Camshaft (inlet valves)   35 Plug

bearings wetted with clean engine oil. Refit the cylinder head as described in **Section 1 : 7**.

1 : 9 *The crankshaft pulley*

Removal and refitment :

Remove the drive belt as described in **Chapter 4, Section 4 : 3**. Remove the pulley retaining bolt and use a puller to withdraw the pulley.

To refit, align the pulley keyway with the drive key and remount the pulley. Torque tighten the retaining bolt to 3.25 to 3.79daNm (24 to 28lbf ft). Refit and tension the drive belt as described in **Chapter 4, Section 4 : 3**.

1 : 10 *The front cover*

Removal :

Remove the radiator as described in **Chapter 4, Section 4 : 4**. Remove the camshaft cover. Remove the pump drive belt as described in **Chapter 4, Section 4 : 3**. Remove the coolant pump pulley. Remove the

crankshaft pulley as described in **Section 1 : 9**, the sump as described in **Section 1 : 11** and the camshaft drive chain tension adjuster.

Refer to **FIG 1 : 12**. Remove the 11 forward facing bolts and the three bolts which secure the front cover to the cylinder head and remove the front cover. Remove the crankshaft oil slinger. Disengage the camshaft drive chain **taking care not to rotate the camshafts or crankshaft** or the camshaft timing will be lost. Refer to **Section 1 : 19** and remove the jackshaft sprocket. Remove the front cover backplate and its gaskets after extracting the single retaining clamp screw immed iately below the coolant pump aperture.

Refitting :

Check the condition of the front oil seal. If there is any doubt about its condition, obtain a new replacement.

Apply Hylomar jointing compound to the upper face of a new cork gasket and locate the gasket on the cylinder head to front cover joint. If a new oil tube has been fitted, it is important that (to maintain the correct level) the vertical height measured from the sump

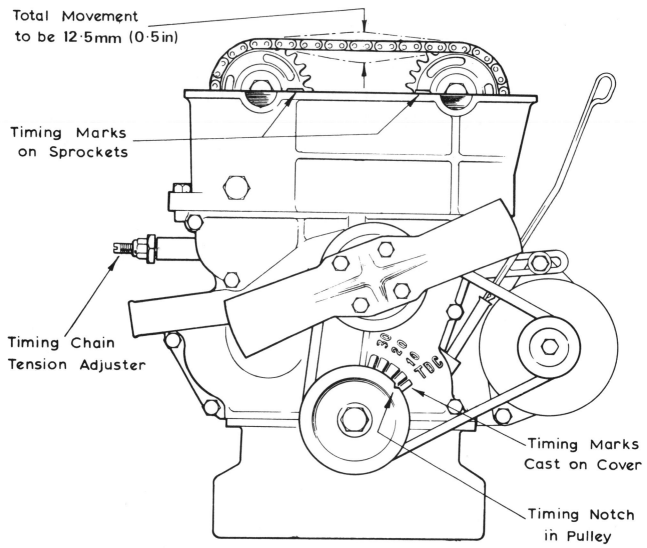

Total Movement to be 12·5mm (0·5in)

Timing Marks on Sprockets

Timing Chain Tension Adjuster

Timing Marks Cast on Cover

Timing Notch in Pulley

FIG 1 : 7   Timing marks

mounting flange to the top of the tube is 104.7mm (4.10in).

Fit the backplate to the cylinder with a new dry paper gasket and retained by the single clamp screw. Before fully tightening the clamp screw, offer up the front cover to the cylinder block. Locate both the coolant pump insert in the front cover and the oil seal on the crankshaft and move the front cover assembly, backplate and gasket to ensure maximum step between the oil sump face on the front cover and the cylinder block sump face and also between the top faces of the front cover and the backplate. This step should not exceed 0.254mm (0.010in) measured by feeler gauge. **Taking care not to move the backplate,** remove the front cover assembly and torque tighten the clamp screw to 0.81 to 1.08daNm (6 to 8lbf ft). Refit the jackshaft sprocket (see **Section 1 : 19**), engage the camshaft drive chain and refit the crankshaft slinger.

Apply 3Ms EC776 jointing compound to the front cover joint faces and fit the cover. It is important to align the cover and refit the the bolts in their correct locations (see **FIG 1 : 12**). Torque tighten the $\frac{1}{4}$in bolts

to 0.68 to 0.95daNm (5 to 7lbf ft) and the $\frac{5}{16}$in bolts to 1.36 to 2.03daNm (10 to 15lbf ft). Refit the camshaft drive chain tension adjuster. Refit the sump as described in **Section 1 : 11**. Refit the crankshaft pulley as described in **Section 1 : 9**. Refit the coolant pump and fan pulley. Refit and tension the belt as described in **Chapter 4, Section 4 : 3**. Adjust the chain tension as described in **Section 1 : 5**. Refit the camshaft cover. Refit the radiator and refill the cooling system as described in **Chapter 4, Sections 4 : 2** and **4 : 4** respectively. Run the engine and check for oil and coolant leaks.

1 : 11 *The sump*

Removal :

Remove the anti-roll bar as described in **Chapter 8. Section 8 : 4**. Remove the drain plug 15 in **FIG 1 : 1** and drain off the engine oil. Position a screw jack under the cylinder block/bellhousing flanges and, with the engine thus supported, release the engine mountings

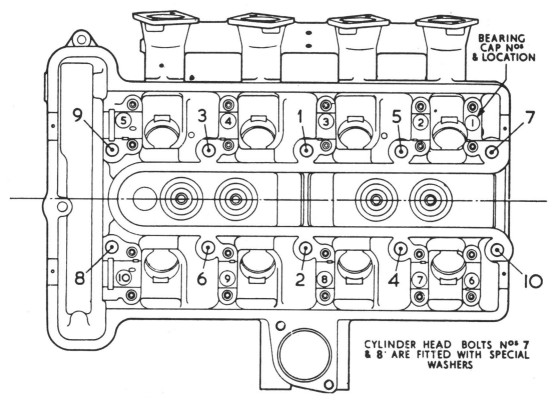

FIG 1 : 8 Cylinder head bolt tightening sequence

and raise the engine with the jack just enough to enable the sump to clear the chassis brace. Remove the sump retaining bolts and dismount the sump. Remove and discard the joint gasket.

Refitting :

Thoroughly clean the interior of the sump and the joint faces. Apply 3Ms EC776 jointing compound to both faces of a new gasket. Refit the sump and torque tighten the retaining bolts to 0.81 to 1.08daNm (6 to 8lbf ft). Reverse the removal sequence for the remaining operations. Refit the drain plug and torque tighten it to 2.71 to 3.38daNm (20 to 25lbf ft). Refill with oil as described in **Section 1 : 2**.

1 : 12 *The camshaft drive chain tensioner*

Removal and refitment :

Remove the camshaft cover and set the engine to the timing position as described in **Section 1 : 5**. Refer to **FIG 1 : 1** and remove the camshaft drive chain tension adjuster by fully unscrewing. Remove the sprocket from the inlet camshaft as described in **Section 1 : 5**.

Refer to **FIG 1 : 6**. Insert a suitable piece of wire with a hooked end into the sprocket bracket 15. Release the pivot bolt 14. Remove the bracket and sprocket assembly by passing it up between the two camshafts. Unscrew the sprocket retainer 18 and separate the sprocket from the bracket.

To assemble and refit, reverse the removal sequence. Torque tighten the sprocket retainer and the pivot bolt to 5.42 to 6.10daNm (40 to 45lbf ft).

1 : 13 *The pistons and rings*

Decarbonising the piston crowns :

If the cylinder head is being serviced as described in **Section 1 : 8**, take the opportunity of decarbonising the piston crowns.

Plug all the holes and passages in the top surface of the cylinder block with clean rag to prevent entry of dirt. Clean the carbon deposits from the piston crowns but leave a ring of carbon round the edge of each piston. Avoid the use of sharp tools which could damage the piston surfaces.

Composite oil control rings :

If oil consumption is excessive (more than 1 litre per 800 kilometres; 1 pint per 250 miles; or 1 USA pint per 210 miles), fitment of composite oil control rings is recommended subject to limited bore wear.

If wear exceeds 0.076mm (0.003in), the cylinder bores should be rebored up to a maximum of 0.381mm (0.015in) oversize and oversize pistons fitted. If wear exceeds 0.076mm (0.003in) in bores which have already been opened out, a new block should be obtained and standard pistons and rings fitted.

Subject to these limitations, composite (two steel rails and one expander ring) oil control rings may be fitted. They are available to suit limited wear standard (Part No 026 E 6003) bores and 0.381mm (0.015in) oversize (Part No 026 E 6004) bores. They must always be fitted **before** fitting the compression rings and the gaps in the upper and lower rails should be positioned 25.4mm (1.0in) either side of the gap in the expander ring.

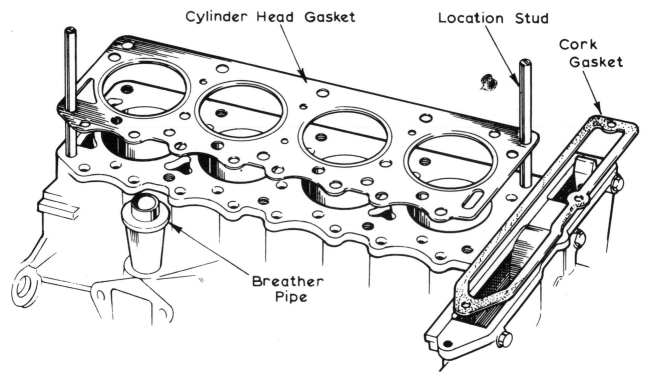

FIG 1 : 9   Cylinder head location studs and gaskets

Piston removal :

Remove the cylinder head as described in **Section 1 : 7**. Remove the sump as described in **Section 1 : 11**. Keeping all parts identified to the positions in which they were fitted, remove the big-end caps as described in **Section 1 : 14**. Push the pistons and connecting rods up and out through the tops of the bores after first cleaning off any ridge of carbon at the top of the bore.

Remove the piston rings carefully to avoid breakages. Remove and discard the gudgeon pin retaining circlips and separate the rods from the pistons by pressing out the gudgeon pins. Clean off all oil and carbon deposits from the piston crowns and ring grooves. Do not use sharp tools which could damage the surfaces. Similarly, clean the piston rings and gudgeon pins.

Piston inspection :

Inspect the pistons for score marks, scuffing, chipped ring grooves and signs of seizure. Reject unserviceable pistons. Check that the compression ring to groove clearances are within the range of 0.041 to 0.091mm (0.0016 to 0.0036in) and that the oil control ring to groove clearances are within the range of 0.046 to 0.097mm (0.0018 to 0.0038in). If groove clearances are excessive with the original rings, recheck with new rings. Reject pistons with oversize groove clearances. Reject piston rings which give oversize groove clearances.

Ring inspection :

Using a piston (crown downwards), press the rings one at a time into the bores from which they were removed. Using feeler gauges, check that compression ring gaps are within the range of 0.229 to 0.356mm (0.009 to 0.014in) and that oil control ring gaps are within the range of 0.254 to 0.508mm (0.010 to 0.020in). Reject rings which have oversize gaps.

Gudgeon pins :

There are two grades of gudgeon pins. Grade A pins have an external diameter of 20.635 to 20.637mm (0.8121 to 0.8125in) and grade B an external diameter of 20.628 to 20.632mm (0.8122 to 0.8123in). Gudgeon pin bores in the pistons are offset by 1.016mm (0.040in) towards the thrust face. The fit with the pistons is classed as finger push fit.

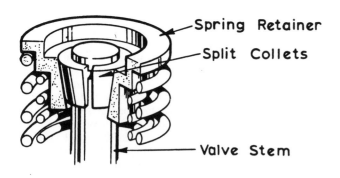

FIG 1 : 10   Valve spring retainer (upper spring seat)

Spring Retainer
Split Collets
Valve Stem

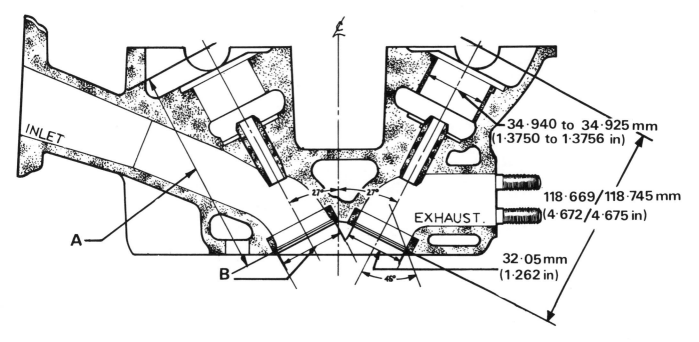

FIG 1 : 11   Valve seat measurements and angles

Key to Fig 1 : 11   A 119.329/119.405mm (4.698/4.701in) or (big valve) 119.838/119.913mm (4.718/4.712in)   **B** 37.16mm (1.467in) or (big valve) 38.10mm (1.500in)

(within figure)
INLET
34·940 to 34·925mm
(1·3750 to 1·3756 in)
118·669/118·745mm
(4·672/4·675 in)
EXHAUST
32·05mm
(1·262 in)
A
B
27° 27°
45°

Selection of new pistons :

Delay selection of new pistons until the cylinder bores have been inspected and measured as described in **Section 1 : 18**. If the cylinder bores are then acceptable, obtain standard new pistons of the appropriate grades to suit the bore diameters. If the cylinder bores have worn in excess of 0.076mm (0.003in) but have not been rebored, have the bores opened out to 0.381mm (0.015in) and obtain oversize pistons and rings to suit.

The desired piston to cylinder bore clearance is 0.068 to 0.083mm (0.0027 to 0.0033in) for A type pistons and 0.076 to 0.091mm (0.0030 to 0.0036in) for C type pistons. Diameters of the four grades of each piston type are quoted in the **Technical Data** section of the **Appendix**.

Piston refitment :

Assemble the pistons to the connecting rods by heating them in water which is almost boiling. This will enable the gudgeon pins to be fitted more easily. Ensure that the FRONT markings on the pistons and rods are on the same side. Retain the gudgeon pins with new circlips.

Position the oil control ring gaps towards the rear and the compression ring gaps at 120° either side. Wet the cylinder bores with clean engine oil and, with the pistons, rings and small-ends also wetted with oil, use a suitable ring clamp and enter the piston assemblies into the bores. Confirm that the FRONT markings are towards the front of the engine and reconnect the big-ends to the crankpins as described in **Section 1 : 14**. Refer to **Sections 1 : 7** and **1 : 11** and complete the reassembly.

1 : 14   *Connecting rods and big-end bearings*

Removing the big-end bearings :

Remove the oil sump as described in **Section 1 : 11**. Turn the crankshaft to bring the relevant piston to the bottom of its stroke. Mark the cap and rod for correct refitting. On early engines, untab the cap bolts. Release the cap bolts by two or three turns and tap them to release the cap. Remove the bolts and dismount the cap. Remove the upper bearing shell from the connecting rod and the lower shell from the cap. Repeat this sequence on the remaining big-ends.

Big-end bearing shells :

Reject bearing shells which are scored or excessively worn. If a bearing failure has occurred, examine the crankpin for transfer of bearing metal and ensure that all oilways are clean and clear. Crankpins (and main journals) may be salvaged by regrinding undersize. 'Undersize' bearing shells will then be required.

The desired running clearance between a connecting rod and its crankpin is 0.013 to 0.059mm (0.0005 to 0.0022in). Connecting rod to crankpin clearances (and crankshaft journal to main bearing clearances) are best measured by using Plastigage, which is a proprietary plastic 'thread', as follows.

1 Select the diameter of Plastigage which covers the clearance to be measured. Place a length of the thread on the journal along its full width.
2 Fit the bearing shell and cap. Torque tighten the cap retaining bolts. The Plastigage will be squeezed down to the clearance dimension of the bearing and its width will increase. **Do not turn the connecting rod or crankshaft while the Plastigage is in position.**

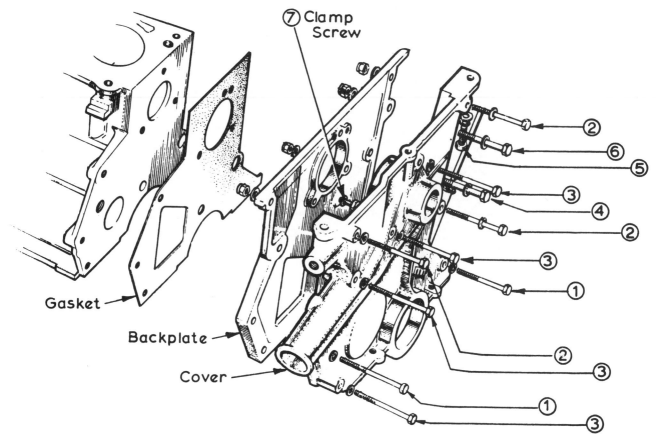

FIG 1 : 12   Front cover mounting details

Key to Fig 1 : 12   1 Dowel bolts 0.25in UNC x 2.50in long   2 Bolt 0.25in UNF x 2.25in long   3 Bolt 0.25in UNC x 2.25in long   4 0.3125in UNC x 2.25in long   5 0.3125in UNC x 1.0in long   6 0.3125in UNF x 1.75in long   7 0.25in UNC x 0.75in long

3 Remove the bearing cap and shell and, using the Plastigage scale provided with the thread, read off the clearances. The maximum width will indicate the minimum clearance and the minimum width, the maximum clearance.

Refitting the big-end bearings :

Lubricate with clean engine oil and fit the upper and lower bearing shells in their appropriate locations. Fit the cap to the connecting rod and torque tighten the bolts to 5.96 to 6.24daNm (44 to 46lbf ft). Note that tab washers are only fitted to early engines (which have four flywheel bolts). Follow the same procedure for the remaining rods.

Connectiong rod removal and refitment :

Removal of the connecting rod/piston assemblies and separation of the rods from the pistons is included in **Section 1 : 13** as also is their reassembly and refitment. Big-end end float should be within the range of 0.101 to 0.254mm (0.004 to 0.010in). **Do not attempt to salvage a bent, twisted or damaged rod, but obtain a new replacement.**

There are two grades: A (silver) have an internal diameter of 20.635 to 20.637mm (0.8124 to 0.8125in); and B (green) which have an internal diameter of 20.637 to 20.642mm (0.8125 to 0.8127in). Gudgeon pin grades and diameters are given in **Section 1 : 13**.

1 : 15 *The main bearings*

Removing the main bearings :

Remove the oil sump as described in **Section 1 : 11**. Mark each main bearing cap (if not already marked) and the cylinder block so that the caps may be refitted in their original positions. Remove No 1 (front) main bearing cap and withdraw the upper bearing shell by pushing out and turning the crankshaft at the same time. Withdraw the lower bearing shell from its cap. **Do not remove the next bearing cap until the first has been refitted.**

Main bearing shells :

Reject bearing shells which are scored or excessively worn. If a bearing failure has occurred, examine the journal for transfer of bearing metal and ensure that all oilways are clean and clear. Main journals (and crankpins) may be salvaged by regrinding undersize. 'Undersize' bearing shells will then be required. The maximum permissible main journal regrind is 0.762mm (0.030in) undersize.

The desired running clearance between the crankshaft and the main bearings is 0.038 to 0.076mm (0.0015 to 0.0030in). Main bearing to crankshaft journal clearances (and connecting rod to crankpin clearances) are best measured by using Plastigage as described in **Section 1 : 14**.

Thrust washers :

Crankshaft end float is controlled at the centre main bearing by thrust washers (see **Section 1 : 18**). End float should be within the range of 0.076 to 0.20mm (0.003 to 0.008in).

Refitting main bearings :

Fit the new bearing shells wetted with clean engine oil by reversing the removal sequence. Torque tighten the retaining bolts to 7.48 to 8.14daNm (55 to 60lbf ft). Torque tighten each bearing cap before proceeding to remove the next in sequence. On completion, refit the sump as described in **Section 1 : 11**.

1 : 16 *Removing and refitting the engine*

The engine is removed upwards and forwards out of the engine compartment. Appropriate equipment which is capable of safely supporting the engine weight and allowing the necessary manoeuvres is essential. Identify all pipes, wiring, controls, etc., as they are disconnected and wire or tape to the chassis so that they cannot interfere with the engine.

Removing the engine :

1 Disconnect the battery. Remove the bonnet as described in **Chapter 12, Section 12 : 2**. Remove the radiator as described in **Chapter 4, Section 4 : 4**. Drain off the engine oil as described in **Section 1 : 2**.

2 Disconnect the following: the coolant temperature capillary (early engines) or the sender unit (later engines) wiring, the oil pressure pipe (early engines) or the pressure sender unit (later engines) wiring and the generator or alternator wiring. Uncouple the heater hoses. Disconnect the distributor, the coil and the starter motor wiring. Disconnect the brake servo hose(s) (if fitted) and the headlamp vacuum hose.

3 Dismount the brake servo unit(s) (if fitted). Refer to **Chapter 2, Sections 2 : 6, 2 : 9, 2 : 11 or 2 : 13** as applicable and uncouple the choke and throttle controls and dismount the carburetter air box and air trunking. Disconnect the fuel feed pipe from the pump. Refer to **Section 1 : 21**. On cars with a cast-type manifold and downpipe, remove the downpipe. On cars with a fabricated-type exhaust system, remove both sections of the manifold and downpipe assemblies.

4 Refer to **Chapter 5, Section 5 : 6** and, without uncoupling the hydraulic pipe, withdraw the clutch

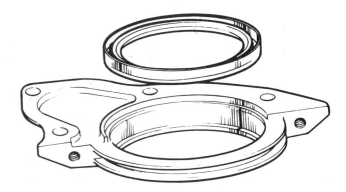

FIG 1 : 13   Rear oil seal and carrier

slave cylinder from its location. Remove the starter motor as described in **Chapter 11, Section 11 : 6**.

5 Attach lifting equipment or arrange a suitable sling and take the weight of the engine. Remove the lower clutch housing bolts and dismount the cover. Use a screw jack to support the gearbox. Remove the bolts which secure the bellhousing to the engine. Refer to **Section 1 : 20** and release the engine mountings.

6 Check that there are no pipes, wiring or controls still bridging the engine with the chassis, manoeuvre the engine forwards off the gearbox mainshaft and lift it up and out of the engine compartment. Take great care not to damage the clutch by letting it foul the splines on the gearbox shaft.

Refitting the engine :

1 Lower the engine into the car and carefully manoeuvre it rearwards to accept the gearbox shaft and pass it through the clutch assembly and into engagement with the crankshaft pilot bearing. Ensure that the upper part of the bellhousing is located on the dowels.

2 Recouple the engine mountings. Note that the engine earthing strap is connected to the lefthand mounting. Refer to **Chapter 5, Section 5 : 5** and fit the engine to bellhousing bolts. Fit the lower cover. Release the engine weight from the lifting equipment and remove the sling or lifting tackle. Remove the screw jack from beneath the gearbox.

3 Fit the carburetter air box and trunking. Reconnect and adjust the choke and throttle cables. Refit the clutch slave cylinder and adjust the release mechanism as described in **Chapter 5, Sections 5 : 3** and **5 : 6** respectively. It will not be necessary to bleed the clutch system if the hydraulic pipe was not disconnected.

4 Refer to **Section 1 : 21**. Reverse the removal sequence and refit the exhaust system. On cars with a cast-type manifold and downpipe, discard the gasket from the manifold to downpipe joint (if one was fitted) and use Holt's 'Firegum' as a jointing material instead. Refit the brake servo unit(s) (if fitted) and bleed the braking system as described in **Chapter 10, Section 10 : 12**.

5 Reconnect the headlamps vacuum hose and the brake servo vacuum hose(s) (if fitted). Reconnect the wiring to the distributor, the coil and to the

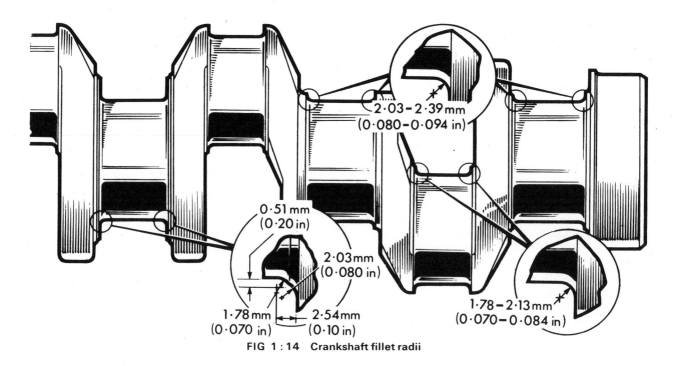

FIG 1 : 14   Crankshaft fillet radii

generator or alternator. Reconnect the oil pressure pipe or the pressure sender wiring. Refit the coolant capillary or the coolant sender unit wiring. Couple the fuel feed pipe to the pump.

6 Install the radiator and refill the cooling system as described in **Chapter 4, Sections 4 : 2** and **4 : 4** respectively. Refill the engine sump as described in **Section 1 : 2**. Refit the bonnet.

7 Reconnect the battery. Check that nothing has been left unfitted or disconnected, start the engine and check for oil and coolant leaks. Adjust the ignition timing as described in **Chapter 3, Section 3 : 5**. Adjust the idling speed as described in **Chapter 2, Sections 2 : 5, 2 : 8, 2 : 11** or **2 : 12**.

1 : 17 *The flywheel*

Removing the flywheel :

Remove the engine as described in **Section 1 : 16**. Remove the clutch assembly from the flywheel as described in **Chapter 5, Section 5 : 4**. Remove the retaining bolts (four on early engines, six on later engines) and dismount the flywheel.

Slight damage or scoring of the rear face may be corrected by judicious machining. Severe damage will dictate the fitment of a new flywheel. Slight damage to the ring gearteeth may be corrected by blending. Severe damage will dictate the renewal of the ring gear.

Renewing the ring gear :

Cut between two adjacent teeth with a hacksaw and split the ring gear with a chisel. Under no circumstances should any attempt be made to press the ring gear off the flywheel.

Thoroughly clean the periphery of the flywheel and the internal diameter of the new ring gear. Heat the ring gear evenly to a temperature **not exceeding** 316°C. Fit the ring gear to the flywheel with the chamfers on the leading edges of the teeth relative to the normal direction of rotation. Allow the assembly to cool naturally in air. **Do not quench.**

Refitting the flywheel :

To ensure true running, thoroughly clean the crankshaft and flywheel mating surfaces before positioning the flywheel squarely on the crankshaft. Fit the retaining bolts and torque tighten them to 6.10 to 6.78daNm (45 to 50lbf ft). Check the lateral run-out using a dial indicator. This should not exceed 0.101mm (0.004in). The ring gear run-out should not exceed 0.406mm (0.016in) laterally or 0.152mm (0.006in) radially. Refit the clutch assembly as described in **Chapter 5, Section 5 : 5**. Refit the engine as described in **Section 1 : 16**.

1 : 18 *The crankshaft and cylinder block*

Rear oil seal renewal :

Remove the engine as described in **Section 1 : 16**. Remove the oil sump and the flywheel as described in **Sections 1 : 11** and **1 : 17** respectively. Remove the retaining bolts and withdraw the rear oil seal carrier from the cylinder block. Remove the oil seal from the carrier. Clean off old gasket and jointing compound.

Fit a new seal to the carrier. From engine No LP7799, a one-piece seal (see **FIG 1 : 13**) was introduced. Apply 3Ms EC776 jointing compound and fit a new gasket. Fit the retaining bolts and locate the carrier squarely on the cylinder block before torque tightening to 1.63 to 2.03daNm (12 to 15lbf ft). Refit the flywheel and sump as described in **Sections 1 : 11** and **1 : 17** respectively. Refit the engine as described in **Section 1 : 16**.

Crankshaft sprocket removal and refitment :

Remove the engine as described in **Section 1 : 16**. Remove the front cover as described in **Section 1 : 10**.

Using a suitable puller, withdraw the crankshaft sprocket.

Use a new key when refitting. Ensure that the keyway and the key are aligned and press the sprocket onto the crankshaft with the long boss towards the front main bearing journal. Refit the front cover and refit the engine as described in **Sections 1 : 10** and **1 : 16** respectively.

Crankshaft removal :

Remove the engine as described in **Section 1 : 16**. Remove the camshaft cover. Set the engine to the timing position as described in **Section 1 : 5**. Remove the front cover as described in **Section 1 : 10**. Remove the sump as described in **Section 1 : 11**. Release the camshaft drive chain tension and disengage the chain. Remove the rear oil seal and carrier as described earlier.

Identify and remove the big-end bearing caps as described in **Section 1 : 14** and push the pistons up into the bores. Identify the main bearing caps and remove their retaining bolts. Lift off the caps. Lift out the crankshaft. Collect and identify the bearing shells and the thrust washers. Keep all parts identified for refitting (if serviceable) to their original positions.

If, as stated in relevant earlier sections, there has been a main or a big-end bearing failure, the crankshaft must be checked for damage and for transfer of bearing metal. The oilways must be checked and, if necessary, flushed with clean engine oil to ensure that they are clean and clear. Crankshafts with worn or scored crankpin or main journals may, as indicated in the relevant sections, be reground undersize. The fillet radii must, on regrinding, be correct as shown in **FIG 1 : 14**.

Crankshaft refitment :

Reverse the removal sequence, not forgetting to ensure that the crankshaft is in the timing position before refitting the chain. Fit new main bearing shells and big-end shells or, if the original shells are serviceable and the clearances acceptable, refit the original shells as described in **Sections 1 : 14** and **1 : 15** respectively. Check the clearances using Plastigage as described in **Section 1 : 14**. Fit the thrust washers with their oil grooves towards the crankshaft flanges as shown in **FIG 1 : 15**. Check the end float between the crankshaft and the thrust washers. The total end float should be within the range of 0.076 to 0.203mm (0.003 to 0.008in). If necessary, adjust by fitting thicker or thinner thrust washers.

Pilot bearing :

The pilot or spigot bearing is located in the tail of the crankshaft. Commencing at engine No 18500, a needle roller bearing was introduced. This bearing is prepacked with grease and requires no further lubrication. Earlier crankshafts may be bored out from 20.960/20.990mm (0.8252/0.8264in) to 20.980/21.005mm (0.8260/0.8270 in). P7137 (insertion) and CP7600/7 (extractor) tools are required for fitting and renewing the needle roller bearing.

The cylinder block :

The cylinder bores may be inspected and measured after removal of the pistons and connecting rods as

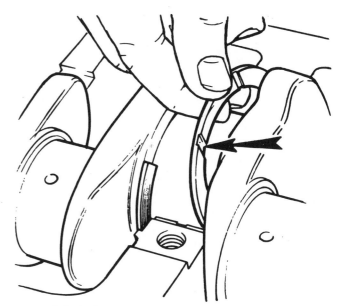

FIG 1 : 15   Fitting crankshaft thrust washers

described in **Section 1 : 13** or, if the engine is being completely overhauled, after stripping and removing the crankshaft. If the bores are to be honed or rebored, the block must be stripped and, after the machining operations, the block and all oilways and passages must be very thoroughly cleaned and flushed before rebuilding the engine. A cracked block must be rejected and a new replacement obtained.

To assess the reboring or honing requirement, measure round the bores at four places at top, middle and bottom stroke positions to build up a complete picture of bore wear, ovality and taper. Slight scoring may require no more than honing of the bores. If oil consumption was high but wear is less than 0.076mm (0.003in), composite piston rings (see **Section 1 : 13**) may be fitted. If wear exceeds this, reboring and the fitment of oversize pistons is indicated. Each bore should be machined at least to a diameter which will correct the ovality, taper, scoring, etc., and the final rebore diameter should be the actual diameter of the oversize piston plus the desired piston to bore clearance as specified in **Section 1 : 13.**.

1 : 19 The jackshaft and bearings

Removing the jackshaft :

Remove the engine as described in **Section 1 : 16**. Remove the camshaft cover and set the engine to the timing position as described in **Section 1 : 5**. Remove the front cover as described in **Section 1 : 10**. Refer to **Section 1 : 3** and remove the oil pump and filter assembly. Remove the distributor as described in **Chapter 3, Section 3 : 4**. Remove the fuel pump as described in **Chapter 2, Section 2 : 4**. Disengage the camshaft drive chain.

Refer to **FIG 1 : 6**. Untab and remove the jackshaft sprocket retaining bolts. Dismount the sprocket and distance piece. Untab and remove two retaining bolts and withdraw the jackshaft thrust plate. Withdraw the jackshaft.

To renew the jackshaft bearings, the use of tool P6031 and adaptors P6032 and P6033 is essential. Extract the old bushes. Ensure that the oil holes in the new bushes and in the cylinder block align. The splits in the bushes must be upwards and outwards at 45° to the vertical. On completion of the fitment of the new bushes, check that the oilways are clean and clear. If access to the special tools cannot be arranged, have the work carried out by a fully equipped agent.

Refitting the jackshaft :

If the oil gallery plugs were removed, apply a sealing compound to them before refitting. Fit a new dowel and slide the jackshaft into position. Use a new tabwasher and fit the thrust plate into its groove in the shaft. Torque tighten the two bolts to 0.68 to 0.95daNm (5 to 7lbf ft). Check the shaft end float. This should be within the range of 0.063 to 0.190mm (0.0025 to 0.0075in) and is adjusted by fitting a thicker or thinner thrust plate. When the end float is correct, bend up the tabs to lock the retaining bolts.

Refit the jackshaft sprocket and spacer. Use a new tabwasher and torque tighten the retaining bolts to 1.63 to 2.03daNm (12 to 15lbf ft). The remaining operations are the reverse of the removal sequence. Refer, as necessary, to the relevant chapter and section for details. Ensure that the camshaft drive chain is correctly tensioned as described in **Section 1 : 5**. Check and adjust the ignition timing as described in **Chapter 3, Section 3 : 5**. Refit the engine.

1 : 20 *The engine mountings*

Renewing the mountings :

Raise and support the front of the car. Support the engine with a jack. Remove the righthand mounting and fit the new raplacement. Repeat the sequence on the lefthand mounting. Note that the engine earthing strap is connected to this mounting. Remove the engine support jack and lower the car.

1 : 21 *The exhaust system*

There are a number of variants of the exhaust system between early and later models and it is important that, if new parts or units are required, they should match those being discarded.

Earlier cars are fitted with a cast iron manifold and separate cast iron downpipe. Later cars are fitted with gas-flowed two-part fabricated manifolds and integral fabricated downpipes.

Removing and refitting the cast-type manifold :

Remove either three Allen screws or three nuts from the manifold to downpipe joint. Remove and discard the gasket (if fitted). Remove eight nuts securing the flanges to the cylinder head and ease the manifold off the studs.

Refitment is the reverse of this sequence. **Do not fit a gasket** at the manifold to downpipe joint. Use Holt's 'Firegum' as a jointing material and bolt up immediately.

Removing and refitting the fabricated-type manifolds :

Support the engine on a jack and remove the lefthand engine mounting. Disconnect the Y-box joint from the intermediate pipe. Remove the generator or alternator as described in **Chapter 11, Sections 11 : 4** or **11 : 5**. Remove the eight nuts securing the flanges to cylinder head. Ease the manifolds off the studs, twist to clear the brake servo unit(s) (if fitted) and manoeuvre them from the engine compartment. Note that it may be found expedient to dismount the servo unit(s) (if fitted).

Refitment is the reverse of this sequence. Fit new gaskets at the head joints. Ensure that the engine earthing strap is reconnected to the engine mounting.

1 : 22 *Fault diagnosis*

(a) Engine will not start

1 Defective coil
2 Faulty capacitor
3 Dirty, pitted or incorrectly gapped distributor points
4 Ignition LT or HT wiring loose or insulation defective
5 Water on HT leads
6 Battery discharged, terminals corroded
7 Defective or jammed starter motor
8 Sparking plug leads wrongly connected
9 Vapour lock in fuel pipes
10 Defective fuel pump
11 Overchoking or underchoking
12 Leaking or sticking valve
13 Incorrect valve timing
14 Incorrect ignition timing

(b) Engine stalls

1 Check 1 to 5 and 10 to 14 in (a)
2 Sparking plugs defective or incorrectly gapped
3 Retarded ignition
4 Mixture too weak
5 Water in fuel system
6 Fuel tank vent blocked
7 Incorrect valve clearances

(c) Engine idles badly

1 Check 2 and 7 in (b)
2 Air leak at manifold joint
3 Incorrectly adjusted carburetters
4 Mixture too rich
5 Worn piston rings
6 Worn valve stems or guides
7 Weak exhaust valve springs

(d) Engine misfires

1 Check 1 to 5, 8, 10 and 12 to 14 in (a)
2 Weak or broken valve springs

(e) Engine overheats (see Chapter 4)

(f) Low compression

1 Check 12 and 13 in (a); 5 and 6 in (c); and 2 in (d)
2 Worn piston ring grooves
3 Scored or worn cylinder bores

(g) Engine lacks power

1 Check 3 and 10 to 14 in (a); 2, 3, 4 and 7 in (b);
  5 and 6 in (c); and 2 in (d). Also check (e) and (f)
2 Fouled sparking plugs
3 Automatic ignition advance inoperative

(h) Burnt valves or seats

1 Check 12 and 13 in (a); 7 in (b); and 2 in (d). Also
  check (e)
2 Excessive carbon round valve seats

(i) Sticking valves

1 Check 7 in (b); 2 in (d)
2 Bent valve stem
3 Scored valve stem or guide

(j) Excessive cylinder wear

1 Check 11 in (a)
2 Lack of oil
3 Dirty oil
4 Broken or gummed up piston rings
5 Connecting rod bent

(k) Excessive oil consumption

1 Check 5 and 6 in (c). Also check (j)
2 Ring gaps too wide

3 Piston oil return holes blocked
4 Scored cylinder bores
5 Oil level too high
6 External oil leaks

(l) Main bearing or big-end bearing failure

1 Check 2 and 5 in (j)
2 Restricted or blocked oilway(s)
3 Worn journals or crankpins
4 Loose bearing cap
5 Extremely low oil pressure

(m) Internal coolant leakage

1 Cracked cylinder block or head
2 Defective head to block gasket

(n) Poor coolant circulation (see Chapter 4)

(o) High fuel consumption (see Chapter 2)

(p) Engine vibration

1 Loose generator or alternator
2 Engine mountings loose or defective
3 Misfiring due to carburation, ignition or mechanical
  faults

NOTES

CHAPTER 2

THE FUEL SYSTEM

2 : 1 Description

Fuel is drawn from a rear mounted tank by a mechanical diaphragm type pump. Fuel level in the tank is indicated on a gauge in the instrument panel. The contents gauge operates electrically from a float-type sender unit fitted in the rear wall of the fuel tank. Different models are fitted with differing fuel tank capacities which are quoted in the **Technical Data** section of the **Appendix**.

The fuel pump is mounted on the righthand side of the engine and is operated from an eccentric on the jackshaft. The pump incorporates a gauze screen and an inverted sediment bowl. Pressure fuel is fed to the carburetters via a branched pipe. Twin side draught carburetters are fitted to all models. These may, depending upon the model, be of Weber, Zenith-Stromberg or Dellorto manufacture. Manual cold starting choke control is fitted to all carburetter types.

It should be noted that the ignition timing differs from model to model and depends upon the carburetters fitted. Ignition timing relevant to each specific model is, consequently, quoted in **Sections 2 : 5, 2 : 8, 2 : 11** and **2 : 12**.

A canister-type air cleaner, fitted with a renewable dry paper element, is provided. A flexible trunking connects the cleaner with the carburetter air intakes air box.

Models which are exported to countries in which exhaust emission control is mandatory are provided with an appropriate system in conjunction with special Zenith-Stromberg carburetters. Evaporative loss features are also incorporated in relevant export models.

2 : 2 Servicing

Zenith-Stromberg damper reservoirs :

Every 5000km (3000 miles), release the black cap from the top of each carburetter and withdraw the damper units. The correct oil level is 6.35mm (0.25in) from the top of the centre rod. Top up, if necessary, using clean engine oil.

Servicing schedules and mileage intervals are given in **Chapter 13**. Note, however, that no specific mileage intervals are prescribed for the servicing of Weber or Dellorto carburetters and the procedures described in **Sections 2 : 7** and **2 : 14** should be carried out on an 'as and when necessary' basis.

In dusty terrain, the air cleaner element should be cleaned or renewed at shorter mileage intervals than are recommended in **Chapter 13**. Similarly, if fuel supplies are dirty, it will be prudent to clean the fuel pump gauze screen and sediment bowl more frequently than at the stated servicing intervals.

2 : 3 Air cleaner

The components of the cleaner assembly are shown in **FIG 2 : 1**.

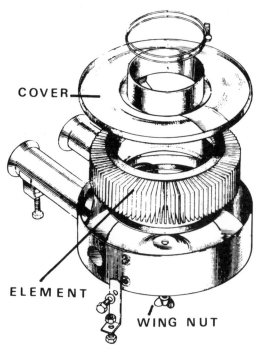

FIG 2:1   Components of the air cleaner

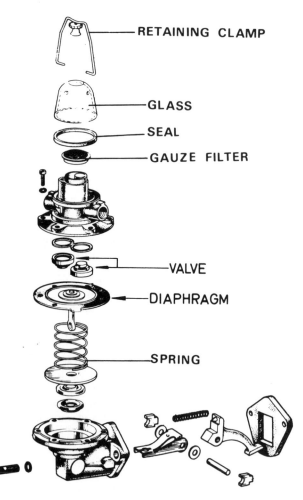

FIG 2:2   Components of the fuel pump

Element removal and refitment :

Remove the front grille. Uncouple the air trunking by releasing the large clip. Remove the retaining bolts and withdraw the cleaner from the car. Invert the canister, remove the wing nut and dismount the cover. Withdraw the element.

Clean the interior of the canister and cover. If the element has been in use for a limited mileage and provided that it is intact, it may be refitted after cleaning by tapping it gently to dislodge dust, etc. At the recommended mileage, however, discard the element and the sealing rings, fit new sealing rings (supplied with the element) to the new element and reassemble and install the unit by reversing the removal sequence.

Water contamination :

If it is found that, on a horizontally mounted cleaner, the element is contaminated by water, provide drainage by drilling a 19.05mm (0.75in) diameter hole in the cover as close to the periphery as possible. On later models the canister is mounted vertically.

2 : 4 *The fuel pump*

The components of the fuel pump are shown in **FIG 2 : 2**.

Filter cleaning :

Unscrew the sediment bowl retainer clamp, lift off the bowl and withdraw the gauze filter screen. Carefully wash the filter in clean petrol and flush all traces of sediment from the chamber and bowl. Renew the screen if damaged or it will not clean adequately. Renew the sealing gasket unless that removed is in perfect condition.

To reassemble, reverse the screen removal sequence.

Testing the fuel pump :

If it is suspected that fuel is not reaching the carburetters, ensure that the fuel tank venting system is not blocked before testing the pump.

Disconnect a carburetter feed pipe and, with a container under the pipe end, turn the engine over a few times by the starter motor and watch for fuel squirting from the pipe. Reduced flow from the pump may be due to a clogged filter screen or to a partially blocked pipe. Clean the filter screen as described earlier. An obstructed pipe may be cleared by using compressed air. Disconnect the pipes from the pump and carburetters. **Do not pass compressed air through the pump or the valves will be damaged.** Remove the tank filler cap before blowing through the tank to pump pipe. Limited fuel delivery may also be due to an air leak in the (suction) tank to pump pipe.

The pump itself may be defective due to dirt under the valves, faulty valve seatings or a punctured diaphragm. To correct these faults the pump must be removed and dismantled.

Fuel pump removal and refitment :

Uncouple the feed and delivery pipes from the pump. Blank off the pipe ends to preclude entry of dirt. Remove the two bolts and spring washers which retain the pump to the cylinder block. Dismount the pump and discard the joint gasket.

Before refitting the pump, thoroughly clean the pump and cylinder block joint faces. Fit a new gasket (hold it in place with a smear of grease), insert the rocker arm into the block so that it lies against the jackshaft eccentric. Fit the spring washers and bolts. Torque tighten the bolts to 1.63 to 2.03daNm (12 to 15lbf ft). Ensure that the pipe joints are clean before coupling them to the pump. Run the engine and check for oil and fuel leaks.

Dismantling the pump :

Clean the exterior of the pump and scribe a line across the body flanges so that they may be aligned on reassembly. Remove the filter screen as described earlier. Remove the screws and washers and separate the upper from the lower body.

It should be possible to blow air (by mouth) through the inlet valve but not to suck air out and vice versa on the outlet valve. The valve assemblies are 'staked' in position and, to remove a valve, the staking must be relieved. The valves, as assemblies, are identical and interchangeable.

Turn the diaphragm and pullrod assembly through 90°, disengage the rod from the link in the rocker arm assembly and remove the diaphragm assembly. Note that the diaphragm cannot be separated from the rod. Remove the diaphragm return spring and (if fitted) the oil seal retaining washer and seal.

If the rocker arm pin is firm in the body, it need not be removed unless there is undue wear in the pin or associated parts. The arm and associated parts are located by two retainers which are fitted into slots. The retainers are held by punched indentations at each end of the retaining pins. If it is necessary to remove the arm assembly, hold the arm firmly in a vice and with two flat bars 30.5cm (12in) long inserted one on each side in the gap between the casting and the vice, lever the body away from the arm and pin. Ensure, when doing so, that the bars do not damage the machined face of the body.

Servicing the dismantled pump :

Thoroughly clean all parts in petrol. Ensure, particularly, that the valves are, if they are not being renewed, clean and clear of anything which could prevent them closing fully. Check the diaphragm for hardening, cracking, etc., and examine the lower end of the pullrod for wear where it connects with the rocker arm link. Renew the diaphragm assembly if any part of it is suspect. Renew the return spring if it is corroded or damaged. Renew the oil seal (if fitted). Check the valve assemblies and renew if their fuel tightness is suspect. Discard the old gaskets. Cracked or damaged bodies must be rejected. If the diaphragm joint flanges or the mounting flange is slightly distorted, lapping to restore flatness is acceptable. Renew if there is any excessive distortion.

Assembling the pump :

Reverse the dismantling sequence but note the following points. Ensure that the rocker arm return spring is properly engaged between the locating 'pips' on the casting and arm. If relevant, use new service retainers which, for identification, are copper coloured and are slightly shorter than the original to allow for the restaking. Ensure that, if valves are being renewed, that each is fitted the correct way up. When assembling the diaphragm and bodies, operate the arm until the diaphragm is level with the body flange, fit the upper body (align the scribe marks), fit the screws and spring washers but tighten only until the screw heads engage the washers. Operate the arm to hold the diaphragm at the top of the stroke and, while so held, working diagonally tighten the screws fully. Special care must be taken in maintaining down pressure on the rocker arm while the screws are being fully tightened. When assembly is complete, the edges of the diaphragm should be flush with the body flanges. Any appreciable protrusion of the diaphragm indicates incorrect assembly and the screws should be loosened off and this stage of the assembly repeated.

2 : 5 *Weber carburetter adjustments*

When making adjustments to the carburetters, the engine must be at normal operating temperature and the ignition timing, distributor points, sparking plugs and their gaps and the valve clearances must be in good order. There must be no air leaks at the carburetter to manifold 'O' ring gaskets.

The four mixture control screws, the throttle coupling screw and the idling speed control screw are shown in FIG 2 : 3. Adjustment of idling mixture, idling speed and carburetter synchronisation are carried out concurrently as follows.

1 Remove the air box cover which is retained by a single bolt on earlier models and by three bolts on later models. Removal of the box will have a negligible effect upon the idling speed.

2 Set the four mixture screws three-quarters of a turn open. Start the engine and adjust the rear carburetter throttle screw to give 1000r/min. Synchronise the carburetters using either of the methods described in operations 3 or 4.

3 Using a proprietary carburetter balancing tool (such as the Crypton Synchro Test), adjust the coupling screw until the air flow through each carburetter is the same.

4 Alternatively, hold a length of flexible tubing with one end to the ear and the other at the mouth of each carburetter trumpet in turn. Adjust the coupling screw until the 'hiss' is the same at each carburetter.

5 Adjust each mixture screw in turn. Screw each fully in and unscrew a small amount at a time (not more than an eighth of a turn), waiting about five seconds at each setting. A point will be found which will cause a rise in engine speed and further adjustment will cause the revolutions to drop back again. Adjust each screw to give the maximum rise in revolutions. If a second operator is not available, rig a mirror so that the tachometer can be seen when adjusting the carburetters.

6 During the synchronising and mixture adjustment procedures, it will be necessary to repeatedly adjust the throttle screw to maintain an engine speed of 1000r/min. Repeat the adjustments as necessary until no further improvements can be obtained. Finally, adjust the throttle screw to give an idling speed of 800 to 900r/min. Refit the air box cover.

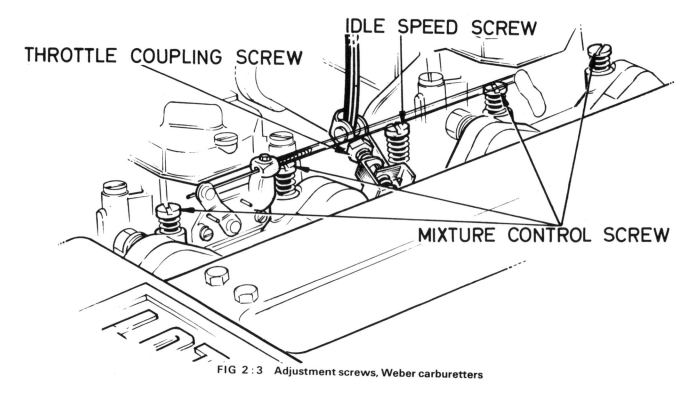

THROTTLE COUPLING SCREW

IDLE SPEED SCREW

MIXTURE CONTROL SCREW

FIG 2:3   Adjustment screws, Weber carburetters

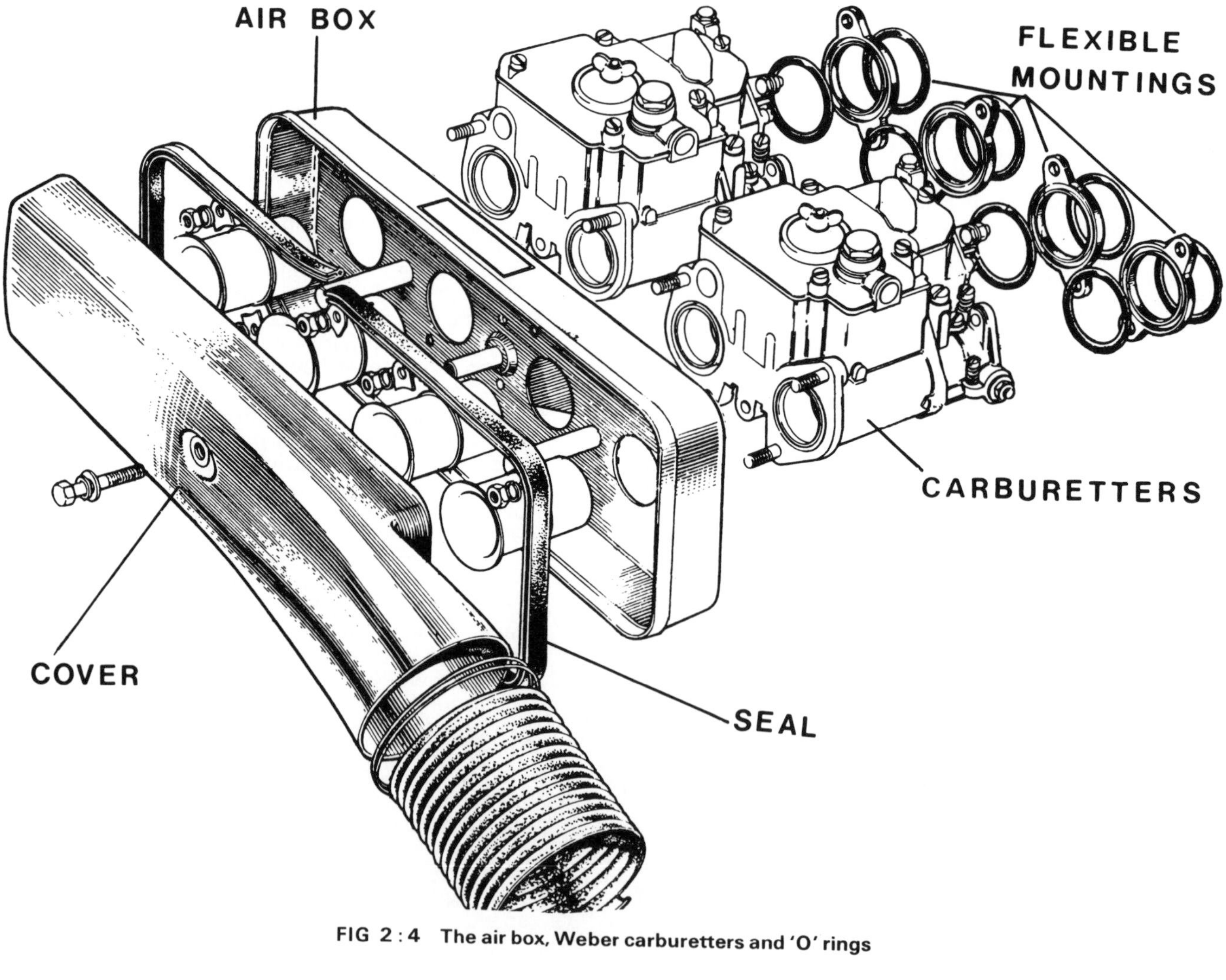

AIR BOX

FLEXIBLE MOUNTINGS

CARBURETTERS

COVER

SEAL

FIG 2:4   The air box, Weber carburetters and 'O' rings

To correct an unbalanced air flow through the throttles in the same carburetter, fit a spanner to each end of the throttle spindle and twist slightly in the relevant direction.

Ignition timing data when Weber carburetters are fitted:

Elan with 'A' type pistons	12° BTDC (static)
Elan with 'C' type pistons	10° BTDC (static)
Elan Sprint	12° BTDC (static)
Elan +2, except 'S 130'	10° BTDC (static)
Elan +2, 'S 130'	12° BTDC (static)

2 : 6 *Weber carburetter removal and refitment*

Removal:

Refer to **FIG 2 : 4**. Release the clip and uncouple the air cleaner trunking from the air box cover. Remove the retaining bolts and dismount the air box cover. Unhook the throttle return spring and disconnect the throttle cable from the carburetters. Uncouple the fuel supply pipes at the carburetters and plug the ends to preclude entry of dirt. Disconnect the choke cable.

Progressively release the carburetter securing nuts. Remove the nuts and washers. Carefully dismount the carburetters as an assembly ensuring that the synchronising link between them is not distorted. Remove the spacers and their 'O' rings from the mounting studs.

Refitment:

Check the condition of the 'O' rings and the spacers. Renew any suspect parts. Fit the spacer assemblies to the mounting studs. Refit the carburetters ensuring that the synchronising linkage is correctly positioned with the lug on the rear carburetter throttle linkage between the spring loaded plunger and adjusting screw on the front carburetter. To each mounting stud fit a double coil spring washer, a flat washer and a nut. Tighten the eight nuts progressively until (using feeler gauges) there is a clearance of 1.02mm (0.040in) between the coils of the spring washers as shown in **FIG 2 : 5**. To ensure that the 'O' rings will not be flattened, do not overtighten the nuts.

Recouple the fuel pipes. Reconnect the controls. Ensure that the choke control on the facia panel is pushed fully 'off' and that the starting device operating levers are also fully in the 'off' position. If not already fitted, fit a new throttle return spring which has a double coil. The Part No is B.26.S.028. Ensure that the the air box to air box cover gasket is in good condition. Refit the air box cover and recouple the flexible trunking.

2 : 7 *Weber carburetter servicing*

Dismount the carburetters as described in **Section 2 : 6**. Refer to **FIG 2 : 4**. Remove the nuts, washers and clamps which secure the trumpets and the air box to the carburetters.

Dismantling a carburetter:

The components of a Weber carburetter are shown in **FIG 2 : 6**. While dismantling, an owner should

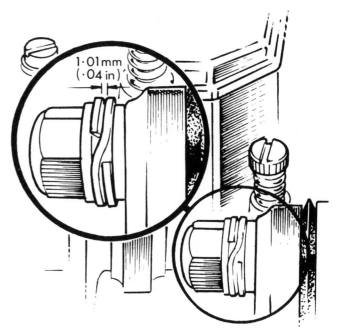

FIG 2 : 5 Clearance between spring washer coils, Weber carburetters

supplement this illustration and the procedure description with his own notes and sketches.

From each barrel, remove the auxiliary venturi 15 followed by the main venturi 14. Unscrew the hexagon headed retainer 93 from the carburetter cover 5 (note the sealing washer 92) and remove the gauze filter 97, taking care not to mislay the brass seat from the top of the filter. Remove the small circular main and idling jet cover 1 retained by a wing nut. Loosen the screws 2 evenly and remove the carburetter cover.

Gently push out the float fulcrum pin 82. The needle valve may now be removed from its seat 87. Withdraw the cover gasket 6 and unscrew the needle valve seat from the cover. Note that a sealing washer 86 is fitted between the seat and the cover.

Remove the accelerator pump from the carburetter body, pull out the inverted U-shaped rod 68 which will withdraw the split retainer 67, spring 69 and piston 70. To dismantle the assembly, compress the spring, slightly rotate the piston and withdraw the hooked end of the control rod followed by the spring and the retainer. Unscrew the accelerator pump inlet valve 79 from the base of the chamber. Shake the valve to ensure that the ball inside the body slides freely.

Remove the idling jet holders 9 (two per carburetter) and withdraw the idling jets 11. Unscrew the emulsion tube holders 7 (two per carburetter). Pull each emulsion tube 10 from its holder. Withdraw the main jet 12 from one end of the tube and the air corrector jet 8 from the other. Remove the accelerator pump delivery valve retaining screws (two per carburetter) and examine the rubber seal around each screw. Extract each pump jet 76 from the body.

Remove the starting jets 80 (two per carbureter). Unscrew the volume control screws 72 and throttle stop screw 73 (if fitted). Examine the springs. The starting device cover 58 on the side of the carburetter

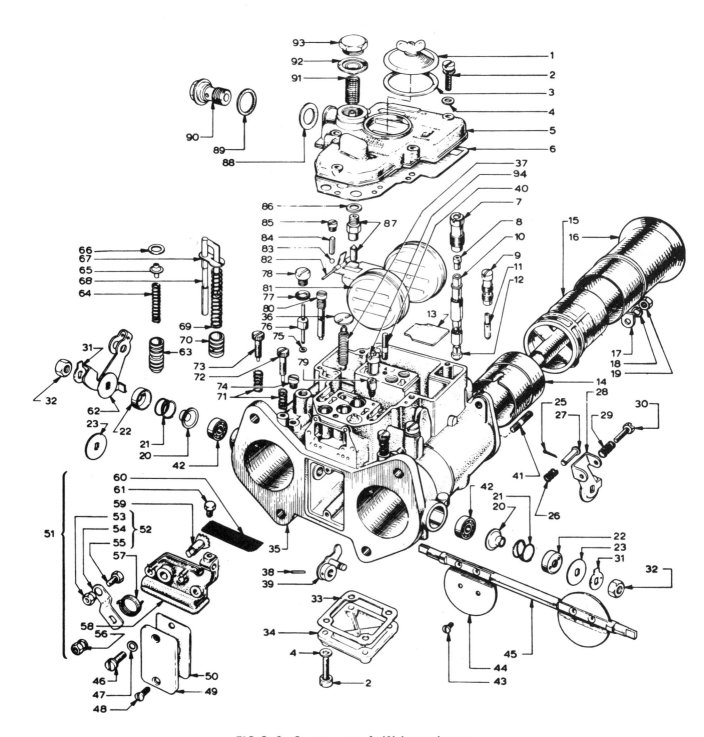

FIG 2 : 6 Components of a Weber carburetter

Key to Fig 2 : 6   1 Cover, jets inspection   2 Screw   3 Gasket, cover   4 Washer   5 Cover, upper body   6 Gasket, cover   7 Holder, emulsion tube   8 Jet, air corrector   9 Holder, idling jet   10 Tube, emulsion   11 Jet, idling   12 Jet, main   13 Plate   14 Choke   15 Venturi   16 Trumpet   17 Plate, fixing   18 Washer, spring   19 Nut   20 Cover, dust   21 Spring   22 Lid   23 Washer, distance   24 Lever assembly   25 Pin, split   26 Spring, throttle control   27 Pin, control lever   28 Lever   29 Spring, control lever   30 Screw, control lever   31 Lockwasher   32 Nut   33 Gasket, bowl   34 Cover, bowl   35 Body, carburetter   36 Plate   37 Spring   38 Pin   39 Lever, pump control   40 Stud, upper body   41 Stud, trumpet to body   42 Bearing   43 Screw, throttle plate   44 Throttle plate   45 Shaft   46 Screw   47 Washer   48 Screw   49 Plate   50 Gasket   51 Control assembly   52 Lever   53 Nut   54 Lever   55 Screw   56 Nut   57 Spring, lever return   58 Cover   59 Shaft, starting   60 Strainer   61 Screw   62 Lever, rear carburetter   63 Valve   64 Spring   65 Guide   66 Circlip   67 Plate, spring retainer   68 Rod, pump control   69 Spring   70 Plunger   71 Spring   72 Volume control screw   73 Screw, throttle adjustment   74 Screw   75 Gasket   76 Jet, pump   77 Gasket   78 Plug   79 Valve inlet   80 Jet starting   81 Float   82 Shaft   83 Ball   84 Plunger   85 Screw   86 Gasket   87 Seat needle valve   88 Gasket   89 Gasket   90 Banjo bolt   91 Filter, upper casing   92 Gasket   93 Plug   94 Valve may be removed after unscrewing the two retaining screws 42 which have spring 43 and flat washers beneath their heads. Carefully prise out the combined starting device piston guide/retainer circlips 66 (two per carburetter). Withdraw the guides 65 and springs 64 and invert the carburetter to extract the starting device valves 63.

Remove the throttle plates 44 (note which way round they are fitted), by removing the two screws 43 securing each plate to the shaft 45. Remove the throttle spindle. Note that a new carburetter body is supplied complete with the throttle spindle, pump operating arm 39, bearings 42, etc. If a new body is to be fitted, these parts need not be dismantled.

If the original body is being retained, removal of the relevant parts is as follows. Bend back the tabwashers 31 and remove the nuts 32 from each end of the spindle. Remove the flat washer 23 from one end and the throttle linkage 62 from the other. Withdraw the plate 49 and gasket 50 secured by two screws 48 from the engine side of the carburetter to gain access to the accelerator pump control arm. Tap out the pin 38 retaining the arm to the spindle. Being careful not to damage the threads, knock out the spindle. This will also remove from one end the spring retainer 22, the spring 21, dust cover 20 and bearing 42. After carefully prising out the spring retainer from the other end, the spring and dust cover can be extracted.

Inspection :

Clean all parts in petrol and inspect for wear or damage. Discard faulty parts. Thoroughly clean all the jets, air bleeds, bleed screws and carburetter passages

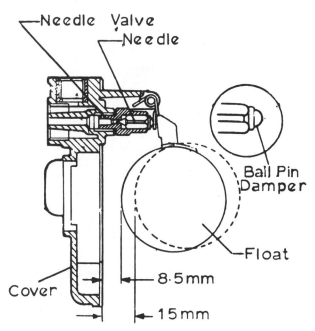

FIG 2 : 7   Float level, Weber carburetter

using compressed air, clean petrol and a small brush. **Do not use cloth as fibres may remain to clog jets or passages. Do not probe the jets as this will ruin their calibration.** If a jet has a blockage which cannot be cleared except by probing, renew the jet.

Renew the float assembly if it is damaged or leaking. Examine all jet seatings and seat faces. Similarly examine the tubes. Inspect all gaskets and seals and

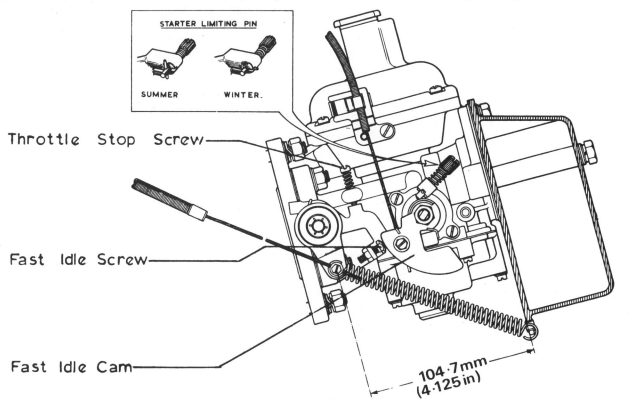

FIG 2 : 8   Adjustment screws, Zenith-Stromberg carburetters

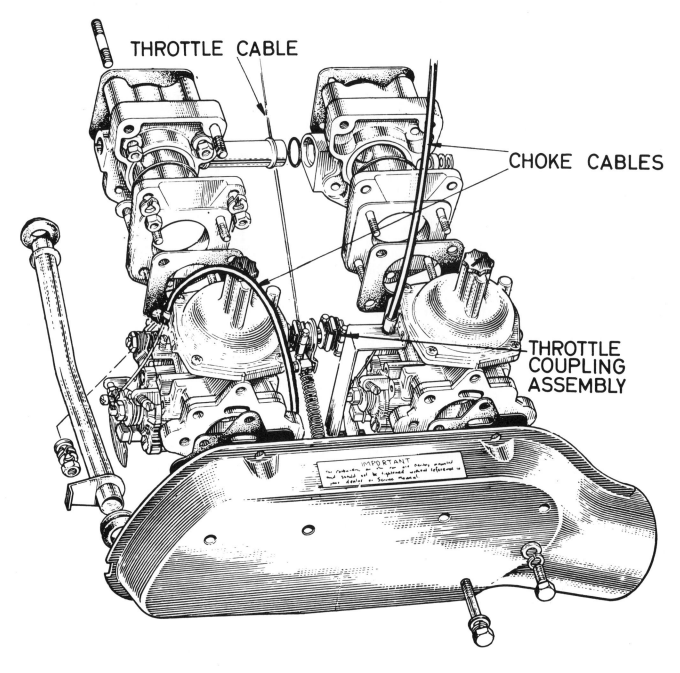

FIG 2:9   The air box, Zenith-Stromberg carburetters and adaptor blocks

renew as necessary. Clean the gauze filter and check that the gauze is not damaged. Shake the accelerator pump valve and confirm that the ball is free to slide.

Reassembling a carburetter :

Reverse the dismantling sequence. An owner should refer to his own notes and sketches but should also note the following points.

If new throttle plates are being fitted, check that the angle on them is stamped 79° 30′. If a throttle plate of a different angle is fitted, the low speed progression will be affected. Do not fully tighten the throttle plate retaining screws until, with the shaft fully closed to centralise the plates in the barrels, it can be confirmed

that they are correctly fitted. Fully tighten the screws but do not peen them until the concentricity has been checked as follows. Using a 0.05mm (0.002in) feeler gauge in the gap between the throttle body and the throttle plate (on the centre line of the plate and at right angles to the spindle) at the progression hole side of the barrel, hold the throttle control lever firmly against the stop screw and adjust the screw until a light pull will withdraw the feeler blade. Now trap the blade on the opposite side of the plate and, if the concentricity is correct, the same effort will withdraw the feeler blade with the stop screw in the same position. If the concentricity is incorrect, loosen the plate retaining screws and adjust the plate position. Repeat the

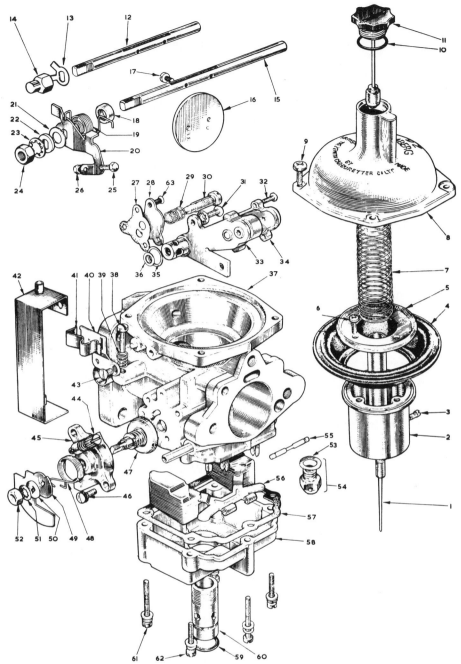

FIG 2 : 10   Components of a Zenith-Stromberg carburetter

Key to Fig 2 : 10   1 Needle   2 Air valve   3 Screw, locking   4 Diaphragm   5 Retaining ring   6 Screw
7 Spring, air valve   8 Cover, top   9 Screw and washer   10 Seal   11 Damper   12 Spindle, front   13 Tabwasher
14 Nut, sleeve   15 Spindle, rear   16 Throttle   17 Screw   18 Seal   19 Spring   20 Lever, throttle   21 Washer
22 Spacer   23 Lockwasher   24 Nut   25 Screw   26 Nut   27 Gasket   28 Plate, sealing   29 Spring
30 Screw   31 Screw   32 Screw   33 Body   34 Cover   35 Gasket   36 Gasket   37 Body   38 Screw
39 Spring   40 Bracket, rear carburetter   41 Clip   42 Bracket, front carburetter   43 Screw, brackets   44 Limiting
pin assembly   45 Housing, starter   46 Screw and washer   47 Starter disc   48 Spring   49 Cam   50 Washer
51 Washer   52 Nut   53 Gasket   54 Needle valve   55 Pin, float   56 Floats   57 Gasket   58 Float chamber
59 'O' ring   60 Plug, centre   61 Screw   62 Screw   63 Screw

procedure on the second plate. When concentricity has been achieved, peen the threaded ends of the screws to lock.

Having achieved throttle plate concentricity, check their synchronisation. Using the same feeler gauge blade, position it between the plate and the body on the progression hole side of the barrel. Hold the throttle control lever hard against the stop screw, adjust the screw until a light pull is required to withdraw the blade. Without disturbing the stop screw, the same effort should be required to withdraw the blade from between the second plate and throttle barrel. If concentricity has been achieved but not synchronisation, a twisted spindle is indicated or that the throttle plates are not identical. A twisted spindle should be corrected by holding one end and applying torque to the other end in the relevant direction.

When fitting the accelerator pump delivery valves, fit a ball 83 first then a weight 84 with the concave face to the ball and, finally, the retaining screws 85.

At the appropriate stage, check the float level. Refer to **FIG 2 : 7** and hold the carburetter cover vertically with the floats hanging down and with the tab which abuts the needle valve in light contact with the ball and perpendicular. If necessary, carefully bend the needle valve tab to achieve the 8.5mm dimension. Carefully bend the other tab to achieve the 15mm dimension (a stroke of 6.5mm).

When assembly has been completed, adjust the volume control screws open by one full turn as a primary setting. The throttle screw should be set one half turn in from the point at which it just contacts the stop lever.

Assemble the two carburetters to the air box and prime the retaining nuts with Loquic Primer N and fit the nuts using Loctite AV. Torque tighten the nuts to 1.08daNm (8lbf ft).

Weber carburetter air trumpets :

Commencing at engine No C22414, the trumpets are sealed with Hylomar SQ.32M compound. This precludes all unfiltered air from leaking into the carburetters. This sealing may be applied to earlier engines. Apply the Hylomar compound round the inner faces of the trumpet shoulders, fill the mating recesses in the carburetter air inlets with Hylomar compound, leave for 10 minutes to allow the compound to partially set and assemble the trumpets and air box to the carburetters.

2 : 8 *Zenith-Stromberg carburetter adjustments*

Starter limiting pins :

There are two positions (winter and summer) of the starter limiting pin which is the spring loaded knurl-headed pin located on the side of each cold start device housing. To adjust, push down and turn through 90°. In the winter position the pin will be horizontal and in the summer position, vertical as shown in the inset to **FIG 2 : 8**.

Idle mixture setting :

Idling mixture is adjusted to very fine limits during manufacture for best quality and driveability at the trimming screw and, consequently, is not a normal service adjustment. If idling mixture is suspect, refer the symptoms to a Lotus agent.

Fast idling :

The fast idling screws are incorporated in the cold start devices. They are factory-set and should not require attention. Should they be disturbed at any time, however, reset as follows.

Remove the carburetters as described in **Section 2 : 9**. Using the shank of a drill (size 0.60mm), in the bottom of the port directly below the spindle, hold the throttle plate open. With the choke in the fully rich position, adjust the fast-idle screw (see **FIG 2 : 8**) until it touches the fast-idle cam. Tighten the locknut securely and remove the drill shank. Refit the carburetter(s) as described in **Section 2 : 9**.

Synchronisation and idling speed setting :

When making these adjustments to the carburetters, the engine must be at normal operating temperature and the ignition timing, distributor points, sparking plugs and their gaps and the valve clearances must be

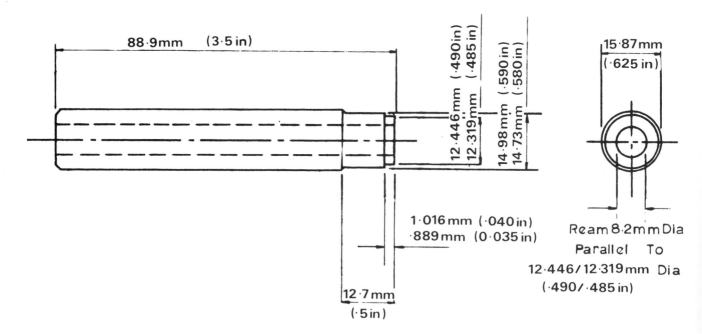

FIG 2 : 11 Lotus tool T339

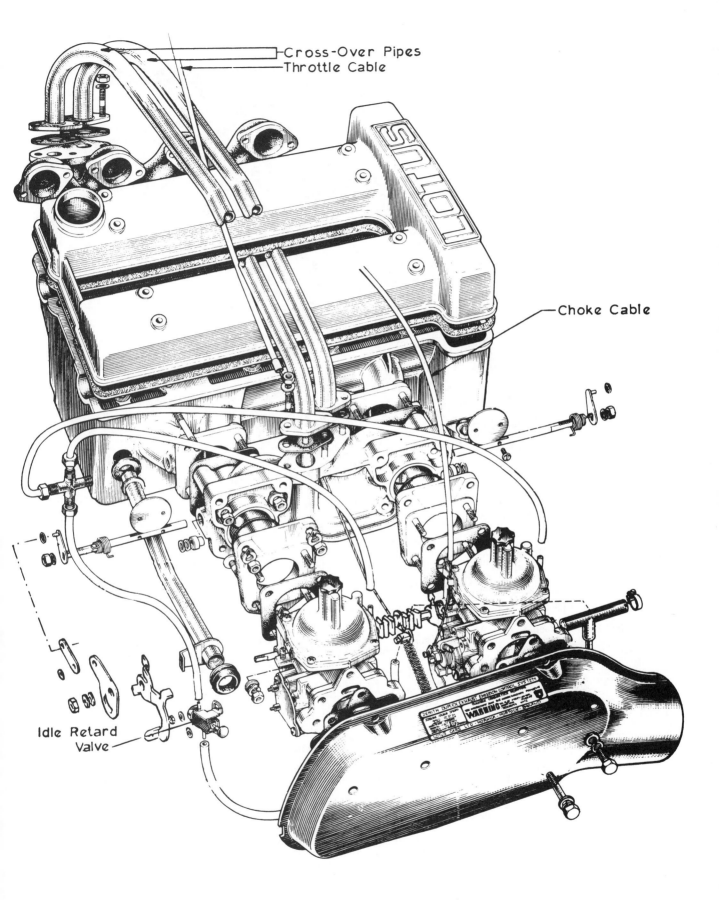

Cross-Over Pipes
Throttle Cable
Choke Cable
Idle Retard Valve

FIG 2 : 12   Exhaust emission control system layout

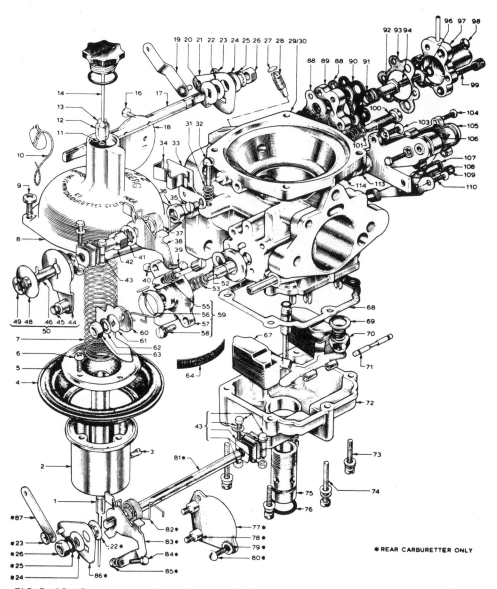

FIG 2:13   Components of an exhaust emission control Zenith-Stromberg carburetter

Key to Fig 2:13   1 Needle   2 Air valve   3 Locking screw   4 Diaphragm   5 Retaining ring   6 Screw   7 Air valve spring   8 Top cover   9 Top cover screw   10 Seal   11 Retaining ring   12 Bushing   13 Washer   14 Damper   16 Throttle screw   17 Spindle, front throttle   18 Throttle   19 Lever, throttle   20 Tabwasher   21 Plate   22 Spacer   23 Lockwasher   24 Washer   25 Lockwasher   26 Nut   27 Plug   28 Screw   29 Body, front carburetter   30 Body, rear carburetter   31 Spring   32 Throttle stop screw   33 Plate   34 Clip   35 Screw   36 Bush   37 Spring   38 Throttle stop lever   39 Fast-idle screw   40 Locknut   41 Lockwasher   42 Sleeve nut   43 Coupling   44 Plate   45 Screw   46 Sleeve   48 Spacing washer   49 Lockwasher   50 Sleeve and plate   52 Clip   53 Spring   55 Spring   56 Pin   57 Housing, starter   58 Housing screw   59 Housing assembly   60 Starter cam   61 Spacer   62 Lockwasher   63 Nut   64 Label   67 Float and arm   68 Gasket   69 Gasket   70 Needle seating   71 Fulcrum pin   72 Float chamber   73 Screw   74 Screw   75 Plug, centre   76 'O' ring   77 Mounting plate   78 Stud   79 Lockwasher   80 Screw   81 Spindle, rear throttle   82 Spring   83 Throttle stop lever   84 Fast-idle screw   85 Locknut   86 Lever mounting plate   87 Throttle lever   88 Gasket   89 Valve body   90 Diaphragm   91 Spring   92 Sleeve nut   93 Gasket   94 Retaining screw   96 'O' ring   97 Throttle bypass valve   98 Retaining screw   99 Retaining screw   100 Adjusting screw   101 Spring, adjusting screw   103 Screw, body   104 Screw, cover   105 Cover   106 Body   107 Valve   108 Bi-metal strip   109 Nut   110 Screw   113 Gasket   114 Gasket

in good order. There must be no leaks at the carburetter to manifold joints.

Refer to **FIG 2:9**. Loosen the throttle coupling W-clip clamps. Unscrew the throttle stop screws (see **FIG 2:8**) to allow the throttle plates to close completely and screw in these stop screws until they just touch the levers. Rotate each stop screw by one and a half turns to open the throttle plates by an exactly

equal amount to provide a datum from which the idling speed and synchronisation can be adjusted. Check that the fast-idle screws are clear of their cams or incorrect synchronisation may result. Check also that the choke lever is fully off against the stop with the choke control pushed fully in. To achieve this, adjust the coupling and cable as necessary. Remove the air box so that direct access to the carburetter inlets is available.

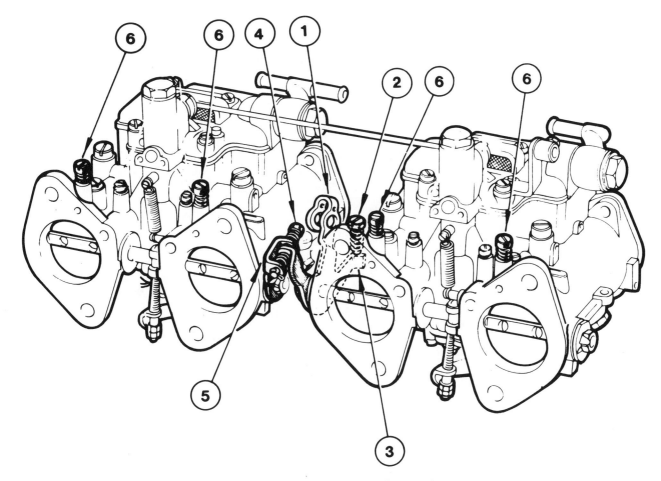

FIG 2:14 Adjustment screws, Dellorto carburetters

Synchronise the carburetters using either of the following methods.

1 Using a proprietary carburetter balancing tool (such as the Crypton Synchro Test), adjust the throttle stop screws until the air flows are equal and the idling speed is 800 to 900r/min. Tighten the throttle coupling clamps.

2 Alternatively, hold a length of flexible tubing with one end to the ear and the other at the mouth of each carburetter in turn. Adjust the throttle stop screws until the 'hiss' is the same at both carburetters and the idling speed is 800 to 900r/min.

Refit the air box and recheck the idling speed which should not be affected to an extent that takes it outside the range of idling speed specified.

Throttle lever setting :

Note that there is lost motion built into the throttle lever and coupling spindle assembly. This allows the throttle spindle to turn when the cold start device (and hence the fast-idle) is operated without pulling the throttle cable return spring.

Ignition timing when Zenith-Stromberg carburetters are fitted :

The static ignition timing for all models with **non-exhaust emission control** Zenith-Stromberg carburetters is 9° BTDC.

The static ignition timing for all models fitted with **exhaust emission control** Zenith-Stromberg carburetters (see **Section 2 : 11**) is 5° BTDC.

2 : 9 Zenith-Stromberg carburetter removal and refitment

Removal :

Release the clip and uncouple the air cleaner trunking from the air box. Remove the retaining bolts and dismount the air box. Discard the gaskets. Disconnect the throttle and choke cables. Uncouple the fuel supply pipe at the T-piece between the carburetters and blank off to preclude entry of dirt. Progressively release and remove the eight carburetter retaining nuts and washers.

Dismount the carburetters as an assembly taking care not to distort the synchronising linkage between them. Remove and discard the joint gaskets. If it is suspected that there is an air leak between the adaptor flanges and the adaptor blocks, check the 'O' rings after removing the securing nuts and dismounting them. New 'O' rings should always be fitted if the flanges have been disturbed and, when refitting the adaptor flange/carburetter assembly to the adaptor blocks, the 'O' rings must be carefully positioned and the nuts adjusted to give a gap of 1.78mm (0.070in) between the parts. To avoid distorting the flanges, do not overtighten the nuts.

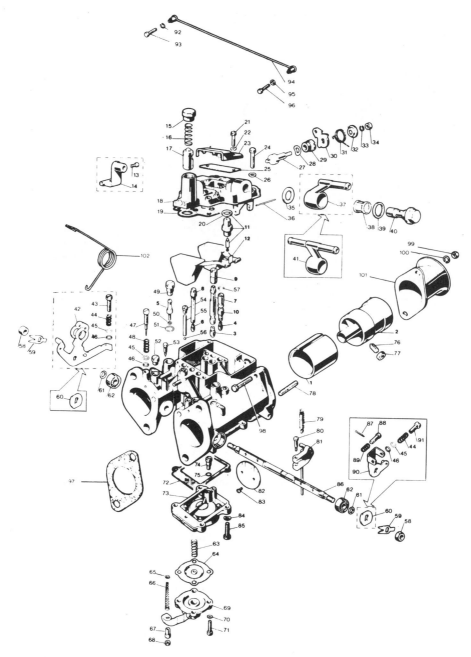

FIG 2 : 15 Components of a Dellorto carburetter

Key to Fig 2 : 15 1 Choke 2 Auxiliary venturi 3 Jet, main 4 Jet, idling 5 Jet, pump 6 Jet, starting 7 Emulsion tube, main 8 Emulsion tube, starting 9 Jet, main air corrector 10 Jet, idling air corrector 11 Needle valve 12 Float 13 Screw, securing choke cable 14 Support, choke cable 15 Plug, starting valve seat 16 Spring, starting valve 17 Starting valve 18 Cover, float chamber 19 Gasket, float chamber cover 20 Gasket, needle valve 21 Screw, jet cover fixing 22 Washer, spring 23 Jet cover 24 Screw, securing float chamber cover 25 Gasket, jet cover 26 Washer, spring 27 Control shaft, starting valve 28 Washer, spring 29 Plug, starting shaft 30 Control lever, starting valve 31 Return spring, starting lever 32 Bush, starting lever return spring 33 Washer, spring 34 Nut 35 Gasket, banjo union (fuel pipe) 36 Float pin 37 Union, banjo (fuel pipe) – rear carburetter 38 Filter, petrol 39 Gasket, plug securing banjo 40 Plug, banjo 41 Union, banjo (fuel pipe) – front carburetter 42 Lever, throttle control 43 Screw, adjusting 44 Spring, adjusting screw 45 Washer, plain 46 Gasket 47 Screw, idling mixture adjustment 48 Spring, screw 49 Plug, pump jet 50 Gasket, pump jet 51 Gasket, pump jet 52 Plug, progression holes inspection 53 Plug, pressure connection 54 Plug, delivery valve seat 55 Plunger, delivery valve 56 Outlet valve 57 Gasket 58 Nut 59 Plate, retaining 60 Spacer 61 Washer, distance 62 Ballbearing 63 Spring, pump diaphragm 64 Pump diaphragm 65 Washer 66 Spring, pump rod 67 Nut 68 Nut 69 Pump cover 70 Washer, spring 71 Screw, pump cover fixing 72 Gasket, pump body 73 Pump body 74 Inlet valve 75 Gasket, inlet valve 76 Screw, auxiliary venturi fixing 77 Nut, fixing screw 78 Stud 79 Spring, throttle shaft return 80 Screw, pump control lever fixing 81 Rod, lever and pump control 82 Throttle 83 Screw, throttle fixing 84 Washer, spring 85 Screw, pump body fixing 86 Shaft, throttle 87 Pin, split 88 Pin, control lever 89 Spring, pin 90 Control lever 91 Screw, control lever 92 Washer, spring 93 Screw, fixing 94 Rod 95 Washer, plain 96 Screw, securing cable 97 Gasket 98 Screw, horn retaining 99 Nut 100 Washer, spring 101 Air horn 102 Throttle spring

Refitment :

Remove all old gasket material from the joint faces. Use new gaskets and fit the carburetters as an assembly. Tighten the nuts progressively to avoid distortion. Reconnect the throttle and choke cables. Recouple the fuel pipe. Use new gaskets and refit the air box. Reconnect the flexible trunking.

2 : 10 *Zenith-Stromberg carburetter servicing*

Remove the carburetters as described in **Section 2 : 9**. The components of a **non-exhaust emission control** carburetter are shown in **FIG 2 : 10**.

Yellow service :

A **Yellow Pack A** is required for each carburetter. Each pack contains a float chamber gasket 57, and 'O' ring 59 for the float chamber plug 60, a needle valve washer 53 and a set of manifold to carburetter gasketing. Proceed as follows.

1 Remove the brass centre plug and drain the float chamber 58. Remove the float chamber screws 61 and washers, withdraw the float chamber vertically away from the body (to clear the float mechanism) and collect the float chamber gasket.

2 Unclip the float pin 55. To ensure correct reassembly, note carefully its top. Withdraw the floats 56. Unscrew the hexagon needle valve body 54 from the carburetter. Remove the 'O' ring from the centre plug and thoroughly clean the parts so far removed.

3 Refit the needle valve into the float chamber cover using the new washer which should have a thickness of 1.6mm and ensure that it is screwed tightly home. Inspect the float assembly for damage or distortion. Fit the float assembly, slide in the pivot pin and check the float height as described at the end of this section. Fit the new gasket, refit the float chamber and tighten the retaining screws working from the centre outwards.

4 Assemble the carburetters to the adaptor flange using new gaskets. Top up the oil level in the damper reservoirs as described in **Section 2 : 2**. Refit the carburetters as described in **Section 2 : 9** and carry out the relevant adjustments as described in **Section 2 : 8**.

Red service :

A **Red Pack B** is required for each carburetter. Each pack contains a float chamber gasket, an 'O' ring, a needle valve, a diaphragm 4, two throttle spindle seals 18, two temperature compensator seals 35 and 36 and a set of flange gasketing. Proceed as follows.

1 Carry out operations 1 and 2 of the Yellow service described earlier. Using the new washer, fit the new needle valve assembly.

2 Unscrew the damper assembly 11 from the cover. Remove the four screws 9 and carefully lift off the cover 8. Remove the air valve return spring 7 and extract the air valve and diaphragm assembly. Avoid the possibility of corrosion to the shaft from perspiration of the hands by lifting upwards with the diaphragm 4.

3 Drain the oil from the damper reservoir. Loosen the metering needle clamping screw 3 until the needle 1 can be withdrawn from the air valve 2. Put this carefully to one side to preclude damage.

4 Remove the four screws 6 which retain the diaphragm retaining ring 5 to the valve. Remove and discard the old diaphragm. Position the new diaphragm with the locating tag recessed into its aperture, align the retaining ring and fit and tighten the four screws tightly.

5 Refit the metering needle with the flat aligned with the locking screw. Using a straightedge laid lightly against the small shoulder on the needle, press the assembly into the air valve until the straightedge aligns the shoulder with the flat face of the valve. The locking screw may now be tightened lightly, taking care not to collapse the needle housing. **Carry out this operation accurately. Shoulder alignment is extremely critical.**

6 Correctly fitted, the needle will be biased towards the throttle and the shoulder of the needle will be exactly flush with the face of the air valve. Check that the needle is correctly fitted by holding the housing and very carefully pulling out the needle. The needle Part No will be seen on its shank.

7 Carefully enter the air valve and diaphragm assembly into the main body. Guide the needle into the jet with a finger in the intake. Locate the outer tag of the diaphragm in the aperture of the top body. To check the assembly, look down the centre of the air valve to confirm that the two depression transfer holes are parallel to the throttle spindle and that the needle is also biased towards the throttle. Refit the air valve return spring.

8 When refitting the cover, hold the air valve with finger or thumb in the intake and slide on the cover, locating the screw holes. Tighten the four cover screws evenly and check the movement of the valve. Freedom of movement over the full travel is essential and, when released from the uppermost position, the air valve should fall with a sharp metallic click onto the carburetter bridge.

9 Top up the damper reservoirs as described in **Section 2 : 2**. Undo the two screws 31 which retain the temperature compensator unit 33 to the main body 37 and withdraw the assembly. Remove the inner seal from the body and the outer seal from the valve. Change both seals and refit the assembly to the carburetter. Tighten the retaining screws evenly.

10 Remove the compensator cover 34 by removing the retaining screws 32 and check the freedom of the valve by lifting it off its seat. On releasing, it should return freely. Do not strain the bi-metal blade or attempt to alter the adjustment. Provided the valve is free, refit the cover and its retaining screws.

11 To renew the throttle spindle seals, remove the levers 20 (if relevant), carefully prise out the old seals (note which way round they are fitted), slide new seals along the spindle and press them into the body recess. The official tool for this operation is Lotus Tool T339 (see **FIG 2 : 11**).

12 Refit the carburetters as described in **Section 2 : 9** and carry out the relevant adjustment as described in **Section 2 : 8**.

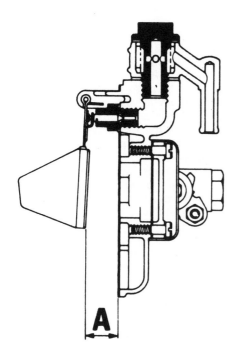

FIG 2 : 16   Float level, Dellorto carburetter

Key to Fig 2 : 16   A See text

Special parts :

Note that the following parts of the carburetter should not be changed or adjusted other than by a qualified service engineer: the jet assembly; the air valve and depression chamber cover; the position of the metering needle; the temperature compensator; and the air valve return spring loading.

With the exception of the air valve return spring which may be renewed if it is damaged, cracked or distorted, if nominated items require renewal or adjustment the relevant sub-assembly or the complete carburetter should be passed to a Lotus agent for attention or return to the makers.

Float height :

With the carburetter removed and the float chamber separated from the main body, invert the body and measure the highest point of the floats above the face of the main body with the fuel inlet needle on its seating. This should be 16 to 17mm. Take great care not to twist or distort the float arms to ensure that a constant fuel level will be maintained.

Should it be necessary to adjust the float height, carefully bend the tag which contacts the end of the needle ensuring that it remains strictly at right angles to the needle in the closed position.

2 : 11 *Exhaust emission control carburetters*

The layout of the exhaust emission control system (which is only available in conjunction with modified Zenith-Stromberg carburetters) is shown in **FIG 2 : 12**. The components of an exhaust emission control carburetter are shown in **FIG 2 : 13**.

The main difference between this and the standard system is in the induction system which is designed to avoid the deposition of wet fuel in the induction manifold. To achieve dry mixture, Zenith Duplex employs a main and a subsidiary gallery from the carburetters to the engine. The subsidiary gallery conducts mixture through an exhaust heated chamber (on the opposite side of the engine from the carburetters) and back to the main gallery. Two sets of throttles are provided. The primary throttles control the mixture supplied via the subsidiary gallery and the secondary throttles via the main gallery. The flow capacity of the primary system covers idling, acceleration up to about 80km/h (50mph), over-run and cruising conditions. At the point at which the primary system begins to restrict flow to the engine, a mechanical linkage picks up the secondary throttle and mixture is supplied via the main gallery. At this point the primary system is bypassed and flow conditions similar to an untreated engine operate.

Exhaust emission control engines are provided with a special ignition distributor which incorporates a vacuum retard capsule arranged to operate only when the throttles are closed (at idling and on over-run). This system is actuated by a valve on the rear carburetter which, when depressed by the throttle lever (in the closed position), connects the distributor vacuum capsule with the manifold depression.

Adjustments :

In addition to the normal adjustments (see **Section 2 : 8**), note that the adjusting screw on the rear carburetter for operation of the valve which actuates the distributor vacuum capsule is factory-set and will not normally require adjustment. Should it be disturbed, however, reset to give approximately 2.3mm (0.09in) movement on the valve plunger when the throttles are closing and approximately 0.4mm (0.016in) free play on the plunger when the throttles are closed.

Ignition timing with exhaust emission control carburetters :

The static ignition timing for an exhaust emission control engine is 5° BTDC.

Servicing :

The servicing procedures described in **Section 2 : 10** apply with, in addition at the mileage intervals stated in **Chapter 13**, renewal of the bypass valve gasket 88. Remove three securing screws 99, dismount the valve 97, discard the old gasket, position the new gasket and refit the valve.

The secondary throttle spindle seals should be renewed at the same time as the primary seals.

It is particularly important on exhaust emission control systems that there should be no air leaks. Gaskets, 'O' rings, and pipe joints and connections must be maintained in good order.

2 : 12 *Dellorto carburetter adjustments*

When making adjustments to the carburetters, the engine must be at normal operating temperature and the ignition timing, distributor points, sparking plugs and their gaps and the valve clearances must be in good order. There must be no air leaks at the carburetter to manifold 'O' ring gaskets.

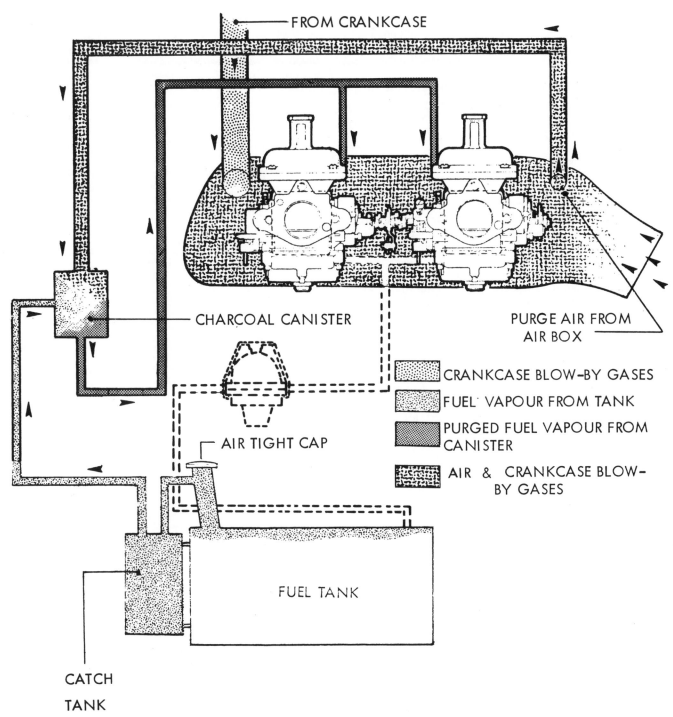

FIG 2:17 Evaporative loss control system layout

Dellorto carburetters are very similar in operation and appearance to Weber carburetters and, as in the case of Weber carburetters, adjustment of idling mixture, idling speed and carburetter synchronisation is carried out concurrently. The procedure is as follows.

1 Refer to **FIG 2:14**. Disconnect the throttle cable from lever 1. Back off the adjusting screw 2 so that it is clear of lever 3.

2 Release screw 4 in lever 5 to ensure that, when pressure is applied to lever 1, perfect closure of all throttle valves in both carburetters is achieved.

3 Still keeping the same pressure on lever 1, adjust screw 4 to hold the lever in that position. The throttle valves should all close perfectly.

4 Give one full turn to screw 2 so that it comes in contact with the lever 3. Fully close the mixture screws 6 then back each off by two full turns. Reconnect the throttle cable to lever 1.

5 Start the engine and allow it to reach normal operating temperature. Using screw 2, adjust the engine idling speed to 800 to 900r/min.

6 If the engine now runs evenly, adjust mixture

screws 6 to obtain regular running on all barrels. Turning the mixture screws inwards weakens the mixture and vice versa. Readjust the idling speed by means of screw 2.

Ignition timing when Dellorto carburetters are fitted

The static ignition timing should be 10° BTDC.

2 : 13 *Dellorto carburetter removal and refitment*

Removal :

Release the clip and separate the flexible trunking from the air box cover. Remove the retaining bolts and dismount the cover. Disconnect the throttle return spring, the throttle cable and the choke cable. Uncouple the fuel pipes from the carburetters and blank off the open ends to preclude entry of dirt.

Progressively release and remove the nuts and washers which secure the carburetters to the manifold. Carefully dismount the carburetters and air box as an assembly. Ensure that the throttle coupling between the carburetters is not strained or distorted. Remove the spacers and their 'O' rings from the mounting studs.

Refitment :

Reverse the removal sequence. Ensure that the 'O' rings are in good condition. Renew them if their serviceability is doubtful. Do not overtighten the retaining nuts or the 'O' rings will be flattened. There should be a clearance of 1.02mm (0.04in) between the spacers and the carburetter flanges.

On completion of refitment, carry out the adjustment procedure described in **Section 2 : 12**.

2 : 14 *Dellorto carburetter servicing*

Generally follow the procedures described in **Section 2 : 7** for the servicing of Weber carburetters, but refer to **FIG 2 : 15** and not to **FIG 2 : 6**.

To check and adjust the float chamber level, refer to **FIG 2 : 16**. With the float chamber cover in the vertical position, the tab should be in light contact with the needle and the dimension **A** (including the joint gasket) should be 14.5 to 15.0mm for DHLA 40 carburetters and 16.6 to 17.0mm for DHLA 40E carburetters. If, with DHLA 40 carburetters, there is persistent flooding, fit a 'Viton' tipped needle valve (B036E60602) and set the level to the DHLA 40E dimension. Adjustment of the level dimension is by carefully bending the tab in the relevant direction.

2 : 15 *Evaporative loss control*

The layout of the evaporative loss control system is shown in **FIG 2 : 17**. The system is designed to eliminate contamination of the atmosphere by evaporated fuel, a mandatory requirement in the USA.

The activated charcoal canister collects fuel vapour given off from the fuel tank vent. The tank filler cap is vapour tight. The catch tank (which cannot be filled through the main filler neck) prevents neat fuel from reaching the charcoal canister in conditions of extreme heat or violent vehicle manoeuvres. The vapour absorbed by the charcoal is purged by clean air while the engine is running via throttle edge drillings in the carburetter.

Ensure that the pipe joints are in good order at all times. At the mileage intervals stated in **Chapter 13**, renew the charcoal canister as a unit. No other servicing is normally required.

2 : 16 *Fault diagnosis*

(a) Insufficient fuel delivered

1 Fuel tank venting restricted or blocked
2 Fuel pipe(s) restricted or blocked
3 Air leak between tank and pump
4 Pump or carburetter filter blocked or restricted
5 Carburetter needle valve stuck
6 Pump valve(s) leaking
7 Pump diaphragm punctured
8 Pump diaphragm spring defective
9 Fuel vapourising in pipes due to heat

(b) Excessive fuel consumption

1 Adjustment(s) required to carburetter(s)
2 Fuel leakage
3 Choke control sticking
4 Carburetter float level(s) high
5 Pump pressure high
6 Dirty air cleaner
7 Idling speed too high
8 Excessively high engine temperature
9 Brakes binding
10 Tyres under-inflated

(c) Idling speed too high

1 Incorrect carburetter adjustment
2 Rich fuel mixture
3 Sticking throttle cable or linkage
4 Worn throttle plates or spindles

(d) Rough idling

1 Check 6 in (b); and 1 in (c)
2 Sparking plugs fouled or defective

(e) No fuel delivered

1 Check 1, 2, 3, 4 and 5 in (a)
2 Fuel tank empty
3 Defective pump or feed pipe

CHAPTER 3

THE IGNITION SYSTEM

3 : 1 Description

The ignition system consists of two circuits, LT (Low Tension) and HT (High Tension). The battery, ignition switch, coil primary winding, contact breaker and capacitor are wired into the primary; the coil secondary winding, sparking plugs and HT leads comprise the secondary HT circuit. The distributor housing carries the contact breaker assembly and centrifugal advance mechanism. The distributor is mounted on the right-hand side of the engine and is driven at half crankshaft speed from a skew gear on the jackshaft (see **Chapter 1, FIG 1 : 1**).

The distributor shaft turns the distributor cam and, through the drive plate, rotates the centrifugal weights. The cam can move relative to the shaft through a limited number of degrees. This movement is controlled by the outward centrifugal displacement of the weights acting against the tension of small springs and provides a specific range of ignition advance at increasing engine speeds. The cam lobes are in contact with the rubbing block of the pivoted breaker arm and open the points at timed intervals.

The HT voltage produced by the coil is fed via an HT lead to the centre point of the distributor cap. It is then directed to one of the four cap segments by the rotor arm. As HT surges are directed to one cap segment after another, individual HT cables conduct the current to the sparking plugs. The firing order is 1, 3, 4, 2.

A special cold start ignition coil is available and may be fitted to replace the standard coil. Fitment is covered in **Section 3 : 7**.

Cars which conform to USA exhaust emission control requirements are provided with emission control carburetters (see **Chapter 2, Section 2 : 11**) and are fitted with an ignition distributor which incorporates a vacuum actuated retard mechanism. The ignition is retarded by 5° only when the throttles are closed (at idling and on over-run).

3 : 2 Servicing

Distributor :

At the mileage intervals stated in **Chapter 13** check the condition and gap of the breaker points. Unclip the distributor cap for access.

Adjusting the points gap :

Remove the rotor arm and turn the engine until one of the cam lobes has opened the points to their full extent. Using clean feeler gauges, check the gap as

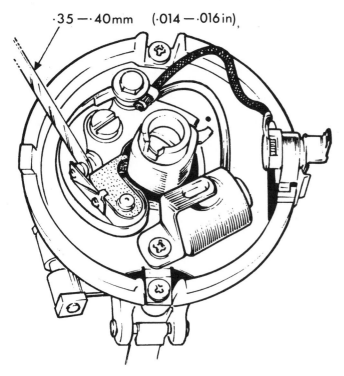

·35 — ·40mm   (·014 — ·016 in)

FIG 3:1   Checking the contact points gap

shown in **FIG 3:1**. The gap should be 0.35mm to 0.40mm (0.014 to 0.016in). To adjust the gap, loosen the fixed contact plate screw, adjust the position of the plate until the gap is correct, retighten the screw and recheck the gap.

Cleaning the points :

Use a fine carborundum stone or a special contact point file to polish the faces of the points and clean off with a cloth moistened in petrol. The pivoted point can be removed to assist cleaning but ensure that the contact faces are square to each other. If the points are badly pitted or burned, fit a new set.

Check that the moving point arm pivots freely. If necessary, remove the arm, polish the pivot with fine emerycloth, clean off and apply a single drop of engine oil to the pivot. Refit the arm.

Renewing the contact points :

Remove the distributor cap and the rotor arm. Remove both points.

Locate a new moving contact on the pivot pin and loosely fit the retaining screw. Locate the fibre washers on the terminal post and pivot pin and fit the breaker arm. Thread the insulating bush into the LT and capacitor lead eyelets before locating it on the terminal post with the end inside the spring eye. Adjust the points gap as described earlier.

Sparking plugs :

Refer to **Section 3 : 6**.

Ignition timing :

At the mileage intervals specified in **Chapter 13**, check the ignition timing with a stroboscopic light as described in **Section 3 : 5** and adjust as necessary.

3 : 3 Ignition faults

If the engine runs unevenly, set it running at about 1000 r/min and, taking care not to touch any metal parts of the plugs or leads, remove and refit each lead from its plug in turn. Doing this to a plug which is firing properly will accentuate the uneven running but will make no difference if the plug is not firing.

Trace the faulty plug, stop the engine and uncouple the plug lead. Restart the engine and carefully hold the lead so that its conductor is about 3mm (⅛in) from the cylinder head. A strong, regular spark will confirm that the fault lies with the sparking plug which should be removed and cleaned as described in **Section 3 : 6** or renewed if faulty.

If the spark is weak or irregular, check the condition of the lead and, if it is cracked or perished, renew it and repeat the test. Check also that the lead is making good contact at the distributor cap and plug terminals. If no improvement results, check that the inside of the distributor cap is clean and dry, that the carbon centre brush can be moved freely against its spring and that there is no sign of 'tracking' which can be seen as a thin black line between the electrodes or to some metal part in contact with the cap. 'Tracking' can only be cured by fitting a new cap.

If the engine will not start at all, check the spark at the plug leads as described earlier and, if no spark occurs when the engine is turned on the starter motor, test the continuity of the LT circuit as described next.

Testing the LT circuit :

Make up a test lamp from two lengths of wire, a bulb holder and a 12-volt 6W bulb. Fit crocodile clips to the ends of the wires. Check that the contact breaker points are clean and correctly set as described earlier and proceed as follows.

Disconnect the thin wire from the distributor terminal. Connect the test lamp between the end of this wire and the terminal. Switch on the ignition and turn the engine on the starter motor. If, when the contacts close, the lamp lights up and goes out when they open, the circuit is in order. If the lamp fails to light up, there is a fault in the LT circuit. Disconnect the lamp and reconnect the wire to the distributor. Use the test lamp to carry out the following tests with the ignition switched on.

Remove the wire from the ignition switch side of the coil and connect the test lamp between the end of this wire and a good earth. If the lamp fails to light up, it indicates a fault in the continuity between the battery and coil or a faulty ignition switch. Reconnect the wire if the lamp lights up.

Disconnect the wire from the coil that connects with the distributor. Connect the test lamp between the coil terminal and earth. If the lamp fails to light up, it indicates a fault in the primary winding and a new coil should be fitted. If the lamp lights up, reconnect it and disconnect its other end from the distributor. If the lamp does not light up when connected between the end of this wire and earth, it indicates a fault in this section of wire.

Capacitor :

The symptoms of a faulty capacitor are usually misfiring and poor starting. Check that the moving contact breaker spring is not weak or broken. If necessary, renew the points as described in **Section 3 : 2**. Remove the distributor cap and, with the ignition switched on, turn the engine with the starter motor. Bad arcing as the points open and close can indicate a defective capacitor. The best method of testing a suspect capacitor is by substitution of a new one.

3 : 4 *Removing and servicing the distributor*

Remove the distributor cap and disconnect the LT lead from the distributor. Remove the distributor clamp retaining bolt and carefully withdraw the distributor from the engine.

Dismantling :

1 Remove the rotor and the contact breaker points. Withdraw the LT terminal block from its slot in the distributor body. Remove the capacitor. Remove two screws and withdraw the contact breaker plate.
2 Disconnect and remove the centrifugal advance springs. Unscrew the centre screw and remove the cam. Remove the centrifugal weights. Drive out the retaining pin and remove the skew gear and thrust washer.
3 If the bearing bush is excessively worn, scored or otherwise unserviceable, use a suitable mandrel at the body end and drive out the bearing bush. The distributor components are shown in **FIG 3 : 2**.

Reassembly :

1 If the bearing bush was removed, soak a new bush in engine oil for 24 hours, insert the small diameter of the bush into the distributor body from the drive end and, using a suitable mandrel, press the bush fully home. Drill the oil hole in the new bush through the hole in the distributor body spigot and remove any burrs, swarf, etc.
2 Locate the spacer washer on the new distributor shaft and insert the shaft into the body. Locate a new thrust washer onto the shaft with the pips towards the gear. Press the new gear onto the shaft until it nips the thrust washer. With the assembly held tightly together, drill the shaft with a No 16 4.5mm (0.177in) diameter drill through the hole in the skew gear and peen-lock the retaining pin. Tap the end of the shaft with a soft hammer to flatten the thrust washer pips and establish the correct end float.
3 Locate the centrifugal weights on the action plate. Fit the cam, engaging the pivot pins in the weights and secure the cam with its centre screw. Fit the centrifugal springs taking care not to over-stretch them.
4 Fit the contact breaker plate and the capacitor. Slide the LT terminal block into its slot in the body. Fit the points and adjust the points gap as described in **Section 3 : 2**. Fit the rotor.

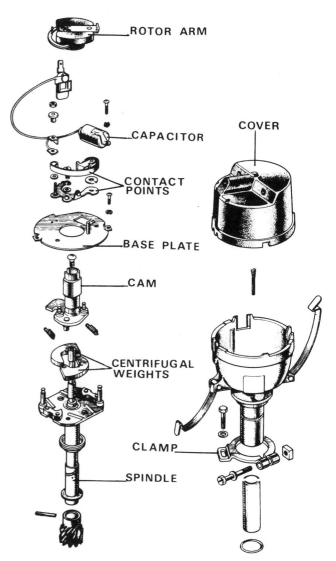

FIG 3 : 2 Components of the distributor

3 : 5 *Fitting and timing the distributor*

The timing marks are shown in **Chapter 1, FIG 1 : 7**.

Turn the engine until No 1 piston is approximately at TDC on the compression stroke (both valves closed). The crankshaft must now be set precisely to the static timing applicable to the carburetters fitted (see **Chapter 2, Sections 2 : 5, 2 : 8, 2 : 11** or **2 : 12**) by selecting top gear, releasing the handbrake and pushing the car backwards or forwards until the notch in the pulley aligns with the specified BTDC angle. Make sure that the car is on level ground and set the handbrake when the engine has been turned to the correct position.

Position the rotor with the electrode towards the distributor clip and fit the distributor with the LT terminal adjacent to the cylinder block. Note that, as the drive gears mesh, the rotor will turn clockwise into alignment with the No 1 HT cap electrode position.

Slacken the bolt and twist the clamp so that the hole is in line with the hole in the cylinder block. Fit and tighten the retaining bolt. Set the ignition timing as described later.

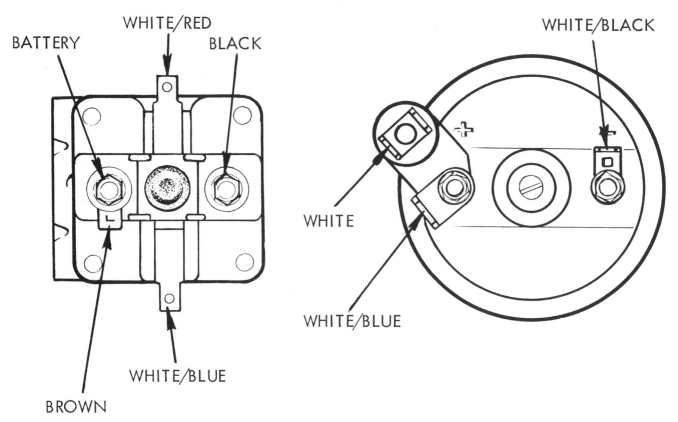

FIG 3:3 Cold start coil and solenoid connections (with generator)

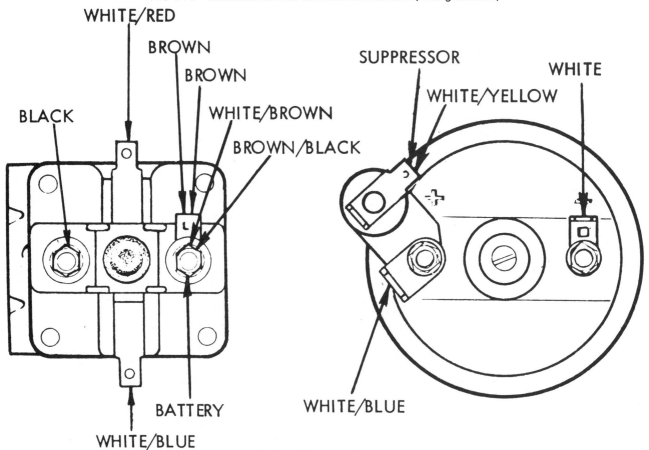

FIG 3:4 Cold start coil and solenoid connections (with alternator)

Static timing with a test lamp :

With the engine correctly set as described earlier, connect a 12-volt test lamp (see **Section 3 : 3**) between the terminal on the side of the distributor and earth. Switch on the ignition, slacken the distributor clamp and turn the distributor body until the lamp just lights. This indicates that the points are just firing No 1 cylinder. Without moving the distributor from this position, tighten the clamp bolt. The timing should now be checked using a stroboscopic light as described later or, if this equipment is not available, the check should be carried out by a suitably equipped service station.

Timing with a stroboscopic light :

This operation is carried out while the engine is running using a special timing light triggered from the No 1 cylinder ignition HT circuit in accordance with the equipment manufacturer's instructions.

Start the engine and allow it to warm up to normal operating temperature. Stop the engine and connect up the timing light. Restart the engine and point the light at the crankshaft pulley adjacent to the timing marks. Progressively increase the engine speed to 2500r/min observing the timing marks to confirm that the centrifugal mechanism advances the timing. At 2500r/min compare the actual timing with that tabulated at the end of this section for the relevant distributor Series number **plus the static timing angle**. Distributor Series numbers relate to the centrifugal advance characteristics and depend upon the car model and the carburetter fitted and reference should be made to **Chapter 2, Section 2 : 5, 2 : 8, 2 : 11,** or **2 : 12**. If necessary, adjust by slackening the clamp and turning the distributor in the appropriate direction. Tighten but do not overtighten the clamp bolt.

Distributor Series number	Centrifugal advance at 2500r/min*
40953	16.8°
41189	14.0°
41189A	14.0°
41225	14.0°
41225A	14.0°
41225 (ECE)	19.0°

*For the total advance, add the relevant static timing angle.

3 : 6 *Sparking plugs*

Recommended types :

If a **non-emission control carburetter** is fitted, use Champion N7Y plugs with their gaps set at 0.51 to 0.58mm (0.020 to 0.023in).

If an **emission control carburetter** is fitted, use Autolite AG32 plugs with their gaps set at 0.63mm (0.025in). For sustained high speed driving use Champion N7Y plugs in Elan models or Autolite AG22 plugs in Elan +2 models. The gap settings should be 0.63mm (0.025in) in each case.

Cleaning and renewal :

Inspect, clean and adjust the points gaps at the mileage intervals specified in **Chapter 13**. Renew the plugs at the mileage intervals recommended noting that this is particularly important in the case of exhaust emission control engines.

Have the sparking plugs cleaned on an abrasive-blasting machine and tested under pressure with the electrodes correctly set to the gap specified earlier. The electrodes should be filed until they are bright and parallel. The gap must always be set by bending the earth electrode. **Do not try to bend the centre electrode.**

If the plugs cannot be screwed in by hand, clean the cylinder head threads with a tap or use an old sparking plug with crosscuts down the threads. Torque tighten plugs to 3.25 to 3.79daNm (24 to 28lbf ft).

Inspection of the deposits on the electrodes can be helpful when tuning. Normally, from mixed periods of high and low speed driving, the deposit will be powdery and range from brown to greyish-tan in colour. There will also be slight wear of the electrodes. Long periods of constant speed driving or low speed city driving will give white or yellowish deposits. Dry, black fluffy deposits are due to incomplete combustion and indicate running with a rich mixture, excessive idling and, possibly, defective ignition. Overheated plugs have a white, blistered look about the centre electrode and the earth electrode may be badly eroded. This may be due to poor cooling, incorrect ignition or sustained high speeds with heavy loads.

Black, wet deposits indicate oil in the combustion chambers from worn piston rings, valve stems or guides. Plugs which run hotter may alleviate the problem but the cure is an engine overhaul.

3 : 7 *Cold start ignition coil*

A special coil is available to replace the standard coil. Fitment is straightforward but the connections differ between cars fitted with a DC generator (see **Chapter 11, Section 11 : 4**) and those fitted with an alternator (see **Chapter 11, Section 11 : 5**). The appropriate connections are shown in **FIGS 3 : 3** and **3 : 4**.

3 : 8 *Fault diagnosis*

(a) Engine will not fire

1 Battery discharged
2 Distributor points dirty, pitted or out of adjustment
3 Distributor cap dirty, cracked or 'tracking'
4 Centre contact not touching rotor arm
5 Faulty wire or loose connection in LT circuit
6 Rotor arm defective
7 Defective coil
8 Broken contact breaker spring
9 Contact breaker points stuck open
10 Defective ignition switch

(b) Engine misfires

1 Check 2, 3, 5 and 7 in (a)
2 Weak contact breaker spring
3 HT cable(s) cracked or perished
4 Sparking plug(s) loose
5 Sparking plug insulation cracked
6 Sparking plug gaps incorrectly set
7 Ignition timing too far advanced
8 Fouled sparking plugs
9 HT cables incorrectly connected

NOTES

CHAPTER 4

THE COOLING SYSTEM

4 : 1 *Description*

The cooling system is pressurised and thermostatically controlled. Coolant circulation is assisted by a belt driven centrifugal pump which is mounted at the front of the engine. A cooling fan draws air through the radiator; it may be either a mechanical unit mounted on the pump pulley or an electrically operated unit.

Coolant circulation is shown diagrammatically in **FIG 4 : 1**. At normal operating temperatures the thermostat is open and coolant returns from the cylinder head to the top of the radiator. At lower temperatures the thermostat is closed and coolant bypasses the radiator and returns to the pump inlet. This provides a rapid warm-up.

4 : 2 *Servicing*

Belt tension :

At the mileage intervals stated in **Chapter 13**, check and, if necessary, tension the pump drive belt as described in **Section 4 : 3**. Renew the belt if its condition is doubtful.

Topping-up the coolant level :

With the engine cool, remove the radiator filler cap and, if necessary, top up to the bottom of the filler neck. Remove the overflow bottle (if fitted) and, after rinsing out, add clean coolant to a capacity of 0.57 litre (1 pint) on Elan or a depth of at least 25mm (1in) on +2 models. The overflow tube must be an airtight fit at both the bottle and the radiator and the end of the tube must be submerged in coolant.

Draining the system :

The cooling system should periodically be drained, flushed and refilled. If antifreeze is in use, it may be collected and filtered for re-use, but it should be discarded after two winters.

Remove the radiator filling cap, set the heater control to maximum heat, open the drain taps at the bottom of the radiator and at the lefthand side of the cylinder block.

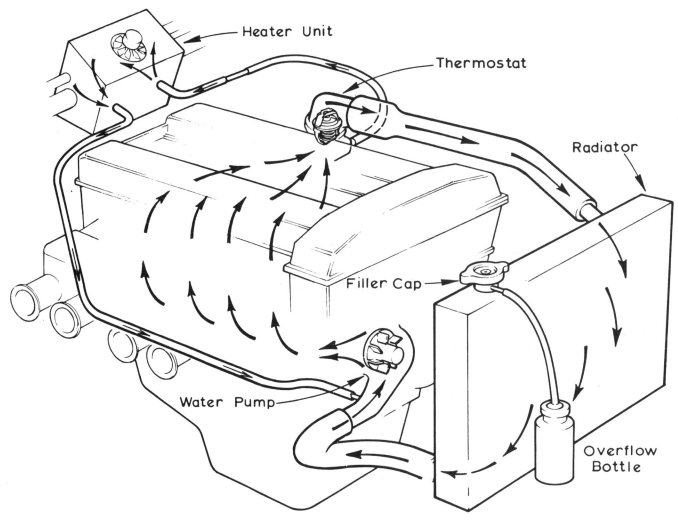

FIG 4 : 1 Diagrammatic layout showing the coolant circulation

Heater Unit

Thermostat

Radiator

Filler Cap

Water Pump

Overflow Bottle

Flushing :

Use a hose to run clean water into the radiator filler until it runs clean at the drain taps. Close the taps, fill the system with water and run the engine until the thermostat opens. Stop the engine and drain the system again before the sediment has time to settle. To avoid burns when removing the cap from a warm radiator, cover the cap with a cloth and remove the cap carefully. Repeat the flushing cycle, close the taps and refill the system with antifreeze (see **Section 4 : 8**).

Filling the system :

Ideally, the front of the car should be raised slightly to ensure that the minimum of air is drawn into the system during filling. Close the drain taps and set the heater control at maximum heat. Fill the system to the level of the radiator filler neck, pinching the radiator top hose while doing so, to expel air. Check the coolant in the overflow bottle (if fitted) as described earlier. Run the engine and check for leaks.

Hoses and clips :

Periodically check the condition of the hoses (including those to and from the heater) and the tightness of their clips.

4 : 3 *Pump drive belt tension and renewal*

Belt tension is correct when it can be deflected a total of 12.5mm ($\frac{1}{2}$in) with firm thumb pressure (see **FIG 4 : 2**). To adjust, loosen the two generator (or alternator) mounting bolts and swivel the unit in the appropriate direction. Tighten the bolts and recheck the tension.

To renew the belt, release the tension fully and disengage the belt from the pulleys. Fit the new belt and tension it as described earlier.

4 : 4 *Radiator removal*

Remove the bonnet as described in **Chapter 12, Section 12 : 2**. Drain off the coolant as described in **Section 4 : 2**. Retain the coolant if antifreeze is in use. Release the clips and pull off the hoses from the top and bottom radiator fittings. Pull off the overflow hose (if fitted). From each side of the radiator, remove the two bolts, nuts and washers which retain it to its mounting brackets. Lift out the radiator taking care that the fan blades do not damage the matrix.

Refitting :

Reverse the removal sequence. Check that the fan is between 3.2 and 5.1mm (0.125 and 0.20in) clear of the radiator matrix. Refill the system as described in **Section 4 : 2**.

4 : 5 *The water pump*

The components of the pump are shown in **FIG 4 : 3**.

Removal :

Refer to **Chapter 1, Section 1 : 10** and remove the engine front cover. With the cover on a bench, withdraw the pump bearing retainer clip from the slot in the housing. Remove the pulley hub from the shaft. Using a suitable press, press the impeller, seal, slinger, shaft and bearing assembly out of the housing. Press the impeller off the shaft. Remove the seal from the shaft. Carefully split the slinger bush with a chisel and detach it from the shaft. Remove the insert from the front cover.

Clean and examine all parts and renew as necessary. Note that a new interchangeable impeller is available with a rubber-backed seal. Ensure that the rubber-backed disc between the impeller and the main seal is fitted correctly. The carbon thrust face of the disc must face the thrust face of the main seal.

Refitting :

Press the shaft and bearing assembly into the housing until the groove in the shaft is aligned with the groove in the housing. Fit a new bearing retainer clip in the bearing and housing groove. Press the pulley hub onto the front end of the shaft until the end of the shaft is flush with the pulley hub face. Fit a new slinger bush, flanged end first, onto the rear of the shaft until the flanged end is between 3.17 and 5.08mm (0.125 and 0.200in) from the end of the bearing. Fit a new seal onto the slinger bush with the carbon thrust face towards the impeller and press into the housing as shown in **FIG 4 : 4**.

Fit new 'O' rings to the insert and fit the insert to the cover. Press the impeller onto the shaft. Ensure that the vanes are undamaged. With the impeller correctly fitted, there should be between 0.51 and 0.76mm (0.02 and 0.03in) clearance between the impeller vanes and the housing. Refit the cover to the engine as described in **Chapter 1, Section 1 : 10**.

4 : 6 *The thermostat*

Removal :

Refer to **Section 4 : 2** and drain off sufficient coolant to lower the level to below that of the thermostat housing. Release the top coolant outlet hose, remove the bolts and washer which retain the outlet to the cylinder head and lift out the thermostat.

Testing :

Clean the thermostat and immerse it in a container of cold water together with a zero to 100°C (212°F) thermometer. Heat the water, keeping it stirred, and note the temperature at which the thermostat opens. The standard unit is set to open at 78°C (173°F). The

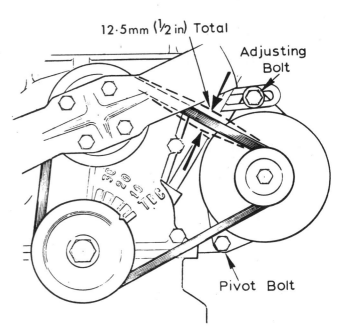

FIG 4 : 2 Drive belt adjustment

unit should close tightly when removed from the hot water and submerged in cold water. Renew the thermostat if it is defective.

Alternative thermostats are available. For hot climates, the setting is 71°C (160°F) and, for cold climates 88°C (190°F).

Refitting :

Reverse the removal sequence.

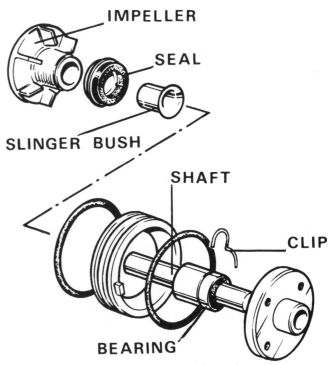

FIG 4 : 3 Components of the coolant pump

4:7 The electric cooling fan

The electric cooling fan is only fitted as standard to certain models but may be installed in other models as described in **Section 4:9**. The fan unit and mounting details are shown in **FIG 4:5**.

Removal:

Dismount the bonnet as described in **Chapter 12, Section 12:2**. Disconnect the battery and release the two motor cables from their connections at the fuse unit and the thermal control switch. Support the fan and motor assembly and release the three bolts securing it to the mounting bracket. The bracket may be removed by releasing the fixings at each side.

Refitting:

Reverse the removal sequence.

Thermal switch:

If the fan does not operate correctly to hold a normal coolant temperature, the thermal switch should be checked and, if necessary, adjusted. If defective, a new thermal switch must be fitted as described later.

The thermal switch should start (cut-in) the motor at a coolant temperature of 90°C (195°F) when either a 71°C or a 78°C thermostat is fitted or at 95°C when an 88°C thermostat is installed. Adjustment of the **Kenlowe** switch is made at the screw shown in **FIG 4:5 (inset)**. **The centre screw on the switch relates to its contact gap setting and must not be touched.**

The following procedures apply only to the **Kenlowe** switch. Refer any problems with an **Otter** switch (see **FIG 4:6**) to a Lotus agent.

Adjustment to cut-in at a higher temperature:

Run the engine at idling until the fan cuts in. When this occurs, turn the adjusting screw anticlockwise until the fan cuts out. Use no undue pressure in either a downward or a sideway direction.

Leave the fan to cut in again at the higher temperature and, if necessary, repeat the adjustment sequence until the correct temperature as shown on the panel gauge is attained.

If the adjusting screw has been turned more than two full turns it may be necessary to turn the screw in a clockwise direction to recalibrate the differential (the range between cut-in and cut-out). It will only be necessary to turn the screw by one half of the last anticlockwise adjustment made.

Adjusting to cut-in at a lower temperature:

Run the engine at idling speed. When the panel gauge reaches the temperature at which the fan is required to cut-in, turn the adjusting screw clockwise until the fan starts. Do not use undue pressure downwards or sideways. Note the amount of adjustment made. If more than one full turn was necessary, the differential may have been extended. To correct this, turn the screw anticlockwise by one third of the clockwise adjustment made. Clockwise adjustment should not exceed three full turns.

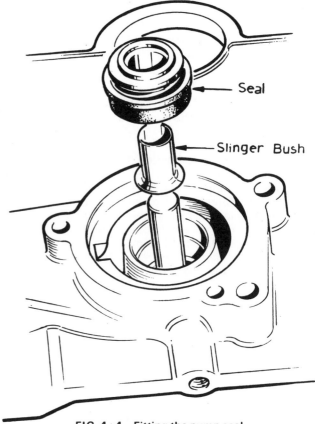

FIG 4:4   Fitting the pump seal

Thermal switch renewal:

The original **Kenlowe** switch is no longer available and, if defective, must be replaced by a current **Otter** switch.

Drain the radiator and disconnect the battery. Refer to **FIG 4:6** and, using a hole saw, cut a 21.43mm ($\frac{27}{32}$in) diameter hole in the front lefthand corner of the top of the radiator. Insert the grommet and fit the new switch. Note that this joint must be dry. Shorten the existing cable to reach the new switch. Attach the two leads to the plug and fit the plug to the switch.

Remove the defective **Kenlowe** switch and seal the hole with the blank provided with the new unit. Refill the cooling system and reconnect the battery.

4:8 Frost precautions

The use of antifreeze at all times is recommended since, apart from it providing protection from frost in relevant conditions, the correct solution will inhibit corrosion in the cooling system. Use an ethylene-glycol type of antifreeze of reputable make in the proportions recommended by the maker for the degree of frost protection required.

The recommended proportions should be measured into a separate container and the cooling system filled from this and not by adding the chemical directly into the radiator. After two winters' use, discard the antifreeze and, after flushing the system as described in **Section 4:2**, refill with fresh solution.

If antifreeze is not used, it must be remembered that the action of the thermostat will delay circulation of

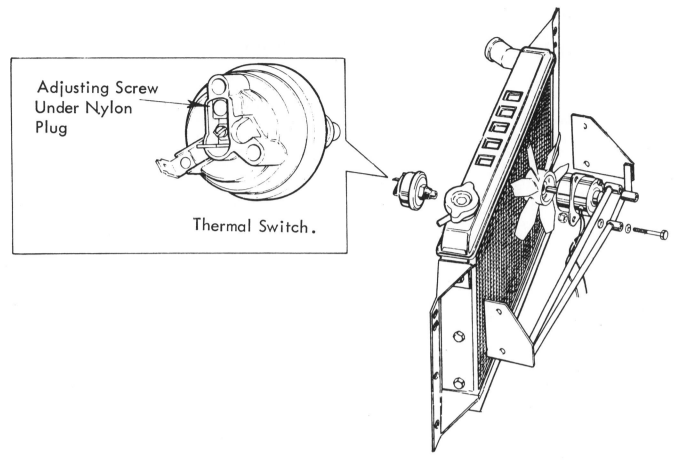

Adjusting Screw
Under Nylon
Plug

Thermal Switch.

FIG 4 : 5 The electric fan and thermal switch

warm coolant to the radiator which may consequently freeze after the engine has been started.

4 : 9 *Modifications*

If necessary to improve engine cooling, the following modifications can be carried out by an owner.

Thermostat of lower rating :

Refer to **Section 4 : 6**.

Outer fan :

An outer fan which converts an existing belt-driven two-blade fan into a four-blade unit may be fitted.

Electric fan conversion :

An electric fan may be fitted to models not so equipped.

Drain the cooling system. Refer to **FIG 4 : 5**. Fit the fan to the motor and bolt the assembly to the mounting bracket so that the fan will be adjacent to the radiator. Bolt the bracket to the radiator using the lower of the two mounting holes and the existing fittings. Drill through the upper mounting hole and attach to the radiator flange with a bolt, washer and self-locking nut at each side.

Cut out a 38mm (1.50in) section from the middle of the top radiator hose and insert the adaptor. Secure

with two clips. Screw the thermal control switch into the adaptor. Ensure that the fit is tight.

The fan motor has two cables. Cut the longer cable to a length of 61cm (24in) and fit a ring terminal to it. Connect this to the main earth bobbin adjacent to the lefthand suspension mounting upright. Connect the other cable to one terminal on the thermal switch. Use the cut piece of cable with 6.35mm (0.25in) 'Lucar' terminal and sleeve fitted to each end to connect between the remaining thermal switch terminal and an 'ignition live' terminal on the fuse box. Check that the fan and switch operate correctly.

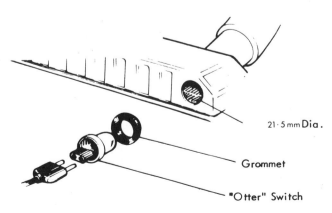

21·5mm Dia.

Grommet

"Otter" Switch

FIG 4 : 6 Fitting a new thermal switch

4 : 10 *Fault diagnosis*

(a) Internal coolant leakage

1 Loose cylinder head nuts
2 Faulty cylinder head gasket'
3 Cracked cylinder head
4 Cracked cylinder block

(b) Poor circulation

1 Radiator matrix blocked
2 Engine cooling passages restricted
3 Low coolant level
4 Slack drive belt
5 Defective thermostat
6 Perished or collapsed hose(s)

(c) Corrosion

1 Impurities in the coolant
2 Infrequent draining and flushing

(d) Overheating

1 Check (b)
2 Low oil level, sludge in sump
3 Faulty radiator cap seal
4 Tight engine
5 Choked exhaust system
6 Slipping clutch
7 Incorrect valve timing
8 Incorrect ignition timing
9 Mixture too weak
10 Electric fan (if fitted) inoperative

(e) Electric fan inoperative

1 Fuse blown
2 Thermal switch defective or setting incorrect
3 Discontinuity in wiring
4 Fan motor defective

CHAPTER 5

THE CLUTCH

5 : 1 Description

The clutch is a single dry-plate assembly and is mounted on the flywheel. The driven plate operates directly on the rear face of the flywheel, the actuating force being provided to the pressure plate by a diaphragm spring.

When the clutch is engaged, the driven plate, which is splined to the gearbox input shaft, is nipped between the pressure plate and the flywheel, is caused to rotate with the flywheel and transmits torque to the gearbox. The clutch is disengaged when the pressure plate is withdrawn from the driven plate by the clutch pedal being depressed. The clutch pedal operates the clutch release lever hydraulically by actuating the piston in the master cylinder and forcing fluid via a pipeline to actuate a piston in the slave cylinder which is mounted on the clutch housing as shown in **FIG 5 : 1**. The release bearing is a special ballbearing with an elongated outer ring which presses directly against the diaphragm spring when the clutch is being disengaged. The bearing is mounted on the release arm which pivots at the gearbox casing. The components of the clutch and release mechanism are shown in **FIG 5 : 2**.

Access to the clutch requires removal of the engine from the car as described in **Chapter 1, Section 1 : 16**.

5 : 2 Servicing

At the mileage intervals recommended in **Chapter 13**, check the fluid level in the master cylinder reservoir. Top up, if necessary, to within 12.5mm (0.50in) of the top. Clean off around the reservoir cap before removing it and check that the air vent is clear. Use only Castrol Girling Brake and Clutch fluid (crimson) as used in the braking system.

At the recommended mileage intervals, check the clutch free play as described in **Section 5 : 3** and adjust if necessary. Also check this adjustment if the clutch fails to engage or disengage correctly.

5 : 3 Clutch adjustment

Refer to **FIG 5 : 1**. The clutch is correctly adjusted when the clearance between the slave cylinder pushrod adjusting nut and the release arm is 2.03mm (0.08in) after the pedal has returned from a full length of travel.

To adjust, disconnect the retracting spring, release the locknut and, holding the pushrod from turning by

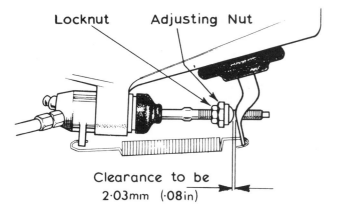

FIG 5 : 1 Clutch adjustment

the flats provided, turn the adjusting nut until the required clearance is obtained. Tighten the locknut and reconnect the retracting spring.

5 : 4 *Removing and dismantling the clutch*

1 Refer to **Chapter 1, Section 1 : 16** and remove the engine from the car. Dismount the clutch assembly by progressively releasing the six bolts which secure the clutch cover to the flywheel and withdraw the assembly from the locating dowels.

2 Refer to **FIG 5 : 2**. Disconnect the retracting spring on the slave cylinder, remove the rubber gaiter from the arm and clutch housing, noting carefully the way in which it is assembled. Remove the two springs from the clutch fork.

3 Remove the clutch bearing with the bearing retainer. Remove the release fork bearing link and the release arm by withdrawing into the clutch housing.

4 Hold the release bearing and hub with the bearing facing downwards and tap the hub sharply on a block of wood to release the bearing from the hub.

Servicing :

Thoroughly clean all parts except for the driven plate and the release bearing. The bearing must only be wiped clean as solvents would wash out the internal lubrication.

The clutch cover, spring and pressure plate assembly is an integral unit and no dismantling of it should be attempted. If any part of it is defective, the assembly

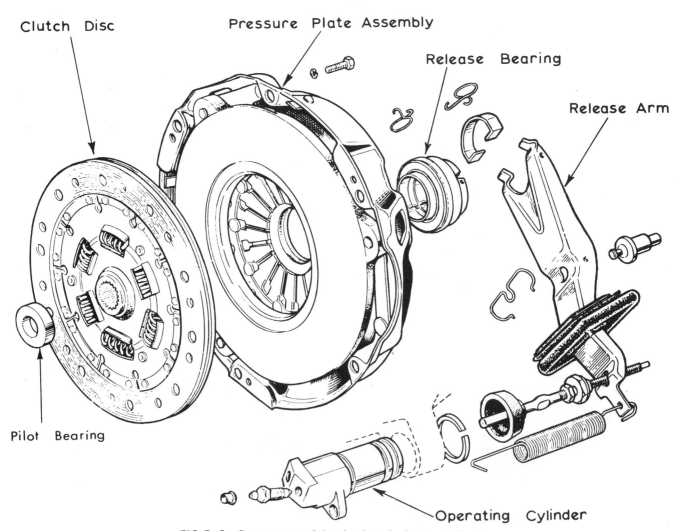

FIG 5 : 2 Components of the clutch and release mechanism

must be renewed as a complete unit. If the assembly is being renewed, fit a new driven plate at the same time.

Inspect the rear face of the flywheel with which the driven plate mates. Small marks on the surface are acceptable. Deeper scoring may be removed by judicious machining or the flywheel should be renewed. Check the pressure plate for scoring or damage. Check that the face is flat and true. Check the diaphragm spring for cracks or excessive wear of the fingers. Check the release bearing for roughness when it is pressed and turned by hand.

Check the driven plate for loose rivets and broken or very loose hub springs. The friction linings should be well proud of the rivets and have a light colour with a polished glaze through which the material grain is clearly visible. A dark glazed deposit indicates oil on the facings. This contamination cannot be corrected and a new or refaced plate must be fitted. Any signs of oil in the clutch dictates examination of the crankshaft rear oil seal as described in **Chapter 1, Section 1 : 18**.

5 : 5 *Assembling and refitting the clutch*

1 Fit the release bearing onto the hub with the bearing facing forwards (see **FIGS 5 : 2** and **5 : 3**). Ensure that the bearing is pressed squarely onto the hub shoulder. Refit it to the release arm following the reverse of the removal sequence and greasing the points shown in **FIG 5 : 3**.

2 The driven plate must be aligned with a dummy mainshaft tool when it is refitted against the flywheel. Fit the special tool through the clutch assembly and the driven plate and offer up the whole unit to the flywheel. Engage the tool into the crankshaft pilot bush.

3 Locate the assembly on the dowels. Fit the bolts and tighten them alternately and evenly. Finally, torque tighten them to 1.63 to 2.03daNm (12 to 15lbf ft). Remove the alignment tool. Refit the engine as described in **Chapter 1, Section 1 : 16**. On completion, adjust the clutch free play as described in **Section 5 : 3**.

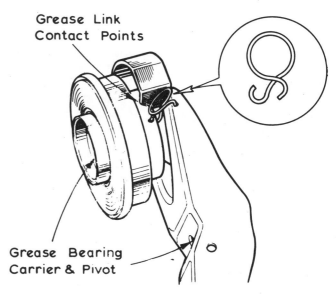

FIG 5 : 3   Release mechanism grease points

5 : 6 *Servicing the hydraulic system*

The components of the master cylinder are shown in **FIGS 5 : 4** and **5 : 5** and those of the slave cylinder in **FIG 5 : 6**.

Master cylinder removal, Elan models :

Uncouple the hydraulic pipe from the master cylinder and blank off to preclude entry of dirt and loss of fluid. Remove the splitpin and the clevis pin and separate the pushrod from the clutch pedal. Remove the retaining nuts and dismount the master cylinder.

Note that this procedure also applies to the removal of the brake master cylinder on Elan (but not on Elan +2) models.

Master cylinder removal, Elan +2 models :

Remove the pedal box as described in **Chapter 10, Section 10 : 10**. With the pedal box assembly on a

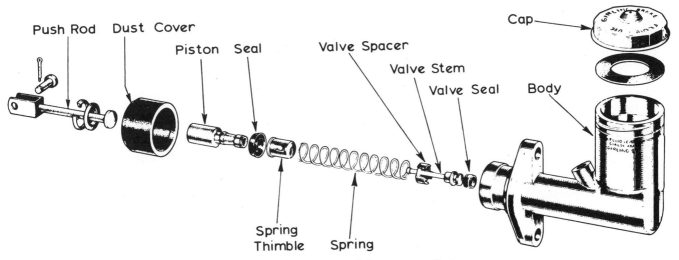

FIG 5 : 4   Components of the master cylinder

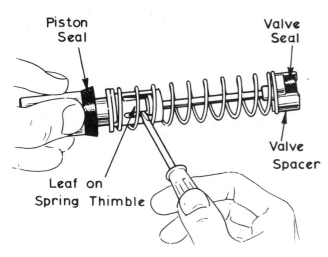

FIG 5 : 5   Dismantling the piston seals

bench, remove the retaining nuts and bolts and dismount the master cylinder from the pedal box.

Overhauling the master cylinder :

Note that the dismantling and reassembly procedures which follow also apply to the master cylinder of the single line braking system.

Dismantling the master cylinder :

Use long-nosed pliers and remove the retaining circlip. Extract the dished washer and the pushrod. Withdraw the plunger assembly. Dismantle the plunger assembly by lifting the thimble leaf over the shouldered end of the plunger as shown in **FIG 5 : 5**. Depress the plunger return spring and allow the valve stem to slide through the elongated hole in the thimble so releasing the spring load. Remove the thimble, spring and valve complete. Detach the valve spacer. Collect the spacer spring washer from under the valve head. Remove the seal.

Thoroughly clean all internal parts in hydraulic fluid or in methylated spirit. Inspect for excessive wear, scoring, corrosion or distortion and renew as necessary. Discard all seals and fit new parts from the appropriate service kit.

Assembling the master cylinder :

Observe absolute cleanliness to preclude contamination by grease, oil or dirt. Assemble all internal parts wetted with hydraulic fluid.

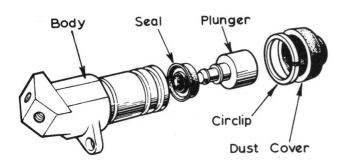

FIG 5 : 6   Components of the slave cylinder

Refit the valve seal so that the flat side is correctly seated on the valve head. Locate the spring washer with the domed side against the underside of the valve head and held in position by the valve spacer (the legs of which face towards the valve seal). Refit the plunger return spring and depress it until the valve stem engages through the elongated hole of the thimble. Ensure that the stem is correctly located in the centre of the thimble. Check that the spring is still central on the spacer. Fit a new plunger seal with the flat face against the the plunger face. Fit a new plunger end seal.

Insert the smaller end of the plunger into the thimble until the thimble leaf engages under the shoulder. Press home the thimble leaf. Insert the plunger assembly into the cylinder bore. Fit the pushrod, washer and circlip. Check that the circlip is fully engaged in its groove.

Refitting the master cylinder, Elan and Elan +2 models :

Reverse the removal sequence in each case. On completion of the refitment, bleed the clutch system as described in **Section 5 : 7** and, additionally in the case of Elan +2 models, bleed the braking system as described in **Chapter 10, Section 10 : 12**.

Slave cylinder removal :

Disconnect the retracting spring. Remove the circlip securing the cylinder in the lug on the clutch housing. Uncouple the hydraulic pipe and blank off to prevent loss of fluid. Remove the dust cover. Hold the pushrod and pull the cylinder forward from its location.

Dismantling the slave cylinder :

Apply low pressure air to the cylinder pipe connection and gently blow out the piston. Pull the seal from its location on the spigot end of the piston. Discard the seal.

Clean the internal parts in hydraulic fluid or in methylated spirit. Reject damaged, scored or excessively worn parts.

Assembling the slave cylinder :

Observe absolute cleanliness to preclude contamination by grease, oil or dirt. Assemble all internal parts wetted with hydraulic fluid.

Fit a new seal to the piston. Fit the piston into the cylinder inserting the spigot end with the seal attached first. Fit a new dust cover to the open end of the cylinder.

Refitting the slave cylinder :

Push the cylinder into its location and, at the same time, insert the pushrod. Fit the retaining circlip. Ensure that it is fully engaged in its groove. Bleed the clutch system as described in **Section 5 : 7**. Adjust the free play as described in **Section 5 : 3**.

5 : 7 Bleeding the system

This procedure, for which two operators are required, is only necessary if air has entered the hydraulic system. This may result from the fluid level in the reservoir having fallen too low; because the system has been drained of old fluid or because part of the system has been dismantled.

The need for bleeding the clutch system may be indicated by a failure of the clutch to release properly when the pedal is fully depressed. Check, however, that the cause is not incorrect free play adjustment (see **Section 5 : 3**).

Fill the reservoir with approved fluid. Attach a length of tubing to the bleed screw on the slave cylinder and submerge the other end in a glass jar partially filled with hydraulic fluid. Open the bleed screw by three-quarters of a turn. Have a second operator pump the clutch pedal using slow, full strokes until the fluid flowing into the jar is free of air bubbles. The master cylinder reservoir must be kept topped up during this procedure to prevent the entry of further air. Finally, after a downward stroke of the pedal, tighten the bleed screw and remove the bleed tube. Check the operation of the clutch and, if this is still not satisfactory, repeat the bleeding operation. On completion, top up the master cylinder reservoir fluid level.

Do not re-use fluid drained from the system unless it is absolutely clean, has been in use for less than a year and has been allowed to stand for at least 24 hours to ensure de-aeration. Keep fluid in a clean airtight container to prevent it from absorbing moisture.

5 : 8 *Fault diagnosis*

(a) Drag or spin

1 Oil or grease on the driven plate linings
2 Leaking master cylinder, slave cylinder or hose
3 Driven plate binding on hub splines
4 Distorted driven plate
5 Warped or damaged pressure plate
6 Broken driven plate linings
7 Air in the hydraulic system

(b) Fierceness or snatch

1 Check 1, 2, 4 and 5 in (a)
2 Worn driven plate linings

(c) Slip

1 Check 1 in (a); and 2 in (b)
2 Weak diaphragm spring
3 Seized piston in slave cylinder
4 No clutch free play

(d) Judder

1 Check 1 and 4 in (a)
2 Pressure plate warped
3 Driven plate linings unevenly worn
4 Bent or worn gearbox mainshaft
5 Excessively worn driven plate hub splines
6 Buckled driven plate
7 Faulty engine or gearbox mountings

(e) Tick or knock

1 Check 4 and 5 in (d)
2 Worn release bearing
3 Loose flywheel

(f) Rattle

1 Loose slave cylinder
2 Broken springs in driven plate hub
3 Worn release mechanism
4 Excessive backlash in transmission
5 Wear in transmission bearings
6 Release bearing loose
7 Retracting spring broken

NOTES

CHAPTER 6

THE GEARBOX

6 : 1 *Description*

Elan models are equipped with a 4-speed and reverse gearbox. Elan +2 models are provided with either the same 4-speed gearbox or with a 5-speed and reverse box. Synchromesh engagement is incorporated on all forward gears in both boxes.

The gearbox is bolted to the clutch bellhousing which, in turn, is secured to the engine. The gearbox cannot be dismounted from the car as a separate assembly. The engine and the gearbox must be removed as a unit (see **Chapter 1, Section 1 : 16**). The gearbox may then be separated if it is to be dismantled for repair or overhaul. Unless an owner has experience of gearbox overhaul work and has access to the relevant tools and to a suitable press, he should pass a defective box to a Lotus agent for overhaul.

The input shaft to the gearbox is splined into the hub of the clutch driven plate and its extreme forward end is spigoted into the pilot bearing in the tail of the crankshaft.

The external components and the gearchange linkage of the 4-speed gearbox are shown in **FIG 6 : 1** and its gears and shafts are shown in **FIG 6 : 2**. A partial cut-away section through the 5-speed gearbox and the gearchange linkage are shown in **FIG 6 : 3**. Gear ratios are quoted in the **Technical Data** section of the **Appendix**.

6 : 2 *Servicing*

In both 4-speed and 5-speed gearboxes, a combined filler and level plug is provided in the lefthand wall of the gearbox casing. A drain plug is located in the bottom of the casing. Maintain the correct oil level which is up to the bottom of the filler plug orifice. Use an EP80 oil of reputable brand. At the mileage intervals specified in **Chapter 13**, the gearbox should be drained, preferably when the oil is warm after a run, and refilled with new lubricant. Clean off and remove both drain and filler plugs. (These are square-headed on Elan models and socket-headed on Elan +2 models.) After draining, refit the drain plug, fill the box to the correct level and refit the filler plug. Torque tighten both plugs to 3.38 to 4.07 daNm (25 to 30 lbf ft).

6 : 3 *Removing and refitting the 4-speed gearbox*

Removal :

1 Remove the gearchange lever as described in **Section 6 : 6**.

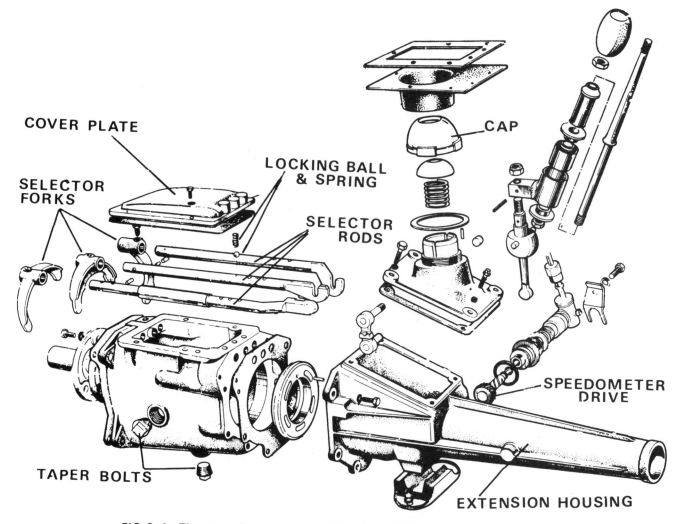

FIG 6 : 1 The external components and the selector linkage of the 4-speed gearbox

2 Refer to **Chapter 1, Section 1 : 16** and carry out operations 1 to 4 inclusive of the engine removal sequence. Refer to **Chapter 7, Section 7 : 3** and dismount the propeller shaft.

3 Disconnect the speedometer drive cable and the reversing light switch wiring from the gearbox. Attach lifting gear or a suitable sling and take the weight of the engine and gearbox unit. Release the engine mountings.

4 Check that there are no pipes, wiring or controls still linking the engine and gearbox unit with the chassis and manoeuvre the unit forwards and out of the car.

5 Remove the bolts which retain the bellhousing to the engine and, taking care not to damage the clutch or the gearbox input shaft, withdraw the bellhousing and gearbox from the engine. Remove the retaining bolts and separate the gearbox from the bellhousing.

Refitment :

Reverse the removal sequence. Torque tighten the gearbox to bellhousing bolts to 5.42 to 6.10daNm (40 to 45lbf ft).

6 : 4 Dismantling the 4-speed gearbox

FIGS 6 : 1, 6 : 2, 6 : 4, 6 : 5 and **6 : 6** apply to the 4-speed gearbox but the operator should supplement these illustrations and the procedure description with notes and sketches of his own.

1 Remove the gearbox as described in **Section 6 : 3**. Drain off the oil if this was not done earlier. Set the gears in neutral. Remove the retaining bolts and washers and (see **FIG 6 : 4**) carefully lift off the coverplate. Ensure that the selector shaft locking springs which are located in the coverplate are not lost when the plate is removed. Collect these locking springs.

2 Confirm that the gears are in neutral and unlock the wire from the bolt heads. Remove the square-headed taper bolts which secure the selector forks to the selector shaft. Withdraw the third and top selector shaft rearwards while supporting the selector shaft sleeve. Lift out the sleeve.

3 Withdraw the first and second selector shaft after turning it through 90°. Remove the floating pin from the cross drilling at the forward end of the shaft. Withdraw the reverse selector shaft rearwards

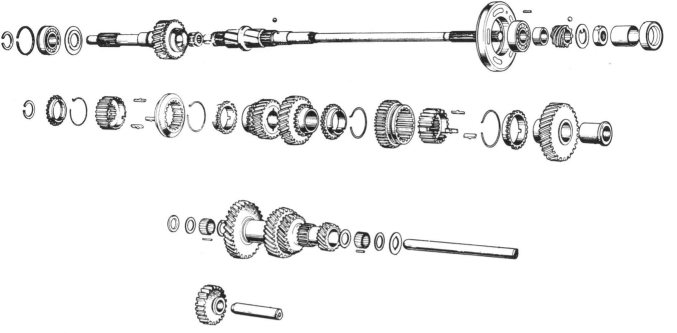

FIG 6:2 Assembly of the internal components of the 4-speed gearbox

and rotate it through 90° in a clockwise direction to prevent it from fouling the extension housing. Lift the selector forks from the locating grooves in their respective gears. If necessary, remove the interlock plungers from their locations in the gearbox casing.

4 Remove the bolts and washers which secure the extension housing to the box casing and withdraw the housing and mainshaft assembly. Remove the speedometer driven gear and bearing from the housing. From the front face of the box, using a brass drift, drive the layshaft rearwards until it is just clear of the casing. Using a dummy layshaft of appropriate length, push the layshaft completely out of the box casing. The layshaft gear assembly and dummy shaft will now lie at the bottom of the box. Withdraw the mainshaft assembly rearwards.

5 Release the main drive gear bearing retainer by removing three bolts and washers. Withdraw the retainer, the large circlip and the paper gasket. Carefully tap out the main drive gear. Lift out the layshaft assembly (containing the dummy shaft) and the two thrust washers. The layshaft runs on 20 needle rollers at each end. A small retaining washer is located on each side of each set of rollers. Push out the dummy shaft, remove the washers and collect the needle rollers.

6 Using tool P7043 as shown in **FIG 6:5** or an equivalent extractor, withdraw the reverse idler shaft. Untab and remove the nut, tabwasher and speedometer gear. Extract the locating ball and remove the spacer. Remove the circlip from the forward end of the mainshaft. Press the mainshaft out of the third and top synchroniser and third gear while supporting the mainshaft from beneath. Press off the mainshaft together with the sandwich plate mainshaft bearing and first gear bush. Remove the

first gear bush locating ball. Press off the second gear and the first and second synchroniser assembly from the mainshaft.

7 The synchroniser hubs, sleeves and the mainshaft are mated. Mating marks as shown in **FIG 6:6** are etched on the corresponding splines of the hub and sleeve and adjacent to the hub and mainshaft splines. The synchroniser sleeve, three blocking bars, two circular springs and the hub which comprise the unit are serviced as an assembly and note should be taken of the way these parts are fitted and, in particular, of which way each circular spring is fitted and that the two spring tags locate in the same blocker bar.

8 The first gear runs on a hardened steel bush which is lubricated via three holes in the gear adjacent to the dog teeth. Check that these holes are clear. Remove the circlips which secure the main drive gear bearing, support the bearing and press the main gear out of the bearing. Extract the oil seal from the rear of the extension housing, examine the rear bearing bush and, if it requires renewal, press it out in the direction of the interior of the housing.

9 Clean off and inspect all parts for wear and damage. Reject parts which are unserviceable and discard all gaskets, oil seals and tabwashers. Obtain new replacement parts.

6:5 Assembling the 4-speed gearbox

The assembly sequence is the reverse of that described in Section 6:4 for dismantling, but the operator should refer to the notes and sketches made during dismantling and also should note the following points at the appropriate stage of reassembly. Assembly should be carried out with internal parts wetted with clean EP80 gear oil.

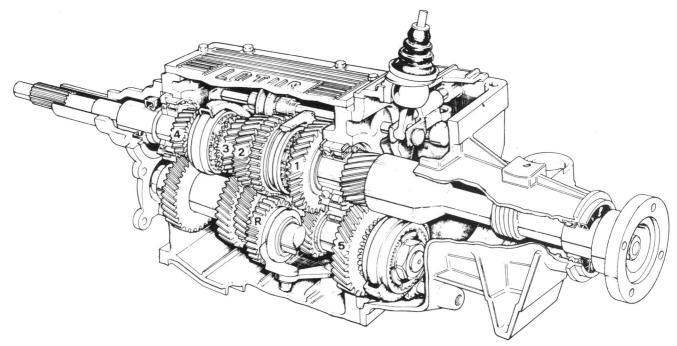

FIG 6 : 3   Cut-away section through the 5-speed gearbox

If the extension housing rear bearing bush is being renewed, enter the new bush into the rear of the housing with the split in the bush uppermost (opposite the groove in the housing bore) and press it squarely into position until the rear of the bush is flush with the deeper recess face in the housing. The rear oil seal lip faces into the housing.

To overhaul the main drive bearing retainer, remove the old oil seal, fit the new seal so that the annular face is located in the channel between the lip and the metal case. Drive the seal into position.

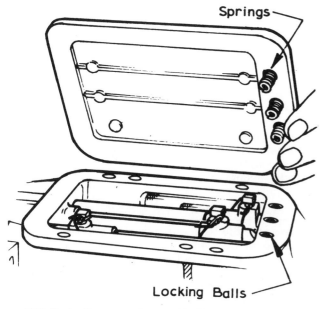

FIG 6 : 4   Detent springs and balls, 4-speed gearbox

Before fitting new synchroniser units, clean the storage preservative from the parts and oil them lightly.

Locate the hardened steel bush in the first gear with the shoulder away from the first gear dog teeth. Ensure that the ball fits in the bush keyway.

Position the sandwich plate on the mainshaft with the dowel hole to the rear. After fitting the bearing, slightly withdraw the plate rearwards to fit over the bearing.

Do not omit the locating ball for the speedometer drive gear. Locate the lockwasher tab on the inner diameter into the groove on the inside of the speedometer drive gear. Torque tighten the nut to 2.71 to 3.38daNm (20 to 25lbf ft) and lock by bending over a section of the outer edge of the lockwasher.

Position the main gear bearing onto the gear with the external circlip groove on the bearing away from the gear. Support the assembly with the main drive gear and press the bearing fully home on the gear. Fit the smaller diameter circlip.

When the layshaft gear cluster has been assembled (with the dummy shaft), locate the thrust washers in position in the gearbox ensuring that the tongues locate in the machined recesses. Take care not to displace the washers when placing the layshaft assembly into the bottom of the box. Fit a string sling at each end of the countershaft to facilitate the later assembly stage.

Cover the main drive gear splines with masking tape to protect the bore of the oil seal when fitting the shaft. Ensure that the oil slot in the retainer aligns with the drain hole in the casing. To preclude oil leaks, apply jointing compound to the three retainer securing bolts before fitting them. Remove the masking tape from the splines.

At the appropriate stage and using the string slings, carefully lift the layshaft assembly into mesh with the mainshaft and main drive gear. Again, take care that the thrust washers are not displaced. Carefully interchange the real layshaft for the dummy shaft. Work from the rear and tap the shaft in. Keep it in contact with the dummy shaft and continue until its front face just protrudes from the front face of the gearbox casing. Ensure that the locking face at the rear of the shaft will align with the recess in the extension housing.

When assembling the selector mechanism, ensure that the interlock plungers are correctly located in the front face of the box. If the interlock plungers were removed, it will be necessary to withdraw the expansion plug from the righthand side of the casing to correctly locate the plungers. Push the plunger into the casing until it is located in the first cross drilling. Locate the other plunger in a similar manner. Fit a new expansion plug.

Ensure that the correct type of locking wire is used to lock the relevant bolt heads.

Before fitting the gearbox coverplate, check that all gears can be selected. Leave the box in neutral. Fit a new gasket and install the selector shaft locking balls and springs. Fit the cover ensuring that the springs are correctly located in the drillings.

Refill the gearbox with new EP80 gear oil either on completion of assembly or after the engine and gearbox have been installed into the car.

6 : 6 *The 4-speed gearchange lever*

From inside the car, remove the tunnel top followed by the gearchange lever grommet. Extract the screws securing the sealing plate and aperture seal. Unscrew the nylon gearchange lever cap and lift out the assembly.

When refitting, use a new gasket between the gearchange cover and the lever cap. Refit the lever assembly. Ensure that the cap is tight by tapping it with a suitable drift. Refit the aperture seal. Note that the shorter flange is towards the facia panel. Fit the sealing plate. Refit the gearchange lever grommet. Refit the tunnel top.

6 : 7 *Removing and refitting the 5-speed gearbox*

Removal:

1 Remove the gearchange lever as described in **Section 6 : 10**.
2 Refer to **Section 6 : 3** and carry out operations 2 to 5 inclusive of the 4-speed gearbox removal procedure.

Refitting:

Reverse the removal sequence. Torque tighten the gearbox to bellhousing bolts to 5.42 to 6.10daNm (40 to 45lbf ft).

6 : 8 *Dismantling the 5-speed gearbox*

Before deciding to dismantle the box, ensure that access to all the special tools and a suitable press can be arranged. **The tools and equipment are essential.**

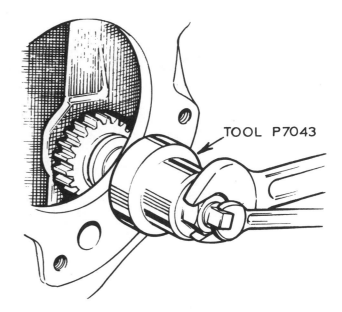

FIG 6 : 5 **Removing the reverse idler gear, 4-speed gearbox**

A partial cut-away section through the 5-speed gearbox is shown in **FIG 6 : 2**. **FIGS 6 : 7** and **6 : 8** show the internal components and **FIGS 6 : 9** to **6 : 15** relate to dismantling and/or reassembly operations. The operator should supplement these illustrations and the procedure description with notes and sketches of his own. These should, in particular, note the order of fitment and which way round ambiguously shaped parts fit so that no doubts will arise on reassembly.

Before commencing to dismantle the gearbox, check the underside adjacent to the Serial Number for the letters 'OS' which indicate that there is one or more

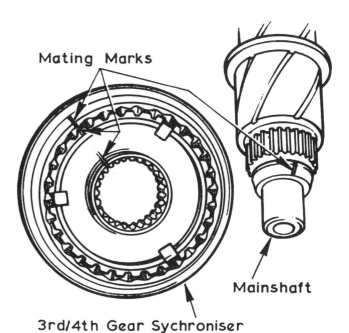

FIG 6 : 6 Synchroniser mating marks, 4-speed gearbox

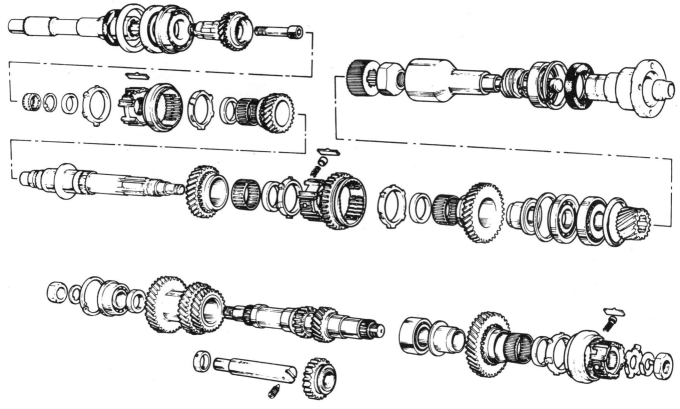

FIG 6 : 7   Assembly of the internal components of the 5-speed gearbox

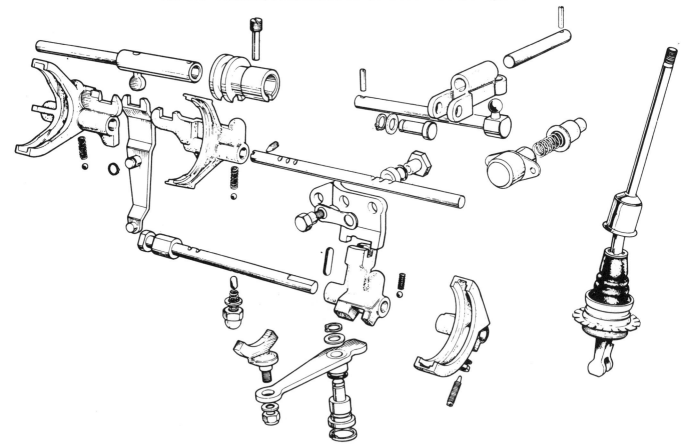

FIG 6 : 8   Selector linkage components, 5-speed gearbox

oversize bearings fitted. When dismantling, note that where an oversize bearing is fitted the letters 'OS', together with the amount of oversize (+0.001in, +0.002in, etc.), will be found stamped adjacent to the bearing bore. In addition to standard sized bearings, four oversizes in 0.001in steps are available. Standard size bearings have a Z after the Part No. Oversize bearings have A, B, C or D after the Part No in ascending order of oversize.

1 Remove four bolts and lift off the gearchange lever cover and gasket. Remove seven bolts (one is inside at **A** in **FIG 6 : 9**), ease the selector link **B** from the selector extension shaft ball end **C** and separate the output shaft housing and its joint gasket from the gearbox. Do not lose the ring dowels.

2 Remove eight bolts and lift off the main cover and its gasket. Remove six bolts and remove the front cover and its gasket. Note that the seal and spacer will be removed with the cover.

Main casing :

3 Refer to **FIG 6 : 10**. Push out the rollpin **A** and remove the shaft extension **B**. Release the locking pin **C** for the interlock spool **D**. Remove the spool and the shaft **E**. Lock any two gears, untab and remove the nuts from both ends of the layshaft. Note that the front nut has a lefthand thread. Remove the nut from the rear of the third motion shaft (this also has a lefthand thread) and, using a suitable puller, withdraw the output shaft adaptor.

4 Select neutral. Refer to **FIG 6 : 11**. Release the bolt securing the 5th gear fork **A**. Remove the fork, the 5th gear synchroniser **B** and baulk ring **C**. Remove the bearing spacer, the 5th gear, its needle bearing and its bearing hub. Keep the hub with its own gear.

5 Push out the rollpin which secures the collar to the reverse idler shaft, release the locating screw (socket-headed at the lefthand rear of the casing) and push the reverse idler gear clear of the laygear. Using puller 18G284 and adaptor 18284AE screwed to the rear end of the layshaft, pull out the layshaft together with the rear bearing. As the layshaft is removed, the laygear and its spacer will drop to the bottom of the casing.

6 Refer to **FIG 6 : 12**. Insert adaptor 18G284AAC/2 between the 4th gear and the 1st motion shaft bearing with the 'thin' face against the bearing. Using puller 18G284 with adaptors 59A, 60A and 61A, withdraw the first motion shaft (of which the 4th gear is a part) and remove the needle bearing and baulk ring.

7 Remove the selector shaft locating screw (socket-headed and on the righthand front of the casing), turn the shaft through 180° and push it out forwards. As the shaft is pushed through the selector forks, insert two dummy shafts 14A into the forks to retain the detent springs and balls. Remove the 1st/2nd and 3rd/4th forks.

8 Remove the three keys from the 3rd/4th synchroniser hub. Remove the circlip which locates the hub and the selective spacer and slide the hub out. Do not misplace the plungers and springs. Slide the 3rd gear forwards, rotate the synchro collar to clear the third motion shaft and remove the collar.

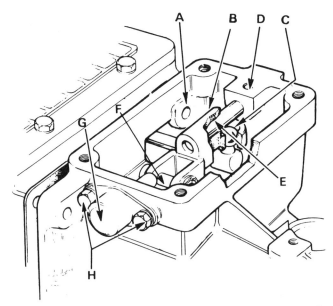

FIG 6 : 9   The extension housing with the cover removed

Key to Fig 6 : 9   **A** Location of the internal securing bolt   **B** Selector link   **C** Selector extension shaft ball end   **D** Rollpin   **E** Linkpin   **F** Operating pin   **G** Plunger assembly   **H** Securing bolts (plunger assembly)

9 Remove the 3rd gear baulk ring, bearing spacer and needle bearing from the third motion shaft. From the rear of the casing, and using drift 18G1155, push out the third motion shaft. This will release the final drive pinion.

10 Remove the bearing hub, bearing, hub spacer, 1st gear baulk ring, 1st/2nd synchroniser assembly, baulk ring, spacer, bearing and 2nd gear. Keep the hub with its own gear.

11 Remove the laygear, spacer and reverse idler gear from the bottom of the casing. Remove the circlip and, using puller 18G248 with adaptor 18G284AL, draw off the front layshaft bearing. Remove the circlip from the third motion shaft rear bearing. Using puller 18G284 with adaptor 18G284AM/1, remove the bearings.

12 From beneath the casing, remove the 5th/reverse selector detent plug (dome-headed), its spring and

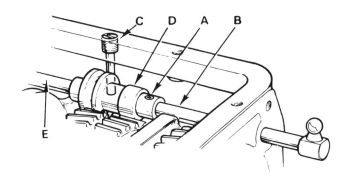

FIG 6 : 10   Interlock spool and selector shaft

Key to Fig 6 : 10   **A** Rollpin   **B** Selector extension shaft   **C** Locking pin   **D** Interlock spool   **E** Selector shaft

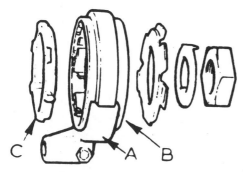

FIG 6 : 11   5th gear synchroniser

Key to Fig 6 : 11   A Selector fork   **B** Synchroniser
assembly   **C** Baulk ring

plunger. Refer to **FIG 6 : 13**. Rotate the 5th/reverse
selector shaft through 180° so that the flat on the
shaft will clear the reverse arm when it is
withdrawn. Using dummy shaft 14A, tap the shaft
out forwards. As the shaft is tapped out, the dummy
shaft will retain the spring, ball and plunger in the
reverse interlock assembly. Note that the core plug
in the casing wall will be displaced from its location.

13 Remove the circlip and washer retaining the reverse
selector lever to its pivot. Remove the exterior
circlip from beneath the casing and withdraw the
pivot complete with its 'O' ring. Remove the
selector lever and interlock. Release the two bolts
and their locking plate which secure the interlock
plate to the casing. Collect the spacers which are
fitted between the plate and the casing. Remove the
sleeve nuts with their 'O' rings from the exterior of
the casing.

Output shaft housing :

14 Remove two bolts on the lefthand side of the
housing and withdraw the 5th/reverse cross-gate
plunger assembly. Remove the single retaining bolt
and remove the speedometer drive assembly. Refer
to **FIG 6 : 9**. Push out rollpin **D** and remove the
linkpin **E** and link **B**.

15 Remove the nut securing the flange to the output
shaft. Press out the shaft with the speedometer
drive gear attached from the flange. Release the
circlip located inside the housing but in front of the
bearing. Withdraw the flange and oil seal. Release
the further circlip and remove the bearing.

First motion shaft assembly :

16 The assembly is made up of two parts: the input
shaft and the first motion shaft with which the 4th
gear is integral. These two shafts are splined
together and retained by a socket-headed bolt.
Remove the bolt. Screw tool 80A into the bolt
location and tighten it. Apply load to the tool head,
press the shafts apart and remove the tool. Remove
the bearings.

Clean off and inspect all components. Clean off old
gasket and jointing compound from the relevant joint
faces. Reject unserviceable parts. Discard all gaskets
and oil seals. Ensure that, if new bearings are required,
the correct oversizes (if applicable) are obtained.

6 : 9 *Assembling the 5-speed gearbox*

Check all threads (particularly those on new
components) for burrs and cleanliness. Similarly, check
all splines (internal and external) and spigots. Assemble
with all internal working surfaces wetted lightly with
clean EP80 gear oil.

Many assembly operations are the reverse of the
dismantling operations, but the following covers
particular procedures and points to be noted. The
operators own notes and sketches should also be
referred to.

First motion shaft :

1 To preclude damage to the cone face rim of the 4th
gear, fit an internal adaptor and position this on the
bed of the press with the shaft vertical. Press on the
roller bearing (flange uppermost) with load applied
only to the bearing inner ring. Follow with the
ballbearing.

2 Ensure that the splines are aligned and slide the
input shaft onto the first motion shaft. Press
together. Apply load only to the spigot end of the
shaft. Apply Loctite to the bolt threads and torque
tighten to 3.53 to 3.79daNm (26 to 28lbf ft).

Third motion shaft :

3 Assemble the relevant components to the shorter
end of the shaft using, initially, the original selective
spacer. The 3rd/4th synchroniser is shown in **FIG
6 : 14**. The oil grooves in this synchroniser assembly
(relieved teeth and recesses on **both** sides of the
outer cone) face towards the 3rd gear. Using feeler
gauges, measure the end float between the shaft
shoulder and the 3rd gear (see **FIG 6 : 15**). If this is
outside the range of 0.13 to 0.20mm (0.005 to
0.008in), fit a thicker or thinner selective spacer.
Ensure that the circlip is correctly engaged.

4 Assemble the relevant components to the longer
end of the shaft. Fit tool 33A behind the selective
hub and, temporarily, fit the nut to retain the tool.
Using feeler gauges, measure the end float between
the hub shoulder and the 1st gear (see **FIG 6 : 15**).
If this is outside the range of 0.13 to 0.20mm
(0.005 to 0.008in), fit a 'thicker' or 'thinner'
selective hub.

Selector forks :

5 Insert tool 29A into the 1st/2nd selector fork until
the end of the tool is level with the ball hole. Insert
the spring and detent ball and, using a pin punch,
hold the ball down against the spring and push the
tool past the ball. Repeat this procedure for the
3rd/4th selector fork. Line up the selector forks and
position them on the synchroniser collars.

Output shaft housing :

6 Use tool 22A to insert the bearing into the housing
from the outside and fit the circlip. Use tool 21A to
fit the oil seal to the housing from outside. Oil the
faces and press the output flange into the bearing.
Fit the inner circlip. The **flat** face of the speedometer
driving gear fits towards the output shaft shoulder.

Insert the shaft into the flange, fit the nut and torque tighten it to 16.27daNm (120lbf ft).

7 Refer to **FIG 6 : 9**. Insert the operating pin **F** into the selector link **B** and secure it with its washer and circlip. Hold the selector link in its relative position, insert linkpin **E** from outside the housing and secure it to the housing with rollpin **D**. Note that this is not the final position of the selector link.

Main casing :

8 Fit the inner snap ring with the step away from the bearing. Fit the two third motion shaft bearings. Select an outer snap ring (refer to the Service Parts List) which will eliminate end float on the bearings. Remove the outer snap ring and the bearings.

9 Fit the 'O' ring to the reverse selector lever pivot pin. From the underside of the casing, drive in the pivot pin and fit the securing circlip. Fit the fork to the lever and secure it with its washer and nut. Fit the lever to the pivot and secure it with its spacer and circlip. Note that from box No 501, the reverse idler gear and its associated parts were modified and can only be fitted as a complete assembly.

10 Using tool 14A, fit the interlock spring and ball as described in operation 5. Fit the interlock and tool into its location ensuring that the lever is located in the lugs of the interlock. Push the tool fully through to retain the ball and spring.

11 Fit the plunger into the selector interlock. Fit the 5th/reverse lever to the interlock plate. Secure with a 'thin' circlip noting that its flat face is towards the end of the pin. Ensure that the plunger is still in position and fit the plate in the selector interlock. In the appropriate order, secure the plate to the casing with the two bolts and retainers (to which new 'O' rings have been fitted), spacers and tabwasher. Torque tighten the bolts to 2.71daNm (20lbf ft).

12 Through the core plug hole, insert the reverse/5th selector shaft and into the selector interlock pushing the 14A tool out. Rotate the shaft during this operation to clear the reverse lever. When in position, turn it back to engage its slot in the reverse operating lever.

13 Temporarily insert the 1st/2nd/3rd/4th selector shaft into its location and a second 1st/2nd/3rd/4th shaft into the upper shaft location. Using a depth gauge across the two shafts, measure the distance to the top front edge of the 5th/reverse lever. If this is less than 10.16 ± 0.127mm (0.40 ± 0.005in), insert appropriate shims between the interlock and its spacers. Shims are available in thicknesses of 0.41mm (0.016in) and 0.61mm (0.024in). The retaining bolts may now be tab locked.

14 From beneath the casing, insert the detent plunger and spring. Fit a new copper washer and the dome-headed plug. Torque tighten the plug to 2.71daNm (20lbf ft). Insert the reverse idler shaft partially. Locate the groove in the idler gear in the reverse selector fork. Using a soft drift, insert the idler shaft through the gear so that the collar may be fitted. The collar rollpin is offset. The longer offset must be towards the gear. Drive the shaft fully

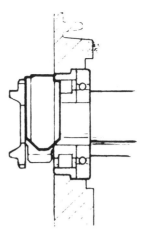

FIG 6 : 12   Adaptor 18G284AAC/2 in position

through until the detent aligns. Apply Wellseal to the grubscrew threads before fitting it. Fit the rollpin through the collar and into the idler shaft.

15 Place the laygear in the bottom of the casing (fourth pinion towards the front). Insert the third motion shaft assembly and the selector forks through the top of the casing and out through the casing wall. Insert tool 31A through the front wall of the casing from outside and secure it to the front of the casing. Remove the nut and tool 33A from the third motion shaft.

16 Use tool 25A to fit the ballbearing (stepped face to the front) and the outer track of the second bearing. Fit the second bearing and the snap ring (with the ring gap **away** from the casing bore cut-out and the step **away** from the bearing). Remove tool 31A.

17 Fit the baulk ring to the flange of the 4th gear (first motion shaft). Place the needle roller bearing (oiled) onto the third motion shaft. Fit the first motion shaft with the aid of the front cover. Enter the outer race of the bearing into the casing, fit the thickest spacer ring into the front cover, lubricate the seal, place the cover in position without its gasket and fit the bolts. Tighten the bolts progressively to pull the cover down evenly and push in the bearing and first motion shaft assembly. Withdraw the bolts and remove the front cover.

18 Insert the layshaft through the lower rear bore with the two machined diameters into the laygear and the splines fully engaged. Use tool 28A to locate the front end of the layshaft. Use tool 25A from outside the casing to fit the rear layshaft bearing flush with the casing. The bearing hub is in two parts, the smaller is fitted first. Remove tool 28A.

19 Fit the spacer to the layshaft with its tapered end towards the laygear. Using tool 19A, fit the front layshaft bearing into the lower bore of the casing with its smaller end diameter towards the laygear. Fit the circlip in front of the bearing. From the front of the casing, insert the 1st/2nd/3rd/4th selector shaft (Part No first) with the indents facing downwards. As the shaft is pushed in, the tool holding the selector forks will be pushed out. Rotate the shaft with a screwdriver through a half turn until the indent is visible when the detent ball will click

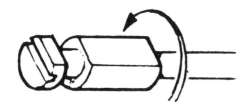

FIG 6:13   Reverse selector shaft

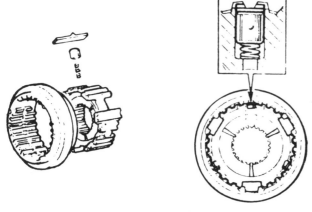

FIG 6:14   3rd/4th synchroniser

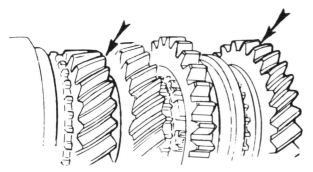

FIG 6:15   End float measuring points

into position. Apply Loctite to the threads and fit the grubscrew.

20 Assemble the 5th gear to its hub with its bearing and spacer. With the assembly inverted (spacer down) on a surface plate, check the end float between the gear and the hub flange. If this is not within the range of 0.13 to 0.20mm (0.005 to 0.008in), fit a 'thicker' or a 'thinner' selective bearing hub. Fit the assembly to the rear of the layshaft. Refer to **FIG 6:11**. Place the selector fork **A** on the fifth synchroniser assembly (relieved teeth and a recess on one side only) **B**. Note that the 'no grooves' face is towards the layshaft. Slide the assembly and its baulk ring **C** onto the layshaft. Ensure that the selector fork also slides onto its shaft at the same time. Align the hole in the fork with the detent on the selector shaft, insert the grubscrew, locknut and washer. Fully tighten the screw and then the locknut. Fit the retaining plate, tabwasher and nut.

21 Fit the fifth pinion to the third motion shaft (machined face towards the bearing). Fit the adaptor and its nut with the cut-outs butting against the pinion. Fit the tabwasher and nut (lefthand thread) to the front end of the layshaft. Select 1st and 3rd gears and torque tighten the nuts as follows: front and rear layshaft nuts, 16.27daNm (120lbf ft); third motion shaft nut, 20.34daNm (150lbf ft). Note that the third motion shaft nut 'flat' edges must be in line with the splines on the adaptor (otherwise the output shaft will foul the nut when assembled). Tab lock both layshaft nuts.

22 Select neutral. Check that the input shaft turns freely. If it does not, tap each end of the layshaft with a soft hammer to centralise the bearings. Repeat this procedure with each gear selected. Check that the first motion shaft bearings are fully entered in their housing bores. To ascertain the correct nip on the bearings, measure (a) the depth of the ring dowel recess in the front wall of the main casing, and (b) in the front cover. Measure (c) the uncompressed thickness of the gasket which will fit between the main casing and the front cover. Select a spacer of thickness a + b + c. Spacers are available of three thicknesses: 5.20 to 5.23mm (RED), 5.24 to 5.27mm (BLACK) and 5.28 to 5.31mm (BLUE).

23 Apply Wellseal to both sides of the front gasket. Lubricate the front cover seal. Fit the cover, gasket and selected spacer. Torque tighten the retaining bolts to 2.03daNm (15lbf ft). Check that all gears rotate freely. Assemble the interlock spool selector assembly using the later type spool which has straight sides to the slot. Insert the assembly into the front shaft hole from the top of the casing. Align the spool with the lugs on the selector forks (see **FIG 6:10**). From the rear wall of the casing insert the selector shaft extension with its ball end uppermost and through into the selector shaft assembly until the rollpin holes align. Support the shafts and insert the rollpin fully. Insert the interlock spool retainer through the top face of the casing and into the spool.

24 Complete the assembly of the gearbox noting the following: apply Wellseal to both faces of all joint gaskets; torque tighten the output housing to gearbox bolts; the selector cover to output housing bolts and the top cover bolts to 2.03daNm (15lbf ft). After fitting the output shaft housing to the main casing, turn the selector link to engage with the selector ball. Refer to **Section 6:10** and fit the gearchange lever. Refer to **FIG 6:9**. Into the hole at the top lefthand side of the output shaft housing, fit the plunger, spring and spacer if these parts were removed. The fitted assembly is **G**. Apply Silastic to the mating face of the housing and secure with its bolts **H** and washers. Before finally tightening the bolts, move the gearchange lever to the left to ensure that the plunger is operating and, with the lever held in this position, fully tighten the bolts.

25 Check that all gears can be selected. Use a new copper washer and apply Wellseal to the threads of the reversing light switch. Select reverse and, using a test lamp, set the switch by rotating it inwards until the contacts close and then by a further half turn. Tighten the locknut. Use Wellseal and refit the displaced core plug.

6 : 10 *The 5-speed gearchange lever*

Remove the circlip which is located just above the rubber bellows. Untab the locking and, using tool 32A to loosen the coupling, unscrew and lift out the lever.

When refitting, note that the threaded part of the lever assembly is of nylon construction and consequently softer than the cover thread. **Take great care not to cross the threads.** Tighten by hand as far as possible (so that crossed threads will be readily noticed) and only use tool 32A to finally tighten the assembly. Bend the tabs to lock.

6 : 11 *Fault diagnosis*

(a) Jumping out of gear

1 Broken selector ball spring
2 Excessively worn selector linkage
3 Worn synchromesh unit(s)
4 Worn gears or dog teeth
5 Loose selector fork(s)

(b) Noisy transmission

1 Check 2, 3, 4 and 5 in (a)

2 Insufficient oil
3 Worn or damaged bearings

(c) Difficulty in engaging gear

1 Check 2, 3 and 5 in (a)
2 Clutch hydraulic system requires bleeding (see **Chapter 5**)
3 Incorrect clutch adjustment (see **Chapter 5**)
4 Defective gearchange linkage

(d) Oil leaks

1 Worn or damaged oil seal(s)
2 Defective gasket, damaged joint face
3 Oil level too high
4 Loose drain or filler plug
5 Cracked casing

(e) No drive when gear is engaged

1 Defective clutch (see **Chapter 5**)
2 Stripped input shaft splines
3 Broken gearbox shaft
4 Stripped gearteeth

NOTES

CHAPTER 7

THE PROPELLER SHAFT, FINAL DRIVE AND REAR SUSPENSION

7 : 1 Description

Track width and other dimensions differ between Elan and Elan +2 models. The differences are shown in the keys to **FIG 7 : 1**.

A propeller shaft which incorporates a sliding joint and two universal joints connects the gearbox with the final drive. Each universal joint consists of a spider, two yokes and four needle roller bearing assemblies.

The final drive unit is flexibly mounted. It carries a conventional crownwheel and pinion, a differential gearing assembly and short output shafts which are splined into the differential side gears and have finger-type coupling flanges. Intermediate shafts take the drive from the output shafts to the rear wheels. Each intermediate shaft is fitted with two flexible couplings which provide full universal rotational drive.

The rear suspension is fully independent. The Chapman-type struts incorporate coil springs and telescopic dampers in concentric units. Wide-based wishbones are fitted. These provide both longitudinal and lateral location of the rear wheel bearing housings. The rear housings carry the outboard stub shafts and the spring/damper unit lower mountings. The upper spring/damper unit mountings are by Lotocone flexible mountings.

FIG 7 : 1 shows the layout of the rear suspension and final drive. **FIG 7 : 2** shows the components of the rear suspension assembly.

7 : 2 Servicing

Tyres :

Except for tyre pressures which are given later, the maintenance operations and mileage intervals quoted in **Chapter 8, Section 8 : 2** for front tyres also apply to rear tyres.

For speeds up to 160km/h (100mph) the rear pressure should be 1.59 bar (23lb/sq in) for Elan models and 1.66 bar (24lb/sq in) for Elan +2 models. For sustained speeds above 100mph, increase the inflation pressure by 0.41 bar (6lb/sq in) in each case.

Final drive unit :

At the mileage intervals stated in **Chapter 13**, check the oil level in the final drive gearbox. The correct level is up to the bottom of the filler orifice which is arrowed in **FIG 7 : 3**.

At the mileage intervals stated in **Chapter 13**, drain the unit (the drain plug is in the lower front of the casing). Use a good quality flushing oil and, after

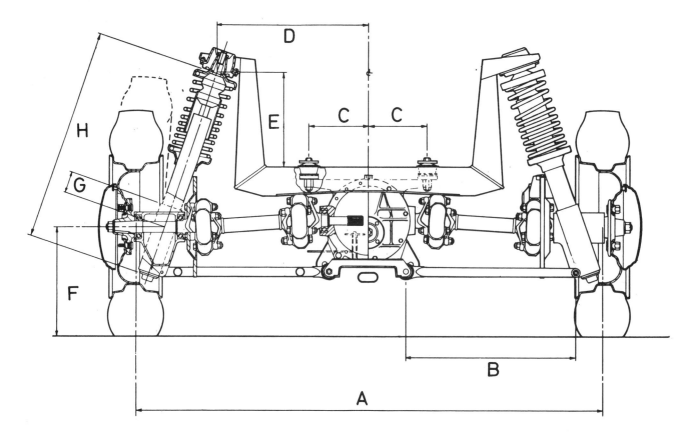

FIG 7 : 1   Rear suspension and final drive, Elan and Elan +2 models. Dimensions are in millimetres (inches)

Key to Fig 7 : 1
Elan models :   **A** Series 1 and 2 1230 (48.44), Series 3 and 4 1195 (47.06)   **B** 450.08 (17.72)   **C** 152.4 (6.0)
D 386.08 (15.2)   **E** 254.0 (10.0)   **F** 273.05 (10.75)   **G** 53.84 (2.12)   **H** 497.84 (19.6) bump; 574.04 (22.6)
normal ride; 655.32 (25.8) droop
Elan +2 models :   **A** 1397.0 (55.0)   **B** 521.21 (20.52)   **C** 152.4 (6.0)   **D** 449.8 (17.71)   **E** 254.0 (10.0)
F 273.05 (10.75)   **G** 53.84 (2.12)   **H** 497.84 (19.6) bump; 574.04 (22.6) normal ride; 655.32 (25.8) droop

thorough draining, refill with EP90 gear oil of reputable brand. Ensure that the drain and filler plugs are securely refitted.

Propeller shaft :

Regularly check the tightness of the front and rear flange nuts and bolts. At the mileage intervals stated in **Chapter 13**, lubricate the universal joints.

7 : 3 *Propeller shaft*

The sliding spline front universal joint and the rear universal joint components are shown in **FIG 7 : 4**.

Removal :

Mark the rear mating flanges so that they may be refitted in their original positions. Support the gearbox with a jack and remove the gearbox mounting. Remove the nuts and bolts from the rear flanges, withdraw the shaft rearwards from the splined joint while lowering the gearbox slightly and dismount the shaft assembly forwards.

Overhaul :

Refer to **FIG 7 : 4** and, using circlip pliers, remove the circlips from the universal joint bearings. Remove the

needle roller bearings by tapping the radius of the yoke lightly with a copper hammer. If a bearing is stubborn, gently drift out the bearing race from inside with a small diameter bar. Take care not to drop the needle rollers.

The parts most likely to be worn after long usage are the bearing races and the spider journals. Discard parts which are loose, distorted or which show excessive load markings. No oversize journals or races are available. It is essential that the bearing races are a light drive fit in the yoke trunnions. Renew the yoke if the bores have worn oval. In case of wear in the fixed yoke, a new tubular assembly will be required.

Reassembly :

Renew the cork gaskets and their retainers. They may be removed using a tubular drift. The spider journal shoulders should be shellaced prior to fitting the retainers to ensure a good oil seal. Assemble the needle rollers into the bearing races and fill with multi-purpose grease. Smear the walls of the races with grease to retain the needle rollers in position while assembling. Insert the spider in the flange yoke. Using a soft drift slightly smaller than the bore, tap the bearing into position. Repeat on the other three bearings. Fit the circlips and check that they are fully seated in their

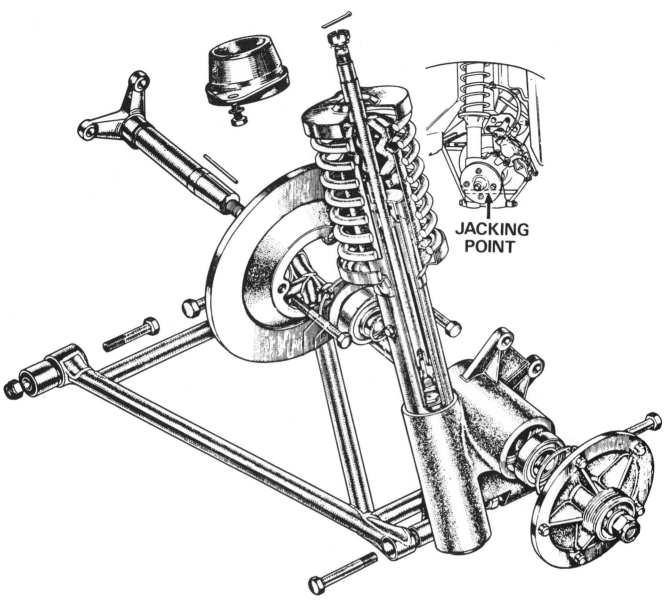

FIG 7 : 2   Rear suspension assembly

JACKING POINT

grooves. If a joint appears to bind, tap it lightly with a wooden mallet.

Refitting :

Reverse the removal sequence. Ensure that the flanges are aligned, clean, and that their spigots are engaged before tightening the coupling nuts and bolts.

7 : 4 *Intermediate drive shaft*

The shaft and rotoflex couplings are shown in **FIG 7 : 5**.

Removal :

Raise the relevant wheel until the rotoflex couplings adopt as true a shape as possible. Place a clamp round the couplings to prevent distortion when they are removed. Remove the three nuts and bolts from the flange at each end of the shaft. Dismount the shaft.

Refitting :

Reverse the removal sequence. Note that washers, if originally fitted under the nuts, should be discarded. All nuts must be of the 'Nyloc' type. Torque tighten the coupling nuts and bolts to 4.75 to 5.42daNm (35 to 40lbf ft). Remove the clamps from round the rotoflex couplings.

7 : 5 *Intermediate drive shaft couplings*

Couplings may be of either rotoflex or of interleaved type.

Removal, rotoflex type couplings :

Remove the intermediate shaft as described in **Section 7 : 4**. Remove the remaining three nuts and bolts securing each coupling. Note that those securing the outer couplings also retain the brake discs.

FIG 7:3   Final drive filler/level plug

Refitting rotoflex couplings :

When fitting new couplings, note that **the metal strap round their diameters must be left intact while fitting the couplings and only removed after the securing nuts and bolts have been fully tightened.**

The metal bosses in the couplings are offset in the rubber. **Correct fitting is with the three 'high' bosses in contact with the flanges of the drive shaft.** Coupling life will be affected if they are incorrectly fitted.

Except for the bolts which secure the brake disc, the coupling and both the outboard and the intermediate shafts, all bolt heads must be towards the road wheel with their heads in contact with the 'low' bosses in the couplings. The correct bolts for nine positions per side are special UNF bolts. **Ensure that if new bolts are**

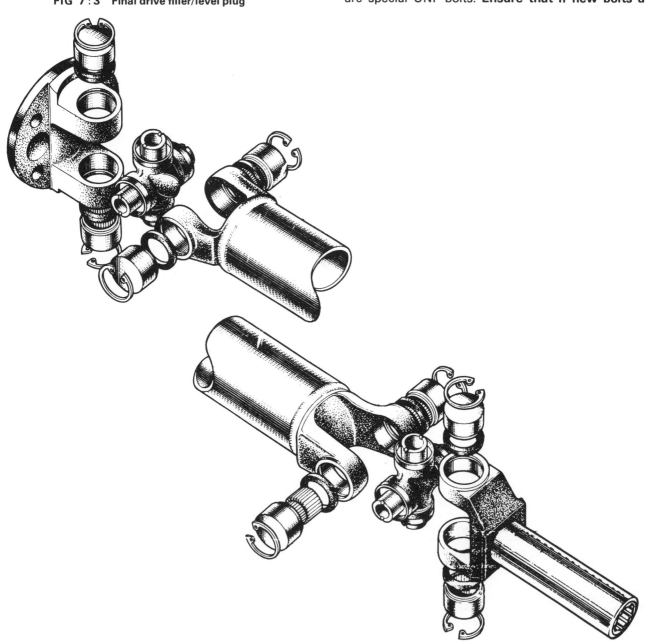

FIG 7:4   Propeller shaft universal joint assembly

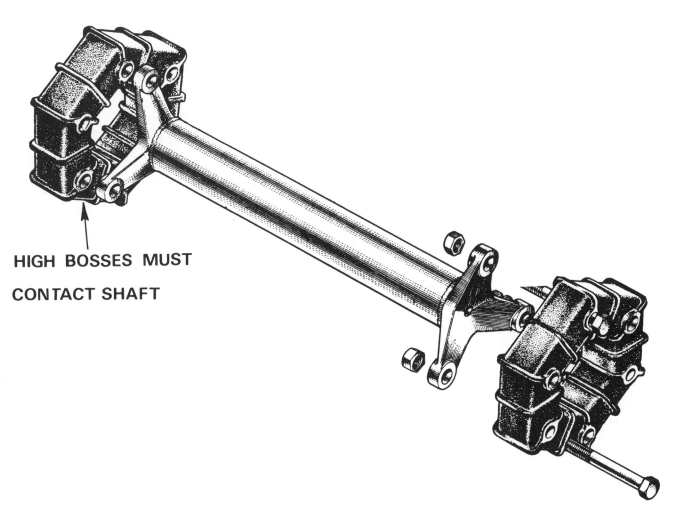

HIGH BOSSES MUST

CONTACT SHAFT

FIG 7 : 5   Intermediate shaft and flexible (rotoflex) couplings

required that they are identical with those being discarded. The other three bolts (making 12 per side) which retain the brake disc, etc., should be 3.25 by $\frac{7}{16}$in in size.

Interleaved couplings :

Interleaved couplings (which reduce 'surge' on acceleration) were introduced at Elan chassis No 8930 and at Elan +2 chassis No 50/1550 and are available to replace rotoflex couplings. They should be fitted, ideally, in sets of four but may be used in matched pairs of two inners and two outers.

7 : 6 *Differential unit*

All dismantling and overhaul operations on the final drive unit should be entrusted to a fully equipped agent. Heavy press equipment is necessary to completely dismantle the unit and special tools and specialised knowledge are required to measure and adjust the backlash in mating gears and to set the various bearing preloads. For reference purposes, the components of a final drive unit are shown in **FIG 7 : 6** but an owner should confine work to removing a defective final drive unit and installing a serviceable assembly.

Removal :

1 Raise the rear of the car and support it on stands. Remove the road wheels (see note in **Chapter 8, Section 8 : 3**). Refer to **Section 7 : 8** and disconnect the lefthand wishbone. Refer to **Section 7 : 5** and remove the rotoflex couplings from the final drive output shafts.

2 Refer to **Section 7 : 3** and uncouple the propeller shaft from the final drive input shaft. Disconnect the forward ends of the torque rods from the chassis.

3 From the inside of the car, pull the backrest centre piece off its concealed clips. Remove the screw from each end. Lift up the lower edge and remove the backrest from the car. On 'S' type cars, release the tags from the parcel tray and fold down the squab. Remove two screws from the upper edge of the tray and lift up the front edge. Remove the two screws which retain the backboard. Lift the seat assembly up and out of the car.

4 Support the final drive unit and, from inside the car, remove the retaining bolt nuts which pass through the chassis rubber mountings. The nuts are located beneath the fuel tank. Withdraw the final drive unit from the lefthand side.

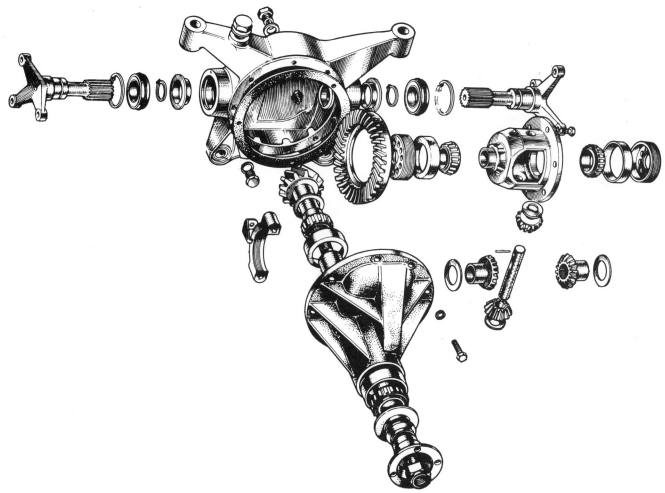

FIG 7 : 6   Components of the final drive unit

Refitment :

Reverse the removal sequence. Torque tighten the torque rod nuts to 2.98 to 3.66daNm (22 to 27lbf ft). Refer to relevant sections for other torque tightening figures.

7 : 7 *Rear hubs and outboard drive shafts*

FIG 7 : 7 shows a cross-section through a rear hub and outboard drive shaft assembly. No routine adjustment to the bearings is required. The procedure for fitting new bearings is as follows.

Removing the bearings :

Raise the rear of the car and support it on stands. Remove the relevant road wheel (see note in **Chapter 8, Section 8 : 3**). Remove the hub securing nut and its washer. Use a puller and draw off the hub. Remove the outboard drive shaft by releasing the three bolts securing it to the rotoflex coupling (see **Section 7 : 5**). Remove the circlip from the inner bearing and push out the drive shaft and inner bearing. Remove the inner bearing locating circlip from the shaft and pull the bearing off the shaft. Remove the outer bearing retaining circlip and drift the bearing from the hub.

Refitment :

Reverse the removal sequence and note that it is necessary to trim flush the surplus seal which stands proud of the outer race on the inner bearing so that the spacer and retaining circlip may be correctly fitted. Although the bearings are of the sealed type, grease should be applied to the internal surfaces of the bearing housing. Locate the outboard drive shaft with the keyway aligned and fit the hub retaining nut and washer. Torque tighten the nut to 13.56 to 14.91daNm (100 to 110lbf ft). Fit the road wheel and lower the car.

Modified hub bearings :

To improve bearing life, modified bearings were fitted at Elan chassis No 45/7743 and 36/7762 (inner) and at chassis No 9095 (outer) and at Elan +2 chassis No 50/0250 (inner) and at chassis No 50/0870 (outer).

7 : 8 *Wishbones*

Removal :

1 Raise and support the rear of the car. Remove the relevant road wheel (see note in **Chapter 8, Section 8 : 3**).

2 Position a screw-type jack below the bearing housing and raise just sufficiently to take the weight off the suspension. Remove the bolts securing the outer ends of the wishbone to the bearing housing.

3 Remove the bolts securing the inner ends of the wishbone to the chassis noting that the bolts are fitted with their heads towards each other. Dismount the wishbone.

Do not attempt to salvage a distorted or damaged wishbone. Fit a new replacement.

Refitment :

Reverse the removal sequence. Ensure that the bolts are fitted the correct way round and torque tighten them to 4.75 to 5.42daNm (35 to 40lbf ft) with the car lowered to the ground and in a **normal ride position.**

Wishbone bush renewal :

The procedure for the renewal of the bushes is as for the front wishbone bushes. Refer to **Chapter 8, Section 8 : 5.**

7 : 9 *Spring and damper units*

Remove the spring and damper unit as follows.

Raise and support the rear of the car. Remove the relevant road wheel (see note in **Chapter 8, Section 8 : 3**). Position a screw-type jack below the bearing housing (see inset in **FIG 7 : 2**) and raise just enough to take the suspension weight. Remove the upper dust shield (if fitted). Refer to **Chapter 10, Sections 10 : 5 and 10 : 9** and remove the brake caliper and disc. Refer to **Section 7 : 8** and remove the bolts securing the outer end of the wishbone to the bearing housing. Push down the wishbone clear of the housing.

Refer to **Section 7 : 7** and remove the outboard drive shaft. From inside the car, remove the grommet concealing the damper upper fixing. Withdraw the splitpin and remove the castellated nut from the damper spindle. Lower the jack slowly as the spring is now free. Lift off the spring abutment, the bump stop and the spring. Dismount the damper and bearing housing assembly.

Refitment :

Clamp the spring and position it on the damper. Fit the bump stop and the spring abutment. Guide the damper spindle through the Lotocone mounting with a piece of wire through the splitpin hole as, using the jack, the assembly is pushed up into its location. Remove the wire and fit the castellated nut but do not tighten it fully at this stage.

Proceed with the reassembly. Leave fitment of the grommet concealing the damper fixing until last. Refer to the relevant sections for refitment procedures and torque tightening figures. With the car lowered and in the **normal ride position**, torque tighten the damper castellated nut to 6.10 to 6.78daNm (45 to 50lbf ft) and lock with a new splitpin.

Damper resilient mountings :

Each Lotocone mounting is retained by two setbolts and spring washers. Access to a mounting requires removal of the damper and spring assembly as

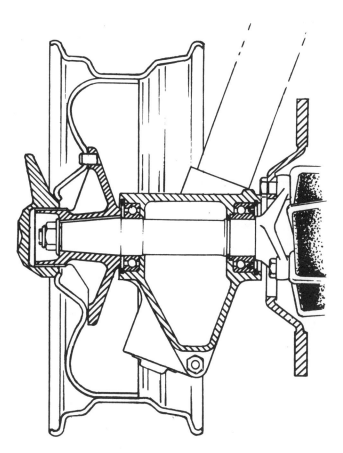

FIG 7 : 7 Cross-section through a rear hub (knock-on type wheel shown)

described earlier. Torque tighten the retaining setscrews to 2.98 to 3.66daNm (22 to 27lbf ft).

Suspension securing nuts :

Refer to **Chapter 8, Section 8 : 10.**

Bump limiting spacers :

These special spacers may be fitted to reduce the possibility of the car 'grounding' when used in rough terrain.

7 : 10 *Track, camber and wheel alignment*

The geometry of the rear suspension cannot be adjusted but, in the event of an accident to the vehicle, it is important to check for distortion and deformation damage by making comparisons with the correct dimensions and angles. Refer to the following data.

Track :

Track and other dimensions are quoted in the keys to **FIG 7 : 1.**

Camber :

The rear camber angle in all Elan and Elan +2 models should be 1° negative to zero.

Wheel alignment :

The rear wheel alignment should be zero to 4.76mm (0.187in) toe-in.

7 : 11 *Fault diagnosis*

(a) Noisy final drive

1 Insufficient or incorrect lubricant
2 Worn bearings
3 Worn gears, incorrect meshing

(b) Excessive backlash

1 Check 2 and 3 in (a)
2 Worn shaft couplings
3 Worn propeller shaft joints or splines

(c) Oil leakage

1 Defective final drive seals
2 Defective final drive gasket or joint face
3 Loose drain or filler plug

(d) Vibration

1 Check 2 and 3 in (b)
2 Propeller shaft bent and out of balance

(e) Rattles

1 Check 3 in (b)
2 Defective rubber bushes
3 Defective or loose damper mounting

(f) 'Settling'

1 Weak or broken spring(s)

CHAPTER 8

THE FRONT SUSPENSION AND HUBS

8 : 1 Description

Track width and other dimensions differ between Elan and Elan +2 models. The differences are shown in the key to **FIG 8 : 1**.

The suspension is fully independent and incorporates coil springs and telescopic damper units. The arrangement is shown in **FIG 8 : 2**. A stub axle carrying a hub is bolted to a vertical link which can pivot between a lower trunnion and an upper ball joint. The trunnion and the ball joint are carried by the lower and upper wishbones respectively. The vertical link carries the steering arm and the brake caliper. The upper and lower wishbones are of different lengths but are interchangeable lefthand to righthand. The vertical link, trunnion, steering arm and hub are handed. An anti-roll bar is secured to the chassis by rubber insulated links and is attached at each end to a damper unit.

8 : 2 Servicing

Tyres:

Regularly check the cold tyre pressures including the spare. For speeds up to 160km/h (100mph), the front pressures should be 1.24 bar (18lb/sq in) for Elan models and 1.38 bar (20lb/sq in) for Elan +

2 models. For sustained speeds above 160km/h (100mph), increase the inflation pressure by 0.41 bar (6lb/sq in) in each case.

Every 3500km (2000 miles), to even out tyre wear, interchange the wheels as follows: fit the spare wheel to the right rear position; the right rear to the left front position; the left front to the left rear position; the left rear to the right front position and the right front to the spare position. At this same mileage interval, have the wheel-balance checked and corrected as necessary. On alloy wheels, use only 'stuck-on' balance weights. On steel wheels, use only 'knock-on' weights.

Vertical links:

At the mileage intervals specified in **Chapter 13**, lubricate both vertical links. Refer to **FIG 8 : 3**. Remove the blanking plug and fit a lubrication nipple. After applying Hypoid 90EP oil, remove the nipple and refit the plug.

Hubs:

At the same mileage intervals, check the front hub bearings. Adjust and lubricate with multi-purpose grease as described in **Section 8 : 3**.

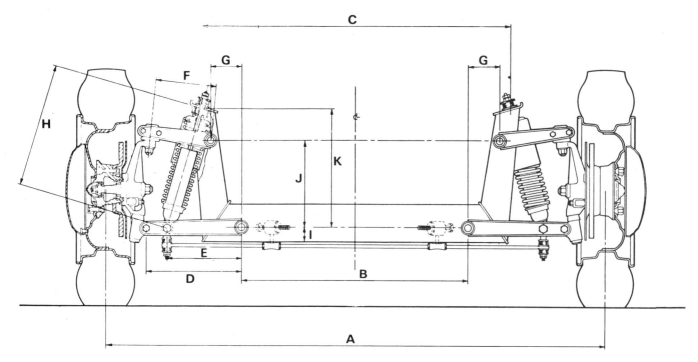

FIG 8:1   Front suspension, Elan and Elan +2 models. Dimensions are in millimetres (inches)

Key to Fig 8:1
Elan models   **A** 1196.34 (47.1)   **B** 551.18 (21.7)   **C** 755.65 (29.75)   **D** 228.6 (9.0)   **E** 177.8 (7.0) **F** 146.05 (5.75)
G 75.18 (2.96)   **H** 343.91 (13.54) droop; 300.73 (11.84) normal ride; 248.66 (9.79) bump   **I** 34.29 (1.35) **J** 208.28 (8.20)
K 286.0 (11.26)
Elan +2 models   **A** 1371.6 (54.0)   **B** 551.18 (21.7)   **C** 755.65 (29.75)   **D** 313.4 (12.34)   **E** 243.6 (9.59)
F 230.4 (9.07)   **G** 75.18 (2.96)   **H** 343.91 (13.54) droop; 300.73 (11.84) normal ride; 248.66 (9.79) bump   **I** 34.29 (1.35)
J 208.28 (8.20)   **K** 286.0 (11.26)

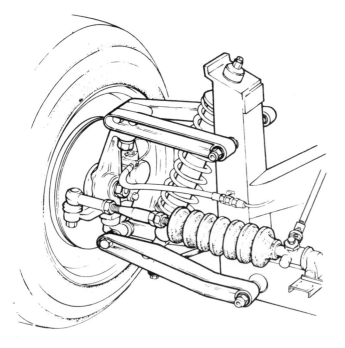

FIG 8:2   A front suspension assembly

8:3 *Wheel hubs*

Note that on 'knock-on' centre lock wheels righthand hubs have righthand threads and lefthand hubs have lefthand threads.

Adjustment:

Raise and support the front of the car. Remove the road wheel. Extract and discard the splitpin locking the hub nut. Mount a dial gauge as shown in **FIG 8:4**. Tighten the hub securing nut until the end float is within the range of 0.05 to 0.10mm (0.002 to 0.004in). Back off the nut by one flat (60°) and relock with a new split-pin. Half fill the hub with multi-purpose grease of reputable brand. Work the grease well past the large washer below the securing nut. Refit the wheel which must be assembled dry. **Do not grease or oil the threads.** With centre-lock wheels, ensure that the drive pegs are fully located before fitting the wheel nuts.

Repeat on the opposite side of the car.

Removal:

Raise and support the front of the car. Remove the road wheel. Disconnect the flexible brake hose at the caliper. Blank off to preclude loss of fluid. Dismount the brake caliper as described in **Chapter 10, Section 10:4**. Remove and discard the hub securing nut split-pin. Remove the nut and washer. Pull off the hub and disc assembly, remove four bolts and separate the hub from the disc. Renew the hub bearings if necessary.

Refitting:

To avoid runout problems, thoroughly clean the hub and disc mating faces. Fit the hub and disc assembly, torque tightening the securing bolts to 2.98 to 3.66daNm (22 to 27lbf ft). Pack the hub with grease and adjust the end float as described earlier. Refit the caliper as described in **Chapter 10, Section 10:4**, reconnect the brake hose and bleed the brakes as described in **Chapter 10, Section 10:12**.

8:4 *The anti-roll bar*

Removal and refitment:

Release the locknuts and remove the nuts and washers securing the bar to the lower ends of the damper units. Note the order in which the bar ends, washers and bushes are fitted (see **FIG 8:5**). Release the nuts and bolts which secure the links to the chassis and dismount the bar. When refitting, reverse the removal sequence.

8:5 *Wishbones*

Refer to **FIG 8:5**.

Lower wishbone removal:

Raise and support the front of the car. Remove the road wheel. Remove the nut and bolt securing the damper to the wishbone. Remove the nut and bolt securing the wishbone to the lower trunnion. Pull the wishbone down and remove the nuts securing the wishbone inner ends to the chassis fulcrum pins.

Refitting a lower wishbone:

Reverse the removal sequence. With the car lowered to the ground and **in the normal ride position,** torque tighten the damper to wishbone nut and bolt and the fulcrum pin nuts to 6.78 to 8.14daNm (50 to 60lbf ft) and the wishbone to trunnion nut and bolt to 4.75daNm (35lbf ft).

Upper wishbone removal:

Raise and support the front of the car. Remove the road wheel. Remove the nuts and bolts securing the outer ends of the wishbone to the upper ball joint. Remove the nuts securing the inner ends of the wishbone to the chassis fulcrum pins and dismount the wishbone assembly.

Refitting an upper wishbone:

Reverse the removal sequence. With the car lowered to the ground and **in the normal ride position,** torque tighten the wishbone to ball joint nuts and bolts to 1.63 to 2.03daNm (12 to 15lbf ft) and the wishbone to fulcrum pin nuts to 6.78 to 8.14daNm (50 to 60lbf ft).

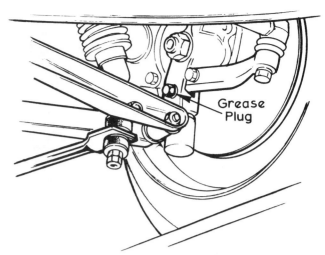

FIG 8:3   A trunnion greasing point

Wishbone bushes, renewal:

Remove the wishbones as described earlier. Use a pilot drift (the outer periphery of which must bear on the outer sleeve of the bush) to press out the bushes. Press in new bushes and refit the wishbones as described earlier.

8:6 *Spring and damper units*

Removing and dismantling a unit:

Remove the complete spring and damper unit as follows.

Refer to **Section 8:4** and remove the nuts securing the anti-roll bar to the dampers. Uncouple the outer ends of the lower wishbones as described in **Section 8:5**. Remove the locknut, nut and washers securing

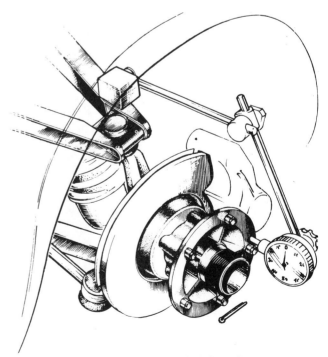

FIG 8:4   Checking hub free play

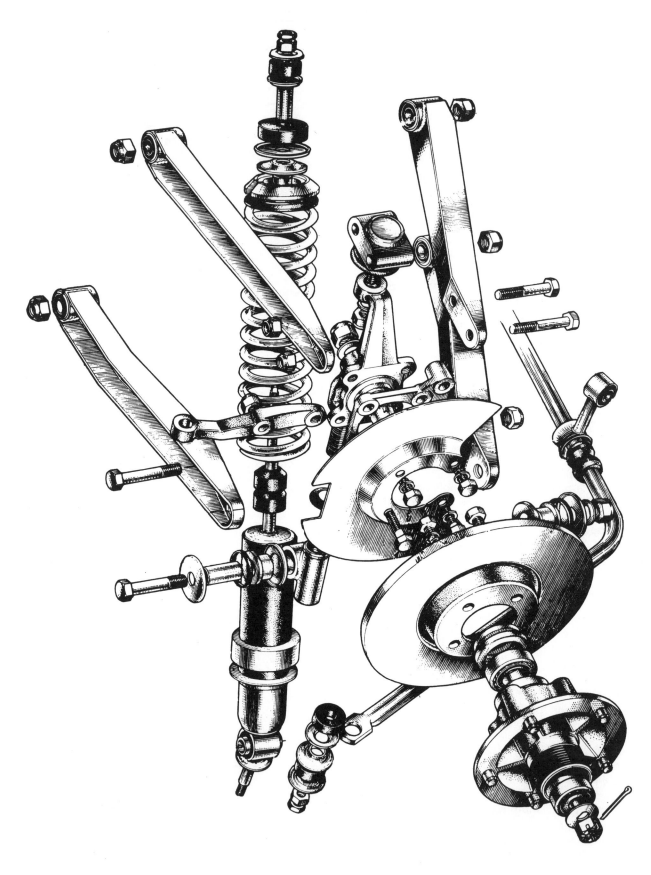

FIG 8 : 5 Front suspension assembly

the upper end of the damper to the chassis (see **FIG 8 : 5**). Collect the washers from the top of the damper spindle (between the top of the damper and the chassis). Using a suitable spring compressing tool, compress the road spring and clamp it in the compressed position. Remove the top spring abutment (which is slotted to clear the damper spindle) and its rubber ring. Lift off the compressed spring, the bump rubber and the lower rubber distance ring. It is not necessary to remove the rubber sleeve from the damper body. New dampers are supplied with the sleeve fitted.

Longer springs are available to increase the front ride height. If used, these springs must be fitted in pairs.

Assembling and refitting a unit :

Push the rubber distance ring fully down to the shoulder on the damper body. Push the bump rubber down the damper spindle until it abuts the damper body. Position the compressed spring followed by the rubber ring and the top spring abutment. Slowly release the compression until the top abutment is correctly located with its spigot inside the top coil of the spring. Refit the seat, washer and mounting rubber onto the damper spindle. Insert the spindle through the mounting hole in the chassis and fit the cup washer (belled end towards the chassis), mounting rubber, cup washer (belled end uppermost), nut and locknut. Refit the outer ends of the lower wishbone to the damper trunnion (see **Section 8 : 5**) and refit the ends of the anti-roll bar to the lower ends of the dampers (see **Section 8 : 4**).

8 : 7 Vertical links

Removal :

Remove the hub as described in **Section 8 : 3**. Release the steering rack ball joint as described in **Chapter 9, Section 9 : 9**. Remove the brake caliper as described in **Chapter 10, Section 10 : 4**. Release the outer ends of the lower and upper wishbones as described in **Section 8 : 5** and dismount the vertical link.

If necessary, the stub axle which is a taper fit in the vertical link may be withdrawn after removal of the retaining nut and washer.

Refitting :

Refit the stub axle if it was removed and torque tighten its retaining nut to 8.81 to 10.17daNm (65 to 75lbf ft).

Reassemble the upper and lower wishbones to the vertical link and the damper to the lower wishbone. Refit the brake caliper and the steering rack ball joint. Refit the wheel hub. Refer to the relevant sections for torque tightening figures.

8 : 8 Upper ball joints

Loosen the nut securing the ball joint to the vertical link but do not remove it at this stage. Refer to **Section 8 : 5** and remove the bolts securing the upper wishbone to the ball joint. Push the wishbone down clear of the joint. Using a soft-faced hammer applied to the loosened nut (to avoid damage to the threads), free the ball joint taper. Remove the nut and withdraw the ball joint.

Refitting :

Reverse the removal sequence. Torque tighten the ball joint retaining nut to 5.15 to 5.69daNm (38 to 42lbf ft).

8 : 9 Lower trunnions

Removal :

Remove the vertical link as described in **Section 8 : 7**. Refer to **Chapter 10, Section 10 : 7** and remove the dust cover and brake caliper mounting plate. Refer to **Chapter 9, Section 9 : 10** and remove the steering arm from the vertical link. Unscrew the trunnion from the vertical link and remove the dust seal.

Refitting :

Fit the dust seal. Using 90EP gear oil, thoroughly lubricate the trunnion before reassembling it to the vertical link. Ensure that the damper mounting hole is parallel to the caliper mounting plate flange. Complete refitting by reversing the removal sequence. Refer to the relevant sections for torque tightening figures.

8 : 10 Modifications

Commencing at Elan chassis No 8797 and at Elan +2 chassis No 50/1436, all suspension securing nuts were changed from 'Stover' or 'Philidas' type to 'Nyloc' type. When 'Nyloc' nuts are being fitted to replace the earlier type nuts, **the bolts must also be renewed.**

8 : 11 Track, camber, castor and kingpin inclination

The geometry of the front suspension cannot be adjusted but, in the event of an accident to the vehicle, it is important to check for distortion and deformation damage by making comparisons with the correct dimensions and angles. Refer to the following data.

Track :

Track and other dimensions are quoted in the keys to **FIG 8 : 1**.

Camber :

The camber angle in Elan series 1 and 2 cars should be zero to $\frac{1}{2}°$ (positive). In Elan series 3 and Elan +2 cars camber should be zero to 1° (positive).

Castor :

The castor angle in Elan cars from chassis No 26/3001 to 26/3061 should be 7° (positive). In Elan cars from chassis No 26/3061 onwards and in Elan +2 cars castor should be $3° \pm \frac{1}{2}$ (positive).

Kingpin inclination :

This is the inclination of the line through the upper ball joint and the lower trunnion (the swivel points). It should be $9° \pm \frac{1}{2}°$ on all models.

8 : 12 *Fault diagnosis*

(a) Wheel wobble

1 Worn or loose hub springs
2 Broken or weak front spring(s)
3 Uneven tyre wear
4 Worn suspension linkage
5 Loose wheel fixings
6 Incorrect tracking

(b) 'Bottoming' of suspension

1 Check 2 in (a)
2 Damper(s) defective
3 Bump stop(s) worn

(c) Heavy steering

1 Defective ball joints
2 Incorrect suspension geometry
3 Tyres under-inflated
4 Steering linkage or unit defective (see **Chapter 9**)

(d) Excessive tyre wear

1 Check 4 and 6 in (a); 2 in (c)
2 Incorrect wheel alignment (see **Chapter 9**)

(e) Rattles

1 Check 2 in (a); 1 in (c)
2 Worn suspension bushes
3 Damper(s) loose
4 Anti-roll bar loose

(f) Excessive rolling

1 Check 2 in (a); 2 in (b); 4 in (e)
2 Anti-roll bar broken

CHAPTER 9

THE STEERING GEAR

9 : 1 *Description*

The layout of the steering gear is shown in **FIG 9 : 1**. The steering unit is a rack and pinion type in which a transverse rack is caused to move laterally when the inner steering column turns a pinion. The steering linkage comprises two links which are axially ball jointed to the ends of the rack. For wheel alignment purposes, they are adjustable in length. The links are ball jointed to the steering arms which are secured to the suspension vertical links. A ball joint at the upper end of each link and a trunnion at each lower end provide the steering pivots.

All models, except early Elan +2 models (which are provided with fixed-type columns), have collapsible-type steering columns. Both types are covered by this manual.

9 : 2 *Servicing*

Steering pivots :

Lubrication of the steering pivots is covered under 'Vertical links' in **Chapter 8, Section 8 : 2**.

Front wheel alignment :

At the mileage intervals stated in **Chapter 13** check and, if necessary, adjust the wheel alignment as described in **Section 9 : 11**.

Steering unit :

At the mileage intervals stated in **Chapter 13** remove the plug shown in **FIG 9 : 2** from the steering unit and fit a grease nipple. Use a gun filled with multi-purpose grease and apply **five strokes only**. Over-greasing may 'balloon' the bellows. Remove the nipple and refit the plug.

9 : 3 *Steering wheel removal and refitment*

Set the front wheels in the straightahead position. Note the orientation of the steering wheel. Prise out the horn push from the wheel, remove the securing nut and pull off the steering wheel.

To refit, align the steering wheel in its original orientation and reverse the removal sequence.

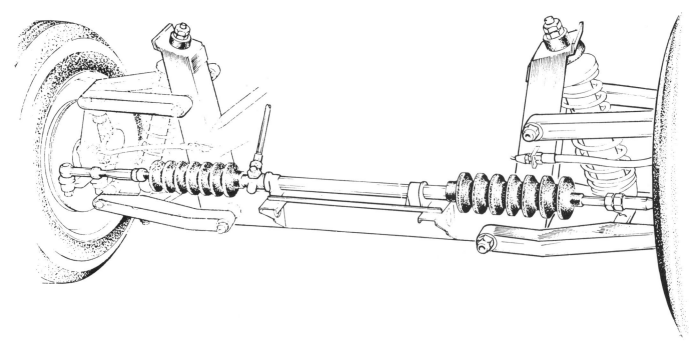

FIG 9 : 1   Layout of the rack and pinion steering gear

9 : 4   *Inner steering column (collapsible-type)*

Removal :

The inner column is removed in two parts, unless the inner and outer columns are removed as a complete assembly.

Refer to **FIG 9 : 3**. Remove the impact clamp and, with a steady pull, withdraw the upper column complete with the steering wheel. Remove the pinch bolt retaining the inner lower column to the steering unit pinion coupling, push the column up into the outer column and, using a suitable rod, continue pushing the lower column upwards until it can be withdrawn into the car interior.

Refitting :

Reverse the removal sequence. The flats on the lower column and the cut-out in the upper column must be aligned to enable the impact clamp to be fitted correctly. Torque tighten the impact clamp to 3.53 to 4.34daNm (26 to 32lbf ft). Check, before tightening the coupling pinch bolt, that there is clearance between the steering wheel hub and the top of the outer column.

9 : 5   *Outer steering column (collapsible-type)*

Removal :

Disconnect the battery. Identify the headlamp dipswitch and the direction indicator switch wiring and their connectors. Disconnect the wiring. Refer to **FIG 9 : 3**. Release the pinch bolt retaining the lower inner column to the steering unit coupling. From below the facia panel, release the nuts securing the upper column clamp. The nuts securing the lower column clamp are accessible from the footwell except in 'S' models in

which access requires removal of the upper fuse unit. Remove the complete steering column from the car. Withdraw the inner column as described in **Section 9 : 4**. Remove the bushes from the outer column.

Refitting :

Fit new nylon bushes (metal reinforcements downwards) to their locations in the outer column with their securing lugs engaged in the holes in the outer column. Refit the inner columns as described in **Section 9 : 4**.

Reinstall the complete column assembly by reversing the removal sequence. Tighten the steering unit pinion to inner column coupling pinch bolt. Check that there is clearance between the steering wheel hub and the top of the outer column.

9 : 6   *Inner steering column (fixed-type)*

FIG 9 : 4 shows the components of the fixed-type steering column assembly.

Removal :

Release the pinch bolt retaining the inner column to the steering unit pinion coupling and, with a steady pull, withdraw the inner column complete with steering wheel.

Refitting :

Reverse the removal sequence. Ensure that the felt bushes at both ends of the outer column do not become displaced. Check that there is clearance between the steering wheel hub and the steering column binnacle. The direction indicator cancellation cam should be horizontal.

9 : 7 *Outer steering column (fixed-type)*

Removal :

Disconnect the battery. From below the binnacle, extract the screws securing it to the upper binnacle and remove both halves. Identify the multi-function switch cables and their connections. Disconnect the cables. Release the pinch bolt retaining the inner column to the steering unit coupling. From below the facia panel, release the clamps which secure the column and withdraw the assembly complete with the steering wheel. Withdraw the inner column and remove the felt bushes from the outer column.

Refitting :

Soak new felt bushes in an EP90 gear oil and insert them into their locations at the ends of the outer column. Do not displace the felt bushes when inserting the inner column. Install the column assembly and loosely attach the securing clamp to the underside of the panel. Tighten the coupling pinch bolt securing the inner column to the steering unit. Ensure that there is clearance between the steering wheel hub and the top of the column. Fully tighten the facia clamp. Reconnect the wiring and refit the binnacle halves. Reconnect the battery.

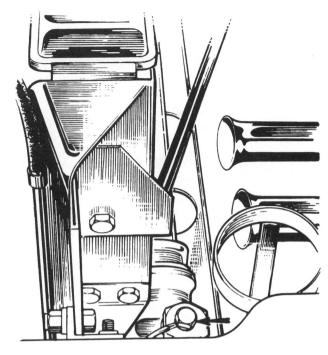

FIG 9 : 2   The steering unit greasing point is arrowed

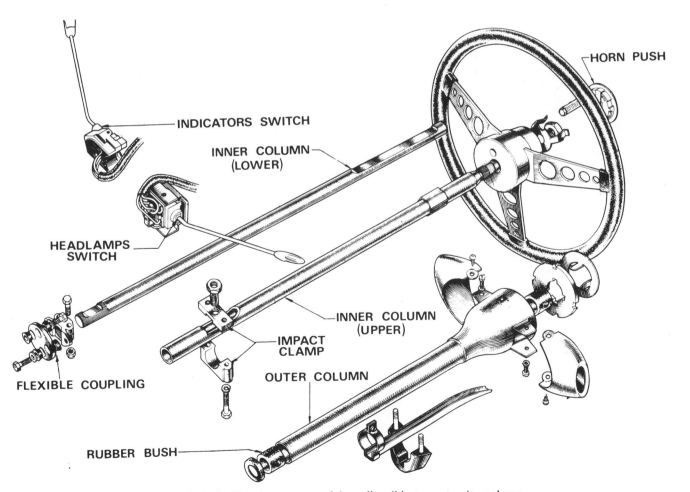

FIG 9 : 3   The components of the collapsible-type steering column

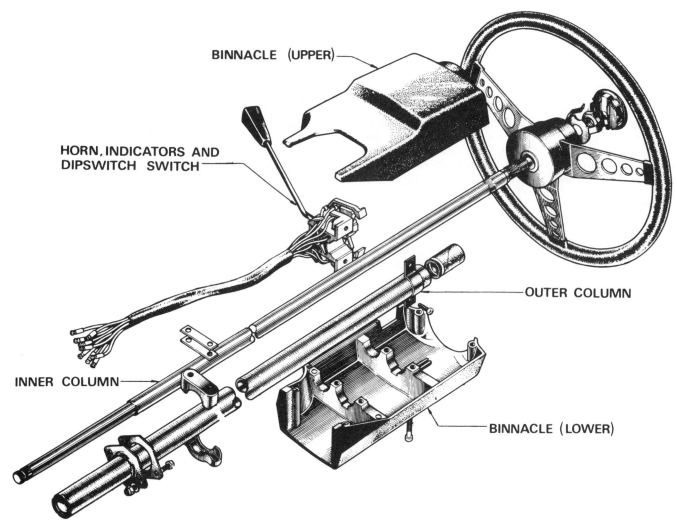

BINNACLE (UPPER)

HORN, INDICATORS AND
DIPSWITCH SWITCH

OUTER COLUMN

INNER COLUMN

BINNACLE (LOWER)

FIG 9 : 4   The components of the fixed-type steering column

9 : 8 *The lock stops*

Limitation of the steering lock is controlled by the locknut shown in **FIG 9 : 5** contacting the rack tube and it is consequently important that dimension 3 in **FIG 9 : 6** is adhered to. If the dimensions specified are achieved and the steering unit is mounted centrally on the chassis, correct steering locks will result.

9 : 9 *The steering unit*

The components of the steering unit are shown in **FIG 9 : 7**.

Removal :

Raise and support the front of the car. Remove the road wheels. Remove the nuts and, using a ball joint extractor, separate the tie rods from the steering arms. Release the coupling pinch bolts securing the inner column to the steering unit.

Remove the nuts and washers securing the unit clamps to the chassis. Identify and collect the packing shims which adjust the unit height. Note the earth strap. Pull the steering unit forwards, disengage the coupling from the inner column and dismount the unit.

Dismantling :

Release the bellows clips and slide both bellows outwards. Slacken the locknuts and unscrew both axial ball joint assemblies from the rack. Withdraw the spring from each end of the rack. Release the tabwasher, unscrew the sleeve nut and remove the tabwasher, shims and cup. Loosen the locknuts and unscrew the outer ball joints from the rods. Remove the locknuts, bellows, clips and cup nut from each tie rod. Remove the locknuts from the rack. Unscrew the cap and remove the shims, spring and pad from the housing.

Remove the circlip and withdraw the pinion assembly, taking care not to lose the dowel peg. Remove the retaining ring, shims, bush and thrust washer. Detach the 'O' ring from the annular groove in the retaining ring. Withdraw the rack and remove the thrust washer and bush from the pinion housing.

Inspection :

After cleaning, examine all parts for wear or damage. Renew as necessary. It is particularly important to check the ball end of the tie rods for 'necking' which, if

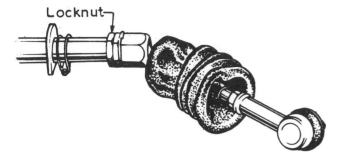

Locknut

FIG 9:5 Limitation of steering lock

it occurs, will be recognised as a groove round the ball to rod waist. **If there is any suggestion of 'necking', renew the tie rods.** If necessary, renew the bush in the end of the rack tube by drifting out the old bush and pressing in a new replacement.

Assembly:

1 Insert the rack into the tube and position the bush and thrust washer into the pinion housing. Assemble the thrust washer, bush and retaining ring to the pinion. Insert the assembly into the pinion housing and secure the pinion with a circlip.

Pinion float adjustment:

2 Set up a dial gauge with its spindle against the end of the pinion shaft. Zero it with the pinion shaft pushed down to its limit. Lift the shaft until the retaining ring contacts the circlip and note the dial reading. This represents the pinion shaft total end float. Remove the circlip and withdraw the pinion shaft assembly. Remove the retaining ring and fit a new 'O' ring into its groove.

3 Make up a shim pack to give minimum end float but with free rotation of the pinion shaft. Shims are available in thicknesses of 0.102mm (0.004in) and 0.254mm (0.010in).

4 Assemble the shim pack and retainer ring to the pinion. Fit the assembly into the housing and finally secure it by fitting the dowel and circlip.

Pinion pressure pad adjustment:

5 Fit the plunger and cap nut to the pinion housing. Tighten the nut to eliminate all end float and, using feeler gauges, measure the clearance between the nut and the housing. Remove the cap nut and plunger. Make up a shim pack equal in thickness to the cap nut to housing clearance **plus** 0.102mm (0.004in).

6 Pack the unit with grease and assemble the cap nut, the shim pack, spring and plunger to the housing and tighten the cap nut. When the nut is correctly adjusted, a torque of 0.18daNm (1.3lbf ft) is required to rotate the pinion. Check and readjust, if necessary, by adding or subtracting shimming from beneath the cap nut.

Tie rod couplings:

7 Refer to **FIG 9:8**. Slide the cup nut over the tie rod and insert the cup into the cup nut. Position the locking tab over the sleeve nut and screw this fully into the cup nut. With the cup nut held in a vice, move the tie rod axially and determine the approximate thickness of shims required. Remove the assembly from the vice. Remove the sleeve nut.

8 Prepare a shim pack slightly thicker than that estimated and fit this in the cup behind the nut. Screw the sleeve nut and locking tab fully into the cup nut. Using feeler gauges, measure the gap between the sleeve nut flange, locking tab and cup nut face. This dimension **plus** 0.05mm (0.002in) is the amount by which the trial shim pack must be **reduced** to give the correct ball end movement. Dismantle the joint and reassemble with the revised thickness of shims taking care not to suddenly tighten the ball joint.

9 Screw the locknut onto the end of the rack so that its position corresponds with the dimensions 3 + 4 + 5 + 3 in **FIG 9:6** (630.43mm (24.82in) between the inner locking faces). Insert the spring into the end of the rack and screw the ball joint assembly as far as possible up to the locknut. Fit the bellows to the rods. Fit the locknuts and outer tie rod ends. Screw them on by exactly 25 turns and tighten the locknuts.

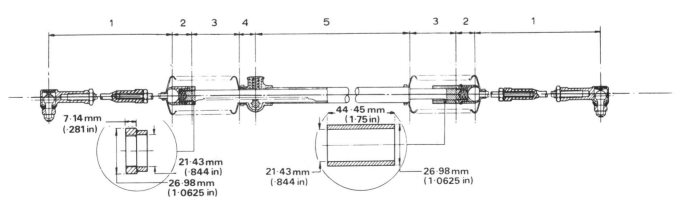

FIG 9:6 Steering gear dimensions

Key to Fig 9:6 1 Elan models, 192.78mm (7.59in); Elan +2 models, 272.54mm (10.73in) 2 34.03mm (1.34in), all models 3 85.85mm (3.38in), all models 4 26.16mm (1.03in), all models 5 432.56mm (17.03in), all models

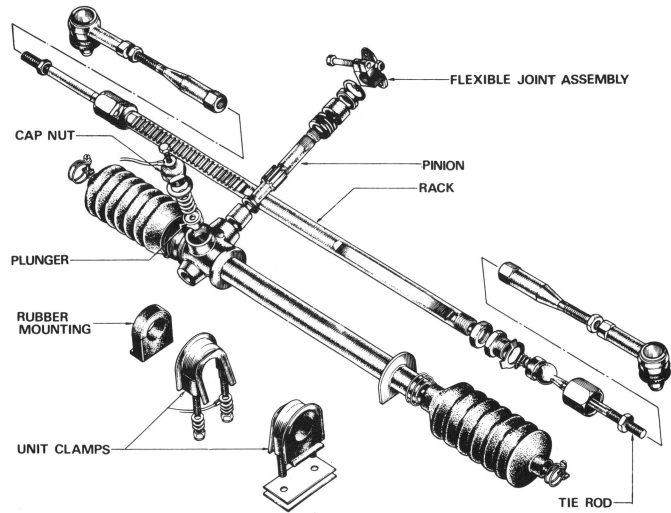

CAP NUT

PLUNGER

RUBBER
MOUNTING

UNIT CLAMPS

FLEXIBLE JOINT ASSEMBLY

PINION

RACK

TIE ROD

FIG 9 : 7   Components of the rack and pinion steering unit

10 Test the adjustment by applying a load of 3.63kg (8.0lb) at the outer end of the tie rod. The rod should articulate freely. If necessary, adjust the shim pack until correct operation is achieved. Shims are available in 0.05mm (0.002in) and 0.254mm (0.010in) thicknesses. When adjustment is correct, lock the assembly by bending the tabwasher over the sleeve nut and the cup nut. Pack the bellows with grease (½oz of multi-purpose grease) and secure them in position with their clips.

Installing the steering unit :

The steering unit shimming heights are marked on the chassis mounting pads. To preclude incorrect steering geometry, adhere to them. A marking of 140 (for example) denotes that, say, three shims of 1.016mm (0.040in) and one shim of 0.508mm (0.020in) will be required. Note that the shimming heights may differ side to side.

Install the assembly with the wheel hubs in the straightahead position. Engage the coupling with the inner steering column. Fit the clamps and their rubber mountings. Ensure that the bolts pass through the shims. Refit the earth strap, washers and nuts. Check

that there is clearance between the steering wheel hub and the top of the outer steering column and fully tighten the coupling pinch bolt. Refit the ball joint ends of the tie rods to the steering arms and torque tighten their nuts to 3.53 to 3.79daNm (26 to 28lbf ft). Refit the road wheels, lower the car and check the wheel alignment as described in **Section 9 : 11**.

9 : 10 *Steering arms*

Removal :

Remove the vertical link as described in **Chapter 8, Section 8 : 7**. Remove the lower two bolts securing the brake disc dust cover, the brake caliper mounting plate and the steering arm to the vertical link.

Refitment :

Reverse the removal sequence. Note that the steering arms are handed left and right. Torque tighten the arm to vertical link bolts to 2.98 to 3.66daNm (22 to 27lbf ft) and refer to the relevant section for other torque tightening figures. Refer to **Section 9 : 11** and check the wheel alignment.

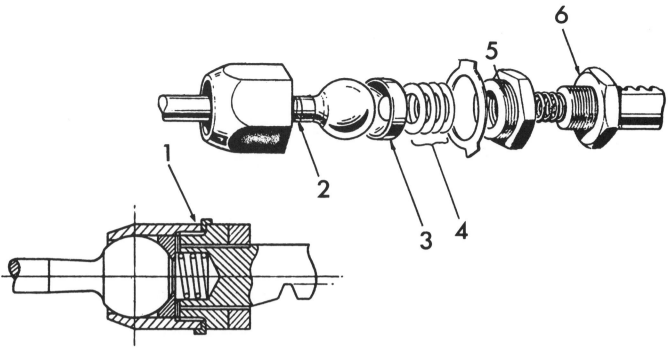

FIG 9 : 8   Rack to tie rod ball joint components

Key to Fig 9 : 8   1 The assembled joint (cross-section)   2 Tie rod   3 Cup   4 Shims   5 Sleeve nut   6 Locknut

9 : 11 *Wheel alignment*

Correct wheel alignment adjustment is most important and it is recommended that the work be entrusted to an agent equipped with the appropriate optical checking equipment. Adjustment is made by turning both tie rods by equal amounts and in the appropriate direction after loosening the locknuts and bellows outer clips. On completion of the adjustment, the locknuts and the clips must be retightened.

Wheel alignment is to specification when the toe-in is 1.60 to 4.76mm (0.062 to 0.187in) on Elan models and zero to 4.76mm (zero to 0.187in) on Elan +2 models.

9 : 12 *Fault diagnosis*

(a) Wheel wobble

1 Wheel(s) out of balance
2 Slack steering connections
3 Incorrect steering geometry
4 Excessive play in steering linkage
5 Defective suspension
6 Worn hub bearings

(b) Wander

1 Check 2, 3 and 4 in (a)
2 Uneven tyre pressures
3 Uneven tyre wear
4 Defective damper(s)

(c) Heavy steering

1 Check 3 in (a)
2 Very low tyre pressures
3 Neglected lubrication
4 Wheels out of track
5 Rack adjustment too tight
6 Inner steering column(s) bent
7 Steering column bushes tight

(d) Lost motion

1 Loose steering wheel, worn splines
2 Worn rack and pinion teeth
3 Worn ball joints
4 Worn wheel pivots
5 Slack pinion bearings
6 Worn inner column to steering unit coupling

NOTES

CHAPTER 10

THE BRAKING SYSTEM

10 : 1 Description

The hydraulic system :

Hydraulically operated front and rear disc brakes are fitted. The three variants of the system are shown in **FIG 10 : 1**. The single line system without servo assistance is shown at **A**. The servo assisted single line system is shown at **B** and the servo assisted dual line system is shown at **C**.

In the single line systems, failure of a hydraulic seal or pipeline will result in potentially rapid failure of the whole system (except of the handbrake). In the dual line system, a seal or pipeline failure in the front brake system leaves the rear brakes operating normally and vice versa. Servo unit failure leaves unassisted braking effort still available to the relevant circuit(s).

A brake failure warning light (with test switch) is incorporated in all models. If this warning light comes on, immediate action must be taken to rectify the fault in the hydraulic system.

Front brakes :

A rigidly mounted caliper straddles each disc. The calipers are twin piston type and each carries two friction pads. Compensation for wear of the friction linings is automatic and functions through the movement of the caliper pistons and seals.

Each caliper is mounted via a mounting plate on a suspension vertical link. A dust shield masks the rear of the brake disc over the area which is not screened by the caliper.

Rear brakes :

The rear calipers are identical in operation to those fitted at the front. Each caliper is mounted on a wheel bearing housing. Dust shields are only fitted to later Elan +2 models.

Vacuum servo unit(s) :

The vacuum servo unit(s) (if fitted) receive fluid from the master cylinder at 'foot pedal' pressure and transfers it to the brake calipers at increased pressure. Power for the pressure boosting is derived from the difference in pressure between atmospheric and the depression (partial vacuum) in the intake manifold.

Handbrake :

The handbrake operates on the rear discs only. Calipers, which are separate and independent from the

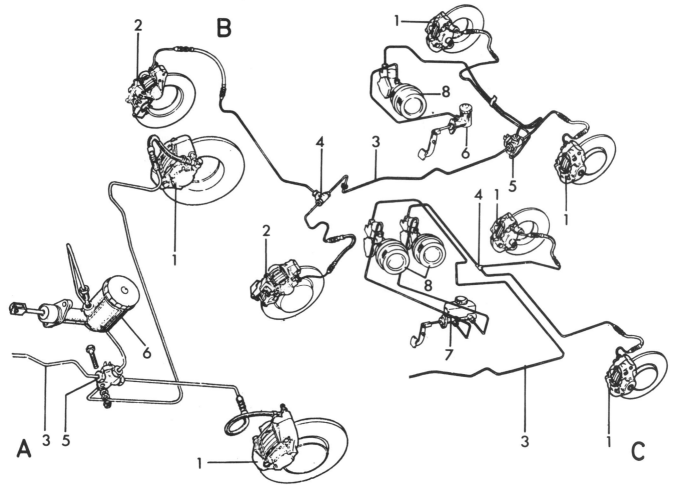

FIG 10 : 1   The variants of the hydraulic braking system

Key to Fig 10 : 1   **A** Single line without servo assistance   **B** Single line with servo assistance   **C** Dual line with servo
assistance   **1** Front brake caliper   **2** Rear brake caliper   **3** Feed to rear calipers   **4** 3-way union   **5** 4-way union
6 Single line master cylinder   **7** Dual line master cylinder   **8** Vacuum servo unit

main calipers, are mechanically applied through a system of cables, rods and levers. Adjustment is required to compensate for pad friction lining wear.

10 : 2 *Servicing*

Master cylinder fluid level :

At the mileage intervals specified in **Chapter 13**, check the fluid level in the master cylinder reservoir. Top up, if necessary, to within 12.5mm (0.50in) of the top. Clean off around the reservoir cap before removing it and check that the air vent is clear. Use only Castrol/Girling Brake and Clutch Universal fluid or a fluid to DOT 3/4. This fluid is also used in the clutch master cylinder.

Caliper pad friction linings :

At the mileage intervals specified in **Chapter 13**, check the thickness of all friction linings. Pads must be renewed before the thickness has worn down to 1.6mm (0.06in). All four pads at the front or at the rear must be renewed at the same time and **never singly or**

only one pair. Renewal procedures are described in **Section 10 : 3**.

Handbrake :

If the handbrake lever movement becomes excessive, adjust as described in **Section 10 : 13**. Renew the pads as described in **Section 10 : 3** before the limit of adjustment is reached.

Vacuum servo unit :

At the mileage intervals specified in **Chapter 13**, renew the servo unit air filter(s) as described in **Section 10 : 14** (if applicable).

Hydraulic system :

At the mileage or time intervals stated in **Chapter 13**, refer to **Sections 10 : 6, 10 : 11** and **10 : 14** and completely overhaul the hydraulic system. In addition to renewing all seals, worn components, etc., renew all hydraulic flexible hoses and (if applicable) vacuum hoses.

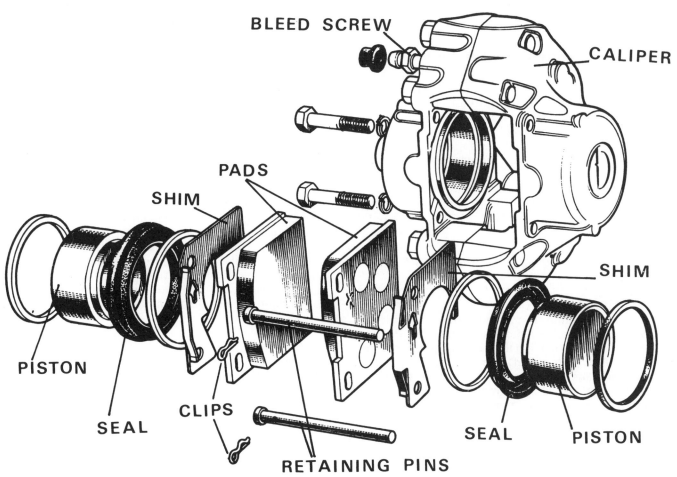

FIG 10 : 2   Components of a front brake caliper

Every 18 months, drain the system and, after flushing, refill with new fluid. The procedure is covered in **Section 10 : 12**.

10 : 3 *Friction pad renewal*

Front brake friction pad renewal :

Raise and support the front of the car. Remove the τoad wheels. Clean off accumulated road dirt from around the brake pads. Remove the pad retaining pin clips, withdraw the retaining pins and, noting how they are fitted, extract the pads and shims. To prevent overflowing, remove a quantity of fluid from the master cylinder reservoir before pressing the caliper pistons back into their bores. Check that the reservoir level does not rise excessively.

Fit the new pads and shims. An arrow, which must point in the direction of forward rotation of the wheel, is marked on the shims. Fit the pins and their clips. Operate the brake pedal several times to bring the pads into adjustment. Check that the pads are free to move slightly (indicating that the pins are not fouling the pads), fit the wheels and lower the car. Top up the reservoir.

Rear brake friction pad renewal :

The procedure is similar to that described earlier for the renewal of front pads. Note, however, that the

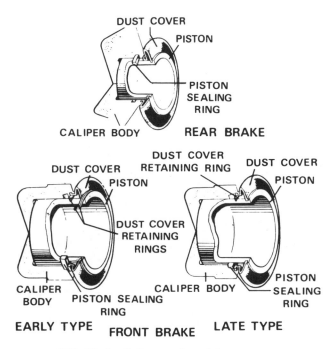

FIG 10 : 3   Caliper seals and dust covers

retaining pins do not pass through the pad plate and that shims are not fitted.

Handbrake friction pad renewal :

Raise and support the rear of the car. Remove the road wheels. Remove the nut, bush and bolt securing the handbrake actuating rod to the caliper operating lever. .Remove the operating lever adjusting nut from its tie rod. Remove the nuts and bolts securing the centralising straps. Swing the clamping levers away from the disc and withdraw the pads from the pivot pins.

Apply a liberal quantity of Girling Brake Grease to all pivot points. Fit the pads by reversing the removal sequence. Adjust as described in **Section 10 : 13** and lower the car.

10 : 4 *Front brake caliper removal and refitment*

Removal :

1 Refer to **Section 10 : 3** and remove the friction pads. If overhaul of the caliper is intended, depress the brake pedal to bring the pistons against the disc. This will facilitate piston removal later.
2 Uncouple the fluid pipe from the caliper and blank off to avoid loss of fluid. From the inner face of the caliper, remove the two mounting bolts and dismount the caliper.

Refitting :

Refit the caliper and torque tighten the two mounting bolts to 2.98 to 3.66daNm (22 to 27lbf ft). The remaining operations are the removal sequence in reverse. On completion, bleed the braking system as described in **Section 10 : 12.**

10 : 5 *Rear brake caliper removal and refitment*

Removal :

1 Carry out operation 1 of the front brake caliper removal procedure described in **Section 10 : 4**.
2 Disconnect the handbrake actuating rod from the operating lever. Note that, on later models, it will be necessary to remove the upper dust shield as described in **Section 10 : 8.**
3 Uncouple the fluid pipe from the caliper and blank off to preclude loss of fluid. From the outer face of the caliper, cut off the locking wire and remove the mounting bolts. Dismount the caliper.

Refitting :

Refit the caliper to the bearing housing and torque tighten the two mounting bolts to 2.98 to 3.66daNm (22 to 27lbf ft). Wire lock the bolts firmly. For the remaining operations, reverse the removal sequence and, finally, bleed the braking system as described in **Section 10 : 12.**

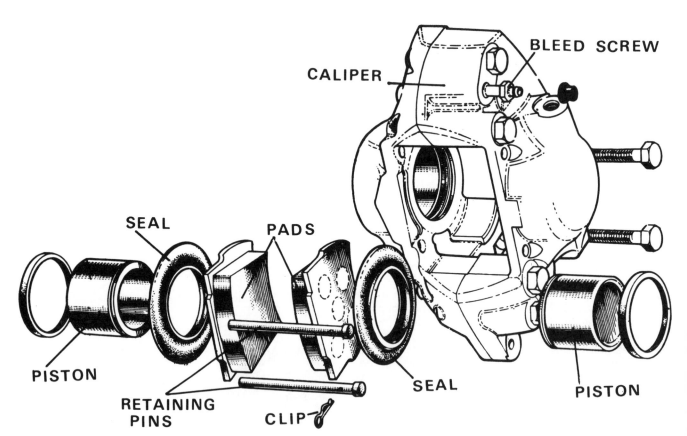

FIG 10 : 4   Components of a rear brake caliper

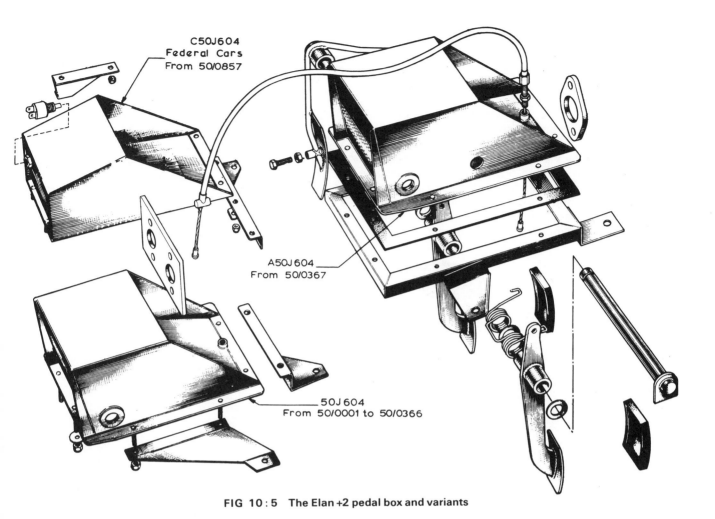

C50J604
Federal Cars
From 50/0857

A50J604
From 50/0367

50J604
From 50/0001 to 50/0366

FIG 10:5   The Elan +2 pedal box and variants

10:6 *Caliper overhaul*

Calipers are made in paired halves bolted together. **Under no circumstances must the halves be separated.**

Dismantling a front caliper:

Dismount the caliper as described in **Section 10:4**. Refer to **FIGS 10:2** and **10:3**. Remove the outer retaining ring (earlier type calipers only). Remove the inner retaining ring and the dust cover. Remove the piston. Withdraw and discard the piston sealing ring. Repeat these operations on the opposite cylinder.

Dismantling a rear caliper:

Dismount the caliper as described in **Section 10:5**. Refer to **FIGS 10:3** and **10:4**. Pull off the dust cover. Remove the piston. Withdraw and discard the piston sealing ring. Repeat these operations on the opposite cylinder.

Inspection and cleaning, front and rear calipers:

Wash the pistons and cylinder bores in clean brake fluid or in methylated spirit. Use no other cleaning agent. Check the pistons and cylinder bores for wear, score marks, corrosion, etc., and renew unserviceable parts. Discard the seals and dust covers and, on reassembly, use new parts from the appropriate service kit.

Assembling, front and rear calipers:

Reverse the dismantling sequence in each case. Assemble with the cylinder bores, piston skirts and piston seals wetted with clean brake fluid.

10:7 *Front caliper mounting plate/dust shield*

Dismount the brake caliper as described in **Section 10:4**. Remove the wheel hub as described in **Chapter 8, Section 8:3**. Refer to **Chapter 8, FIG 8:5** and remove the bolts securing the caliper mounting plate and dust shield to the vertical link. Note that the two lower bolts also retain the steering arm.

Refitting:

Reverse the removal sequence. Torque tighten the mounting plate/dust shield retaining bolts to 2.98 to 3.66daNm (22 to 27lbf ft). For other reassembly procedures and torque tightening figures, refer to **Chapter 8, Section 8:3** and to **Section 10:4**.

10 : 8 *Rear caliper dust shields*

Rear brake dust shields are not fitted to earlier models.

Removal :

Raise and support the car. Remove the relevant road wheel. Remove and discard the four self-locking nuts which secure the upper shield to its mounting bracket. From the upper face of the lower shield, remove the self-tapping screws (and their spire nuts) which secure the shield support clips to the wishbone. Release the locknuts securing the flexible brake hose to the upper mounting bracket and loosen the jubilee clips securing the bracket to the damper. Dismount the shields.

Refitting :

Reverse the removal sequence. Ensure that the flexible hose is not twisted and will not chafe before tightening the locknut. Use new self-locking nuts to secure the upper shield to its mounting bracket.

10 : 9 *Brake discs*

Front brake disc removal and refitment :

Front brake disc removal and refitment is included in the front hub removal and refitment procedures described in **Chapter 8, Section 8 : 3**.

If the disc runout exceeds 0.102mm (0.004in), the cause (distorted disc, dirt between mating faces, maladjusted hub bearing) must be traced and corrected.

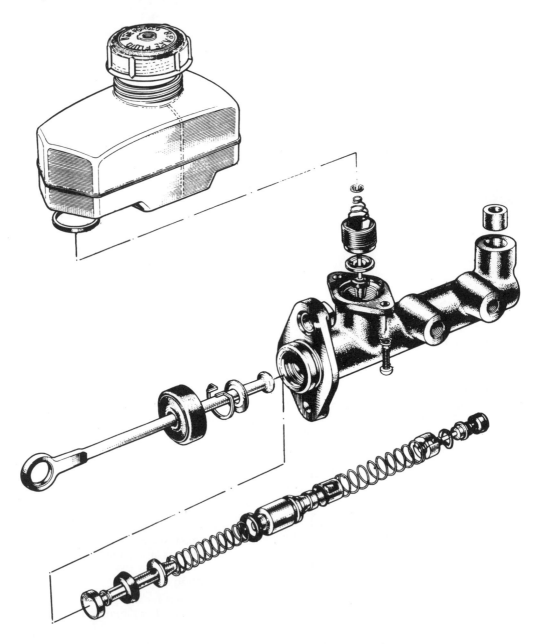

FIG 10 : 6   Assembly of components of the tandem piston (dual line) master cylinder

Rear brake disc removal :

Refer to **Chapter 7, Section 7 : 8** and carry out operations 1 and 2 of the wishbone removal procedure. Remove the brake caliper as described in **Section 10 : 5**. Remove the outboard intermediate shaft outer coupling as described in **Chapter 7, Section 7 : 5**, noting that three of the retaining bolts also secure the brake disc. Turn the disc to clear the outboard drive shaft. Dismount the disc.

Refitting a rear brake disc :

Reverse the removal sequence. Ensure that the mating faces of the disc and outboard drive shaft are scrupulously clean to preclude excessive disc runout. If the runout exceeds 0.102mm (0.004in), trace and correct the cause.

10 : 10 *Pedal box removal and refitment*

The following procedures apply to Elan +2 models only. Three different pedal boxes have been fitted as follows. 50 J604 to chassis Nos 50/0001 to 50/0366, A50 J604 to chassis Nos 50/0367 and onwards and, on models for the USA, C50 J604 to chassis Nos 50/0857 and onwards. Refer to **FIG 10 : 5**.

The removal and refitment procedures are similar for all pedal boxes and are as follows.

Removal (Elan +2 models) :

Uncouple the cable from the accelerator pedal. Uncouple the fluid pipes from the clutch and from the brake master cylinders. Blank off the pipe ends to preclude loss of fluid and entry of dirt. Disconnect the wiring from the stop lamp and from the 'low fluid level' indicator switches. From the upper face of the footwell, remove the nuts securing the pedal box. Withdraw the pedal box as an assembly complete with the master cylinders and pedals. Remove and discard the mounting joint gasket.

Refitting :

. Apply a continuous strip of 'Prestik' to both faces of a new gasket and refit the pedal box assembly to the car by reversing the sequence of the removal operations. Bleed the clutch and braking systems as described in **Chapter 5, Section 5 : 7** and **Section 10 : 12** respectively. Confirm that full travel of the accelerator pedal is available. If necessary, adjust the throttle stop to achieve full travel.

10 : 11 *The master cylinder*

Master cylinders differ between single and dual line systems (see **FIG 10 : 1**). The single line system master cylinder is almost identical with that which operates the clutch release mechanism (see **Chapter 5, Section 5 : 6**).

Removing and refitting the master cylinder, Elan models :

Follow the procedures described in **Chapter 5, Section 5 : 6** for removal and refitment of the clutch

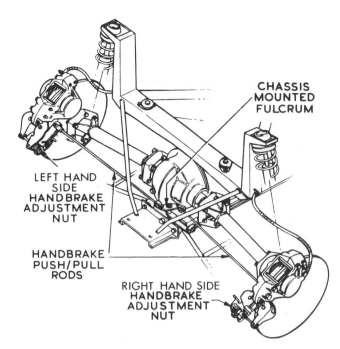

FIG 10 : 7 Layout of handbrake linkage

master cylinder but, in addition, disconnect the wiring from the 'low fluid level' indicator switch on the reservoir cap and, in the case of a dual line master cylinder, two fluid pipes instead of one only. On completion of refitment, bleed the braking system as described in **Section 10 : 12**.

Removing and refitting the master cylinder, Elan +2 models :

The following procedure applies to both single and dual line system master cylinders.

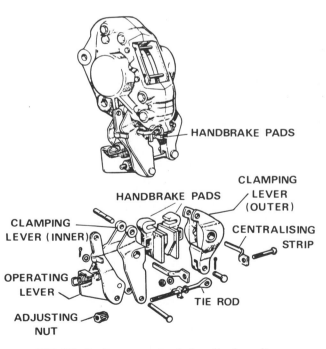

FIG 10 : 8 Components of a handbrake caliper

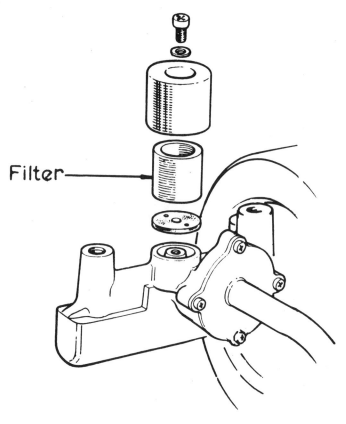

Filter

FIG 10:9 Vacuum servo unit air filter

1 Remove the pedal box as described in **Section 10:10**. Remove the splitpin and clevis pin and separate the master cylinder pushrod from the foot pedal.
2 Remove the retaining nuts and bolts and dismount the master cylinder. Collect and identify any spacers which may have been fitted between the master cylinder flange and the pedal box.
3 Refit by following the removal sequence in reverse. Check that full travel is available at the accelerator pedal. Bleed the brake and clutch systems as described in **Section 10:12** and **Chapter 5, Section 5:7** respectively.

Overhauling the master cylinder:

1 For the single line type master cylinder, follow the procedure described in **Chapter 5, Section 5:6** for the clutch master cylinder. The components are shown in **Chapter 5, FIG 5:4**.
2 For the dual line master cylinder, proceed also as described for the clutch master cylinder in **Chapter 5, Section 5:6**, but note the tandem plunger arrangement. The components are shown in **FIG 10:6**.
3 Discard all seals. Wash all internal parts in new fluid or in methylated spirit. Do not use any other cleaning agent. Inspect the pistons and cylinder bore for excessive wear, scoring or corrosion and other parts for distortion. Renew components as necessary.
4 Assemble with all internal parts wetted with new fluid. Use new seals from the appropriate service kit.

Refer to **Chapter 5, Section 5:6** and (with due regard to the second plunger, spring, etc.) follow the procedure described for reassembly of the clutch master cylinder.

10:12 *Bleeding the system*

This procedure, for which two operators are required, is only necessary if air has entered the system. This may result from the fluid level in the reservoir having fallen too low; because the system has been drained of old fluid or because part of the system has been dismantled. **Do not allow the fluid level in the reservoir to fall below half capacity during the procedure and, when topping up, use only fresh fluid. Do not immediately re-use fluid which has bled from the system as it will be aerated. On relevant models, do not bleed the system with the vacuum servo in operation** (that is with the engine running).

Bleeding procedure:

Clean all dirt from around the relevant bleed screw and remove its dust cap. Attach a bleed tube to the nipple and submerge the free end in a transparent container partially filled with brake fluid. Loosen the bleed screw by about half a turn. Have an assistant pump the brake pedal until fluid emerging from the bleed tube is free of air bubbles. The pumping technique differs for single and dual line systems but, when no further air bubbles emerge, the pedal must be held fully down at the end of a stroke and the bleed screw tightened.

Single line system pumping technique:

Start bleeding at the rear lefthand wheel. Proceed in turn from the wheel farthest from the master cylinder to that nearest to it. The brake pedal should be pumped in a succession of rapid long and short strokes. Push the pedal down through its full stroke and follow with two or three short rapid strokes, then allow it to fly back to its stop with the foot right off.

Dual line system pumping technique:

Bleed the rear brakes first followed by the front brakes. Start bleeding at the lefthand wheel in each case. Use only a light pedal action and do not push the pedal through at the end of its stroke. Do not 'try' the pedal until the system is fully bled. Either action will cause the plunger to move to actuate the brake fail indicator warning light.

If, while bleeding, the plunger operates the warning light, the bleed screw must be closed and a bleed screw in the other circuit must be opened. That is, if bleeding a front brake, open a rear bleed screw and vice versa. A steady pressure must then be applied to the pedal until the warning light goes out. The pressure must then be released immediately and the bleed screw closed otherwise the piston will move too far in the opposite direction and will again have to be reset. When the warning goes out, a 'click' will be felt on the pedal as the piston resets.

Draining and refilling the hydraulic system:

To drain the system, follow the bleeding sequence and open each bleed screw in turn. Fit a bleed tube and pump the brake pedal until no further fluid emerges from the screw. Proceed to the next in order.

Discard the drained fluid :

Flush the system with Castrol/Girling flushing fluid and again drain the system. Fill the reservoir with new fluid straight from the tin. Follow the bleeding procedure, pumping technique and sequence as described earlier for the model being worked on. Keep the reservoir level topped up with new Castrol/Girling Brake and Clutch Universal fluid or any other approved type.

10 : 13 *The handbrake*

The layout of the handbrake linkage at the rear of the car is shown in **FIG 10 : 7**. Caliper components are shown in **FIG 10 : 8**.

Adjustment :

Chock the front wheels and raise the rear of the car. Fully release the handbrake lever. Using feeler gauges and by means of the knurled nuts adjust both calipers to give a maximum clearance of 0.076mm (0.003in) between each disc and each pad. Take up any excess cable slack by means of the adjuster located on the righthand engine mounting support bracket.

Cable renewal :

Fully release the handbrake lever and cable adjusters to give as much cable slack as possible. Pull the cable to free it from its clevis. Loosen the bolt at the forward end of the handbrake lever outer casing. From the upper end of the outer casing, release the pin retaining the handbrake lever, withdraw the lever and release the cable. Remove the cable adjuster and withdraw the cable.

To fit the new cable, reverse the removal sequence. Note that the tube clamping bolt on the forward end of the handbrake lever should only be 'nipped' to tighten as fully tightening it will cause the tube to collapse. Grease all pivot points with Girling Brake grease and adjust the pads as described earlier.

10 : 14 *The vacuum servo*

The function of the vacuum servo unit(s) (if fitted) is described in **Section 10 : 1**. The servo vacuum cylinder is connected to the engine inlet manifold by a hose. Atmospheric air is admitted to the unit via a small filter which must be renewed every 10,000km (6000 miles).

Filter renewal :

Refer to **FIG 10 : 9**. Access to the filter requires the removal of a single screw and washer.

Testing a servo unit :

Switch off the engine and pump the brake pedal several times to clear all vacuum from the unit. Hold a steady light pressure on the pedal and start the engine. If the servo is operating correctly, the brake pedal will move further down without further foot pressure as the vacuum builds up in the system. With the handbrake applied but with the brake pedal released, run the engine up to a medium speed. Turn off the ignition and immediately close the throttle to build up full vacuum. Wait two minutes, then try the brake action with the engine still switched off. Vacuum assistance should be available for at least two operations. If this test fails the non-return valve is faulty. The valve may be either integral with the unit or, as a separate component, it may be in the pipeline between the servo and the inlet manifold.

Overhaul/repair of servo units :

No procedures are prescribed for the overhaul or repair of a servo unit and a defective unit should be removed and a new or exchange replacement unit fitted.

Note, however, that failure of the servo unit does not impair the efficiency of the brakes, but greater foot pedal pressure will be required for the same braking effect.

Routine renewal of servo units :

It is recommended that, as part of the hydraulic system overhaul, the servo unit(s) should be renewed (or exchange replacement(s) fitted) every 65,000km (40,000 miles) or every three years (whichever is reached first).

10 : 15 *Fault diagnosis*

(a) 'Spongy' pedal action

1 Leak in hydraulic system
2 Worn master cylinder
3 Leaking caliper cylinder(s)
4 Air in the system

(b) Excessive pedal movement

1 Check 1 and 4 in (a)
2 Excessive friction pad wear
3 Very low reservoir fluid level
4 Failed front or rear circuit (dual line systems)

(c) Brakes grab or pull to one side

1 Distorted brake disc
2 Wet or oily friction pads
3 Loose caliper
4 Disc loose on hub
5 Worn suspension or steering connections
6 Mixed friction pad linings (different grades)
7 Uneven tyre pressures
8 Seized caliper piston
9 Seized handbrake caliper or linkage

(d) Servo assistance not available (if servo unit(s) fitted)

1 Non-return valve defective
2 Vacuum pipe leaking or displaced
3 Air filter blocked
4 Defective servo unit

NOTES

CHAPTER 11

THE ELECTRICAL EQUIPMENT

11 : 1 *Description*

A range of wiring diagrams is included in the **Technical Data** section of the **Appendix**. Earlier models have the battery **positive** terminal earthed. Later cars have the battery **negative** terminal earthed. Which polarity applies to any given vehicle is readily ascertained by battery inspection. Certain electrical units are interchangeable or adaptable for use with either polarity. Units fitted with electronic devices are not interchangeable and will be irreparably damaged if connected to a car with the opposite polarity to that for which they are intended. **Ensure, when obtaining new or exchange replacement units, that they are suitable for the polarity of the vehicle to which they will be fitted.**

The battery is located behind the passenger seat in Series 1 and 2 Elan models. In all other Elan and Elan +2 models the battery is located in the engine compartment. Fuses are located ·on the bulkhead. The majority of instruments are electrically actuated. The charging circuit may employ either a belt-driven DC generator and control box or a belt-driven AC alternator with an integral rectifier and built-in regulator. A 'no-charge' warning light is provided with both systems.

As the car body is of fibreglass, it is most important to ensure that all earth connections are correctly made. When remaking an earth connection, ensure that the bolt and washer are free from corrosion and lightly smear them with petroleum jelly or silicone grease to inhibit corrosion.

Although information for servicing of electrical equipment is given in this chapter, it must be accepted that it is not sensible to attempt repairs to units which may be seriously defective, electrically or mechanically. Such defective equipment should be replaced by new or exchange replacement units. Testing and adjustment of certain equipment requires specialist facilities and experience.

11 : 2 *The battery*

Depending on the model (see **Section 11 : 1**), either the **positive** or the **negative** battery terminal is earthed. **Do not under any circumstance, reverse the terminal connections.** The connections must be tight on the battery posts and a light coating of petroleum jelly (Vaseline) should be applied to the terminal clamps and posts to retard corrosion and oxidisation.

Keep the fluid in the cells topped up with distilled water to the level of the perforated splash guards.

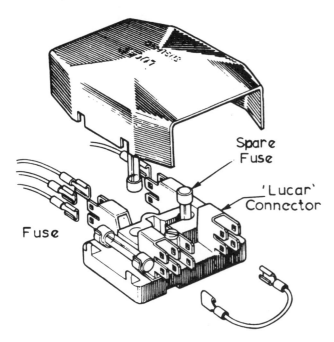

FIG 11:1   A fuse box

Never add undiluted acid. If it is necessary to prepare a new solution of electrolyte due to spillage or loss, add acid to the distilled water. It is highly dangerous to add water to acid.

If the charge state of the battery is suspect, test the electrolyte with a hydrometer. The indications from the specific gravity readings given by the hydrometer are approximately as follows.

	Specific gravity
Cells fully charged	1.270 to 1.290
Cells half charged	1.190 to 1.210
Cells discharged	1.110 to 1.130

These readings will apply when the battery temperature is about 16°C (60°F). For the same cell condition, the specific gravity will increase when the electrolyte temperature is higher than 16°C and vice versa. Add 0.002 for every 3°C (5°F) above 16°C and subtract 0.002 for every 3°C below 16°C.

If the state of the battery is low, take the car for a long daylight run or put the battery on charge at 4 to 5amp. If this does not correct the battery charge state, have the individual cells voltage tested to ascertain whether the battery should be replaced by a new one. If the battery is to be put on charge without dismounting it from the car, disconnect both leads from the battery.

If the battery is to stand for a long period, give it a freshening up charge every month. If left discharged, it will deteriorate and be ruined.

11 : 3 *Fuses and relays*

Fuses :

S-type models are provided with 12 fuses. Other models are provided with two fuses.

If a fuse blows repeatedly, trace the reason for it doing so and, without delay, correct the casual defect. Never fit a replacement fuse of greater capacity than that which has blown since, by doing so, proper circuit protection will be jeopardised.

The circuits protected by the fuses may be traced from the relevant wiring diagram in the **Technical Data** section of the **Appendix**. A fuse unit is shown in **FIG 11 : 1** (see also **FIG 11 : 2** for S-type models). Provision is made for spare fuses. If a spare fuse has to be used, obtain a replacement without delay. A damaged fuse unit cannot be repaired and, after disconnecting the battery earth lead, identify and disconnect the fuse unit wiring, remove the unit and fit a new replacement.

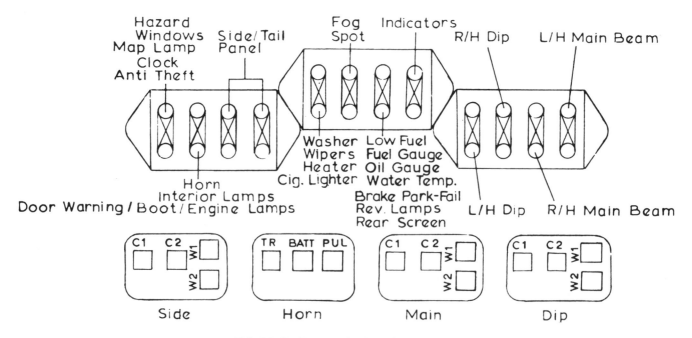

FIG 11 : 2   Fuses and relays, S-type models

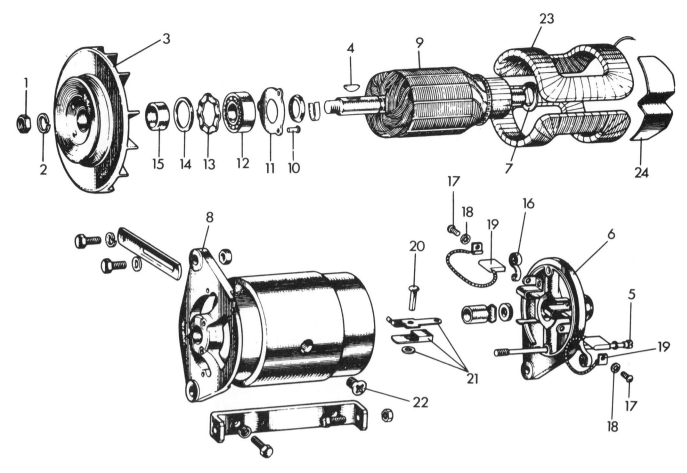

FIG 11 : 3   Components of the DC generator

Key to Fig 11 : 3   1 Nut   2 Washer   3 Driving pulley and fan   4 Key   5 Through bolt   6 Commutator end bracket
7 Washer   8 Drive end bracket   9 Armature   10 Rivet   11 Bearing retaining plate   12 Bearing   13 Corrugated washer
14 Felt washer   15 Bush   16 Brush spring   17 Screw   18 Washer   19 Brush   20 Terminal retainer
21 Terminal, block and washer   22 Pole retaining screw   23 Field coils   24 Shield

Relays :

Refer to **FIG 11 : 2** and/or to the relevant wiring diagram to ascertain the circuits in which relays are employed. Do not attempt to repair a defective relay but fit a new replacement. Before suspecting that a relay is defective, check that the relevant fuse is intact and, using jump wires or a test lamp, confirm that the relevant switch is serviceable and that there is no discontinuity in the wiring.

11 : 4 *The generator and control box*

The Lucas DC generator operates in conjunction with either a type RB 106/2 or a type RB 340 control box.

Maintenance :

Every 20,000km (12,000 miles) or every 12 months, oil the felt ring by injecting a few drops of 10W/30 engine oil into the hole marked 'OIL' at the rear (commutator) end of the generator.

Every 50,000km (30,000 miles), remove the generator for inspection and overhaul of the brush gear.

Tensioning and removal of the drive belt is described in **Chapter 4 Section 4 : 3**.

Testing a generator :

Before suspecting that a generator is unserviceable, confirm that the drive belt is in good condition and that it is correctly tensioned as described in **Chapter 4, Section 4 : 3**. Confirm also that the terminal connections are tight and that the wiring is intact. If these are in order, proceed with the following test procedure.

1 With the engine stationary, switch off all lights and accessories and pull off the connectors from the generator terminal blades. Link the two blades with a short length of wire. **Check whether the car has a positive or a negative earth system** (see **Section 11 : 1**).

2 Start the engine and run at idling speed. For a positive earth car, clip the positive lead of a moving coil zero to 20 range voltmeter to the **D** terminal and the negative lead to a good earthing point on the generator. For a negative earth car, reverse these voltmeter connections.

3 Gradually increase the engine speed. The voltmeter reading should rise rapidly and without fluctuation. Do not race the engine and do not allow the voltmeter reading to reach 20 volts. It will be sufficient to run up to 1500r/min.

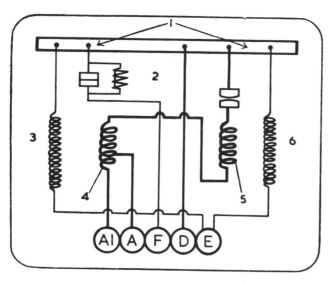

FIG 11:4 RB 106/2 control box circuit

Key to Fig 11:4   1 Frame   2 Field resistance
3 Shunt coil   4 Tapped series coil   5 Series coil
6 Shunt coil

4 If the voltage does not rise rapidly and without fluctuation, remove the radio suppression capacitor (if fitted) from between the output terminals and earth and repeat the test. If the test is now satisfactory, discard the capacitor and fit a new replacement.

5 If the test is still unsatisfactory, note, before removing the generator as described later, if there is excessive sparking at the commutator (an indication that the armature may need renewal).

6 If the test is satisfactory, the generator is serviceable. Remove the wire link and restore the original connections. The charging fault must then be traced to the control box or to the wiring.

Generator removal and refitment :

Identify and disconnect the wiring, remove the adjusting bolt and disengage the drive belt. Remove the

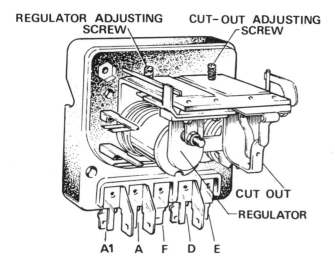

FIG 11:5 The RB 106/2 control box

two pivot bolts and dismount the machine.

To refit, reverse this sequence.

Dismantling a generator :

Unless an owner has the facilities, tools and experience of overhauling electrical machines, he should pass a defective generator to a specialist for overhaul or he should fit a new or an exchange replacement unit.

Refer to **FIG 11:3**. Remove items 1 to 9 in that order. Note that the armature does not have to be pressed out of the drive end bracket unless the bearing 12 or the armature itself has to be renewed. Remove the brushes 19 and their springs 16 from the commutator end bracket. The minimum brush length is 6mm (0.25in). The specified range of brush spring load is 370 to 850g (13 to 30oz). To clean up pits and burns, the commutator may be diamond turned. The refinished diameter must not be less than 36.4mm (1.43in). Clean the slots between the segments but **do not increase the undercuts**. The field resistance should be 6 ohms. Carry out standard insulation and continuity tests. If a new plain bush bearing is required, immerse it in engine oil for 24 hours and **do not ream after fitting**. Check the insulation of the brush holders from the commutator end bracket and ensure that the brush holders are clean and free from burrs and damage which could affect free movement of the brushes.

Reassembling a generator :

Reverse the dismantling sequence. Do not use the drive end bracket as a bearing support when refitting the armature (if it was separated). Ensure that the brushes slide freely in their holders and, if necessary, use a smooth file to ease their fit. Fit the fibre washer(s) and commutator end bracket to the yoke so that the dowel on the bracket locates with the yoke groove and ensure that the brush connectors do not get trapped. Use a thin screwdriver through the ventilator holes to lever the brushes gently into position. On completion of the assembly, lubricate the bush bearing felt as described earlier.

Repolarising a replacement generator :

Install the generator but do not connect the wiring to the **D** and **F** terminals. Determine the earth polarity of the vehicle (see **Section 11:1**). Temporarily connect a jumper lead to the battery positive terminal for a negative earth system vehicle and vice versa for a positive earth system. Flick the other end of the jumper lead several times against the **F** terminal. Disconnect the jumper lead.

The control box :

The control box may either be a two bobbin (voltage regulator and cut-out) type RB 106/2 or a three bobbin (current regulator, voltage regulator and cut-out) type RB 340.

Do not disturb the control box until the testing procedure described earlier has been carried out and has indictated that control box adjustments are required. An owner who does not have experience of control box adjustment or does not have access to first-rate moving coil meters should have a suspect box examined by a specialist to confirm that the box is defective by substituting one known to be serviceable.

Those who have the requisite experience and equipment should refer to **FIGS 11:4, 11:5** and **11:6** which relate to the type RB 106/2 box or to **FIGS 11:7, 11:8** and **11:9** which relate to the type RB 340 box.

Substituting an alternator:

Cars fitted initially with a DC generator may, **if the earthing system is negative earth,** be fitted with an alternator in place of the DC generator.

11:5 *The alternator*

The alternator is a 3-phase AC machine with an integral diode rectifier and built-in regulator. It carries its own cooling fan and is belt driven from the crankshaft.

Observe the following precautions:

1 Never disconnect the regulator or the battery while the alternator is being driven.
2 Never disconnect or dismount the alternator without first disconnecting the battery.
3 Never test the alternator either in the car or on a test bench unless the battery is in circuit. Ensure that the battery is in good condition and fully charged and that the negative is earthed. Never reverse the polarity.

Tests on an alternator which is not charging:

Before suspecting that an alternator is unserviceable, confirm that the drive belt is in good condition and that it is correctly tensioned as described in **Chapter 4, Section 4:3.** Confirm also that the terminal connections are tight and that the wiring is intact. If these are in order, proceed with the following test procedures.

Alternator rated output:

1 Disconnect the battery. Remove the two-piece connector from the alternator. Remove the moulded cover and refit the connector.
2 Disconnect the main cable from the starter motor solenoid. Connect the positive of a zero to 60amp range ammeter to this cable and the negative to the solenoid. Reconnect the battery.
3 Connect a jumper lead between the green cable (f) and the black cable (–) on the regulator. Switch on all the vehicle lights (with the headlamps on main beam). Switch on the ignition and confirm that the warning light is illuminated. Start the engine and slowly increase the speed. At an **alternator** speed of about 1500r/min, the warning light should go out.
4 Increase the engine speed until the alternator is running at 6000r/min. Run for three or four minutes and note the ammeter reading. With a warm alternator this should indicate the rated output of 36amps. This reading may be exceeded if the alternator is cold.
5 If the output differs appreciably from the rated figure, remove the alternator for bench examination. Note, however, that a high resistance in the

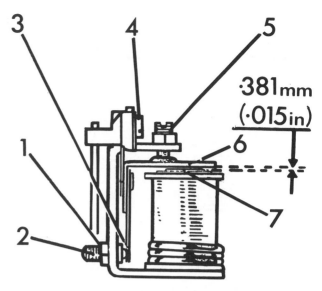

FIG 11:6 Mechanical setting of the regulator (RB 106/2 control box)

Key to Fig 11:6   1 Locknut   2 Voltage adjusting screw
3 Armature tension spring   4 Armature securing screws
5 Fixed contact adjusting screw   6 Armature   7 Core face and shim

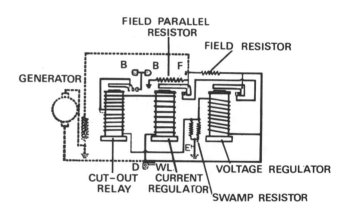

FIG 11:7 RB 340 control box circuit

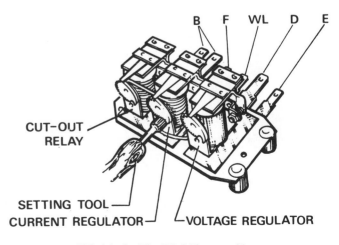

FIG 11:8 The RB 340 control box

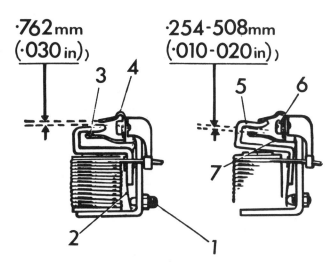

·762mm
(·030 in))

·254-508mm
(·010-020 in))

FIG 11 : 9 Mechanical setting of the cut-out (RB 340 control box)
Key to Fig 11 : 9 1 Cut-out adjusting screw 2 Armature tension spring 3 'Follow through', 0.254 to 0.508mm (0.010 to 0.020in) 4 Stop arm 5 Armature tongue and moving contact 6 Armature securing screws 7 Fixed contact blade

charging circuit (loose, dirty, corroded connections, etc.) will affect the alternator output.

Charging circuit voltage drop test :

6 Connect the red lead of a good quality, low range (allowing accurate readings to 0.25 volt) voltmeter to the alternator main (+) terminal and the black lead to the battery **positive** terminal.

7 Switch on the headlamps on main beam and run the engine to give an alternator speed of 6000r/min. The voltmeter reading should not exceed 0.5 volt. Switch off the lights.

8 Stop the engine and transfer the voltmeter connections to the alternator negative (–) and the battery negative (earth). Repeat operation 7. The voltmeter reading should not exceed 0.25 volt. Switch off the lights.

9 If the readings in operation 7 or operation 8 exceed those specified, a high resistance in the charging circuit is indicated. Trace and rectify this.

Checking the voltage regulator :

10 Ensure that the wiring and connections in the charging circuit are satisfactory (operation 9). Ensure that the battery is well charged (see **Section 11 : 2** and, if it is not, temporarily exchange it for one that is.

11 Connect a good quality (suppressed zero or extended scale type 12 to 15 volt) voltmeter across the battery terminals. Connect a 60amp range ammeter as described in operation 2.

12 Start the engine and run the alternator at about 5000r/min until the ammeter shows an output not exceeding 7.5amp. The voltmeter should then read within the range of 14.1 to 14.5 volts. If the voltage is unstable or outside this range, renew the regulator (it cannot be adjusted and component parts cannot be serviced individually).

Alternator removal and refitment :

Disconnect the battery. Identify and disconnect the alternator wiring. Disengage the drive belt (see **Chapter 4, Section 4 : 3**). Support the alternator, remove the loosened mounting bolts and dismount the machine.

To refit, reverse the removal sequence. Tension the drive belt as described in **Chapter 4, Section 4 : 3**.

Dealing with a defective alternator :

Unless an owner has the appropriate facilities and experience of overhauling electrical machines and some knowledge of electronics, he should pass a defective alternator to a specialist for repair or he should fit a new or an exchange replacement machine.

Those with the requisite experience and knowledge should proceed as follows.

Dismantling the alternator :

The location of the suspected defect will dictate the extent to which the machine requires to be dismantled.

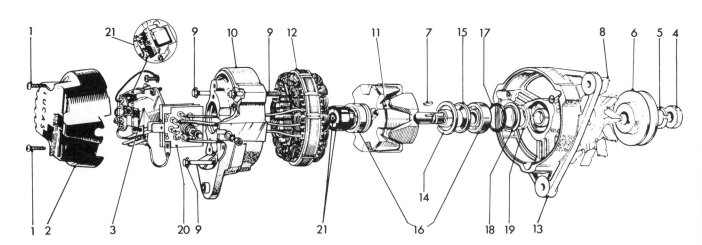

FIG 11 : 10   The AC alternator. Numerals indicate dismantling sequence

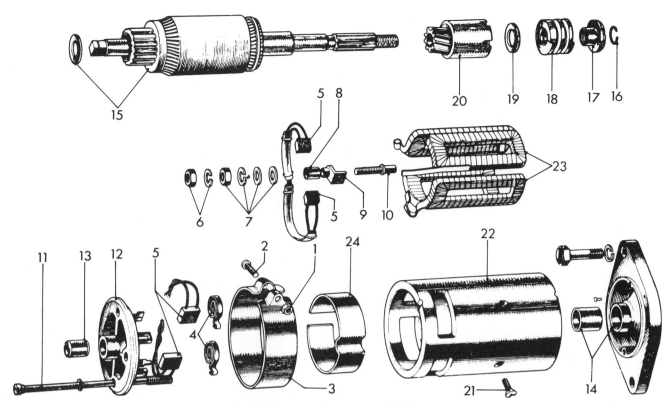

FIG 11 : 11   Components of the type M35G starter motor

Key to Fig 11 : 11   1 Nut   2 Bolt   3 Band   4 Brush springs   5 Brushes   6 Nut and washer   7 Nut and washers
8 Insulated bush   9 Bracket   10 Terminal post   11 Through bolt   12 Commutator end bracket   13 Bush
14 Drive end bracket and bush   15 Armature and washer   16 Jump ring   17 Collar   18 Spring   19 Washer
20 Pinion assembly   21 Pole screw   22 Yoke   23 Field coils   24 Shield

Within that proviso, remove components generally in the order in which they are numbered in **FIG 11 : 10**. If the stator is to be separated from the rectifier, long-nosed pliers should be used as a heat sink when unsoldering the leads from the output diodes. Note carefully the order in which the connections are made.

Inspection and testing :

The length of new brushes is 12.7mm (0.5in). Renew the brushes if the free protrusion from the brush box moulding is less than 5.0mm (0.2in). The brush spring load should be 200 to 280g (7 to 10oz). Slip ring surface defects must **not be corrected by machining** but very fine glass **(not emery)** paper may be used.

The resistance of the rotor winding should be 4.165 ± 5% ohms at 20°C (68°F) and the stator winding resistance should be 0.133 ohms per phase. Use a 15W test lamp and 110 volts DC to check the insulation between a slip ring and a rotor pole and between the stator coils and lamination pack. Check each stator coil for continuity with a 12 volt battery and a test lamp of not less than 36W. If suspect, check the diodes with a 12 volt battery and a 1.5W test lamp. If a diode is defective, renew the complete diode pack. When resoldering, work quickly using only 'M' grade 45/55 tin/lead solder and a very effective heat sink.

Reassembling the alternator :

Reverse the dismantling sequence. Ensure that the slip ring end bearing is positioned fully along the rotor shaft towards the field assembly. Check that the brushes are correctly positioned and ensure that the centre brush is fitted with the special leaf spring. Torque tighten the rectifier retaining nuts to 0.41 to 0.45daNm (3 to 3.3lbf ft) and the through bolts to 0.51 to 0.57daNm (3.75 to 4.17lbf ft). If the rotor and drive end bracket were separated, do not use the end bracket as a support for the bearing whilst fitting the rotor.

11 : 6 The starter motor

Either a type M35G or a type M35J starter motor may be fitted. The components of these machines are shown in **FIGS 11 : 11** and **FIG 11 : 12** respectively. The starter motor is switched via the ignition switch and a bulkhead-mounted solenoid switch. The pinion drive is inertia engaged.

Tests for a starter which does not operate :

Check the condition of the battery and its connections. If these are in order, switch on the lights and operate the starter switch. Current is reaching the starter motor if the lights go dim. If they do not, check

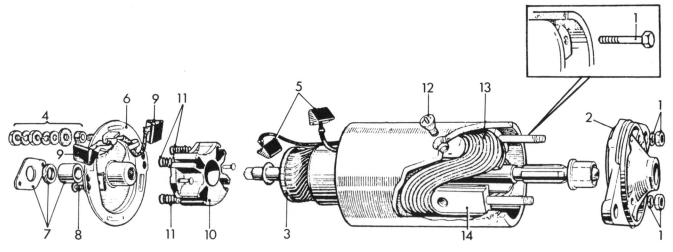

FIG 11 : 12   Components of the type M35J starter motor

Key to Fig 11 : 12   1 Nut and washer (earlier motors) or bolt (later motors)   2 Drive end bracket   3 Armature   4 Terminal nuts and washers   5 Brushes   6 Commutator end bracket   7 Retainer, felt washer and bush   8 Screw   9 Brushes   10 Brush holder   11 Brush springs   12 Pole screw   13 Field coils   14 Pole and (earlier motors) stud

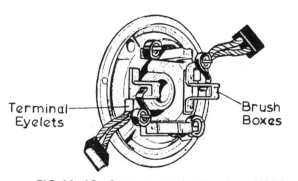

FIG 11 : 13   Starter motor brushes (type M35G)

with a voltmeter or test lamp that there is voltage at the solenoid. If there is, suspect a defective solenoid. If there is not, suspect a defective ignition switch or a discontinuity in the wiring between the ignition switch and the solenoid. If the starter is heard to operate but does not crank the engine, the starter pinion assembly is seized or damaged. If all these points are in order, the starter motor itself is defective and should be removed for investigation.

Removing and refitting the starter motor :

Disconnect the battery. Disconnect the cable to the solenoid. Remove the retaining bolts and dismount the motor.

To refit, reverse the removal sequence.

Servicing the brush gear :

Access to the brushes on the type M35G motor requires only removal of the band cover. Access on the type M35J motor requires removal of the commutator end cover. **FIG 11 : 13** relates to the M35G and **FIG 11 : 14** to the M35J motor.

Renew brushes when they are worn to a length of 8mm (0.31in) in the case of the M35G motor or to 9.5mm (0.373in) in the case of the M35J motor. Sticking brushes should be cleaned with a petrolmoistened cloth and, if necessary, eased with a smooth file. Brush spring load should be 850 to 960g (30 to 34oz) for the M35G machine and 800g (28oz) for the M35J when a new brush is pressed into its guide against its spring to the point at which only 1.5mm (0.06in) is protruding. A push-type spring balance is required for this load measurement. If, on the M35J, the spring loads are appreciably below the 800g (28oz) figure, the end bracket complete with springs and moulding should be renewed.

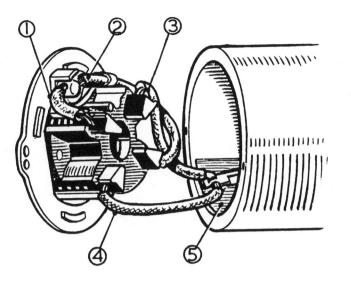

FIG 11 : 14   Starter motor brushes (type M35J)

Key to Fig 11 : 14   1 Short brush flexible C/E bracket
2 Long brush flexible C/E bracket   3 Long brush flexible
field winding   4 Short brush flexible field winding   5 Yoke
insulation piece

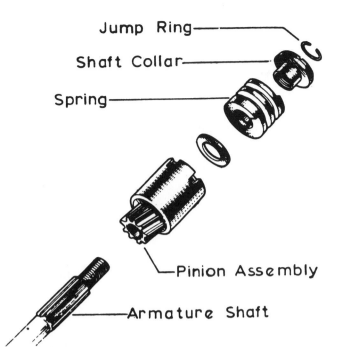

FIG 11 : 15   Starter motor pinion drive

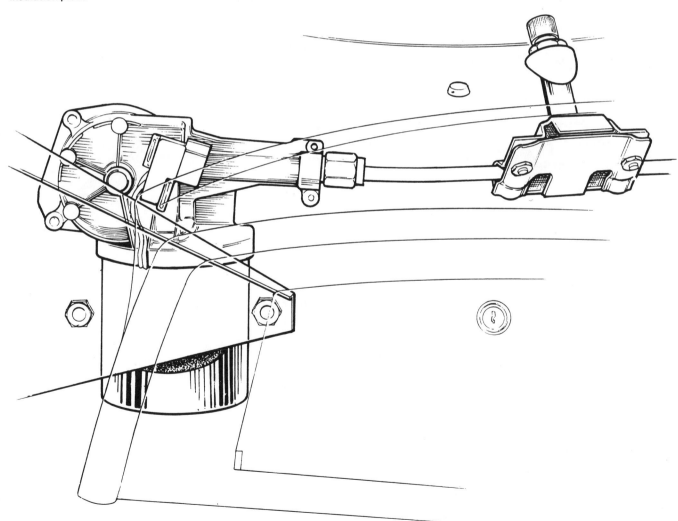

FIG 11 : 16   Windscreen wiper motor and drive (earlier models)

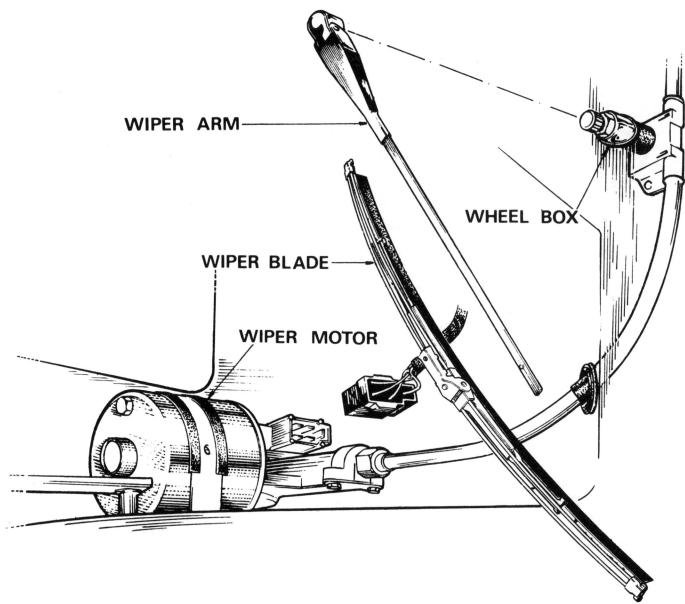

WIPER ARM

WHEEL BOX

WIPER BLADE

WIPER MOTOR

FIG 11 : 17 Windscreen wiper motor and drive (later models)

Dismantling and reassembling a starter motor :

Unless an owner has the facilities, tools and experience of overhauling electrical machines, he should pass a defective starter motor to a specialist for overhaul or he should fit a new or an exchange replacement unit.

Refer to **FIG 11 : 11** or to **FIG 11 : 12** as relevant and dismantle in the order in which the components are numbered.

Reassembly is in general the reverse of the dismantling procedure.

Inspection, servicing and testing :

Check the brushes and their springs as described earlier. Use 110 volt AC and a 15W test lamp to check brush holder and terminal to commutator end bracket insulation. Check the armature and field coil insulation

similarly. Check the field coil continuity with a 12 volt battery and test lamp. Use a 'growler' to check the armature for shortcircuited windings and fit a new armature if a fault is indicated. Inspect the pole shoes for signs of fouling by the armature core. This would indicate a distorted armature and will require a new replacement.

The commutator may, if necessary be lightly skimmed to correct surface defects. Remove only the minimum amount of copper from the diameter or the end face. The minimum thickness of end face copper (type M35J) is 2.0mm (0.08in). The insulation between the commutator segments must not be undercut on either type of motor.

If a new porus bearing bush is being fitted, immerse it in engine oil for 24 hours before pressing it into position with a highly polished mandrel. **Do not machine or**

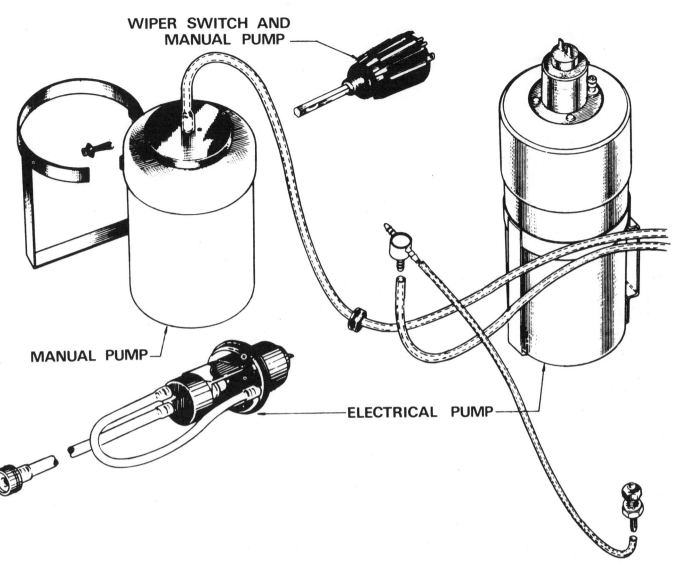

WIPER SWITCH AND
MANUAL PUMP

MANUAL PUMP

ELECTRICAL PUMP

FIG 11 : 18 The manual and electrical versions of the windscreen washers

ream the bore after fitting as this would impair the porosity.

Starter pinion :

Refer to **FIG 11 : 15**. To dismantle, remove the armature from the motor, compress the spring with a suitable clamping device, release the jump ring and withdraw the components from the armature shaft.

Use paraffin to clean the shaft splines and the pinion assembly components. If either the barrel or the screwed sleeve is unserviceable, renew both together. After reassembly, check that the pinion and barrel assembly moves freely on the screwed sleeve.

A seized or jammed pinion can usually be freed by applying a spanner to the commutator end shaft extension.

Starter solenoid :

The solenoid cannot be serviced or repaired and, if defective, must be discarded and a new unit fitted. Dis-

connect the battery before identifying and disconnecting the cables from the solenoid.

11 : 7 *Windscreen washer and wipers*

The earlier type motor and drive are shown in **FIG 11 : 16** and the later type in **FIG 11 : 17**.

Blade renewal :

Lift the blade and arm clear of the windscreen. From beneath, raise the spring clip and pull off the blade. When fitting the new blade, ensure that the locating pip on the arm fully engages the hole in the blade.

Arm removal and refitment :

Lift the spring retaining clip and slide the arm from the spindle.

When refitting, operate and switch off the wipers to bring the spindles to the 'park' position. Refit the arms in the 'park' alignment and check the arc of operation.

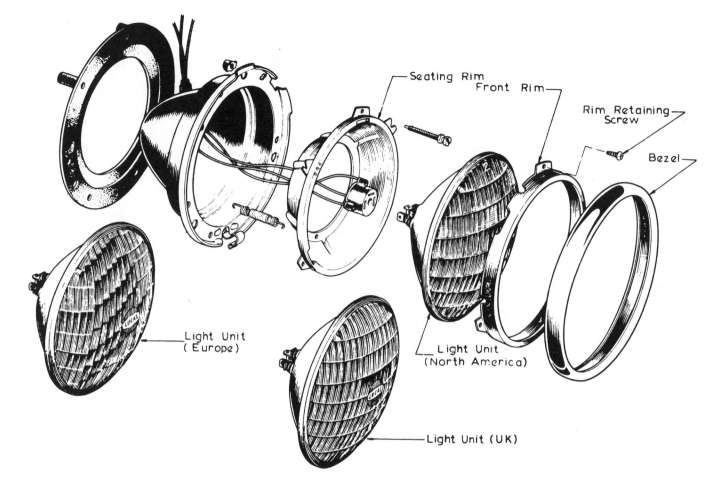

Seating Rim
Front Rim
Rim Retaining Screw
Bezel
Light Unit (Europe)
Light Unit (North America)
Light Unit (UK)

FIG 11 : 19   Sealed beam headlamps

The spindle serrations allow adjustment of the 'park' alignment.

Inoperative or sluggish wipers :

If wipers do not operate, check that the relevant fuse is intact. If it is, check that there is voltage at the motor plug. If not, check the wiper switch and/or the continuity of the wiring. If all these points are in order, the motor itself must be suspect. If the operation is sluggish, suspect a partially seized rack or wheelbox. Note, however, that the higher speed operation may appear sluggish if the windscreen is not **really** wet. The current taken by the motor should not exceed 1.5amps at normal speed or 2.0amps at high speed with the rack and the wheelboxes connected and in good order.

Motor removal and fitment :

Disconnect the battery. Pull out the wiring connector block. Release the bundy tubing coupling nut. Support the motor, remove the screw securing the mounting strap and withdraw the motor complete with the driving rack.

Adequately grease the rack before following the reverse of the removal sequence.

Wheelbox removal and refitment :

Remove the wiper arms and the motor as described earlier. Remove the radio (if fitted). Refer to **Section 11 : 10** and remove the tachometer and the speedometer. Remove the nut, washer and rubber bush from the spindles. From beneath the facia, pull the wheelboxes from their locations and pass them down into the car from behind the glovebox.

To refit, reverse the removal sequence but ensure that the rubber bushes correctly fit the body contour.

Washers :

Depending upon the model and territory, either a manually or an electrically operated washer pump is incorporated. Both versions are shown in **FIG 11 : 18**. No procedures are prescribed for the servicing of the pump or switch and a defective unit should be replaced by a new unit of the appropriate type.

11 : 8 *Headlamp and lighting circuits*

Headlamps :

Variants of the headlamps are shown in **FIGS 11 : 19** and **11 : 20**. The type fitted depends upon the model and country in which the car will operate.

Headlamp bezel removal :

To remove a bezel, insert the tool (see **FIG 11 : 21**) between the bezel and the rim. Slide the tool round to the bottom. Give a sharp tug in an upward direction to pull the bezel clear of the rim.

Headlamp beam alignment :

Access to the trimming screws requires removal of the bezel. The top screw provides vertical adjustment and the side screw provides lateral adjustment.

Beam aiming should always be carried out by an agent who is equipped with an optical type beam setter. Temporarily acceptable, though less accurate, adjustments can be made using a wall or an aiming board marked out with dimensions **A** and **B** as shown in **FIG 11 : 22**. Final setting should always be professionally carried out.

Headlamp vacuum systems :

There are two types of system. In the 'non-failsafe' system the headlamp bowls are held in the closed position by spring pressure and raised by operation of the vacuum cylinder (the vacuum reservoir is formed by the chassis crossmember between the uprights and there is a non-return valve in the vacuum supply pipe from the engine induction manifold). In the 'failsafe' system (the second system), the bowls are held in the raised position by spring pressure if the engine is stationary and closed by the vacuum cylinder when the engine is started (depending upon the position of the facia control). When the engine is switched off, the vacuum system will continue to hold the bowls in the closed position for at least 12 hours provided that the non-return valve and vacuum pipes are not leaking.

11 : 9 *Horns*

Wind-tone horns :

These are electro-magnetically vibrated diaphragm type. They need no maintenance. Adjustment to compensate for wear is carried out at the small screw. Turn the screw anti-clockwise until the horn just fails to sound and then turn back by one quarter of a turn. The aim should be to obtain the best performance for the minimum current.

Air-horns :

These horns operate by vacuum from an adjacent compressor. Every 5000km (3000 miles), apply a few drops of light oil through the orifice marked OIL. Ensure that the vacuum pipes are in good condition and that their connections with the compressor, the Y-piece and the horns are well made. The compressor is energised via a switch and a relay.

11 : 10 *Instruments*

Voltage stabiliser :

This unit is mounted on the rear face of the speedometer in Elan models and, in Elan +2 models, below and to the right or left of the speedometer (RH and LH drive

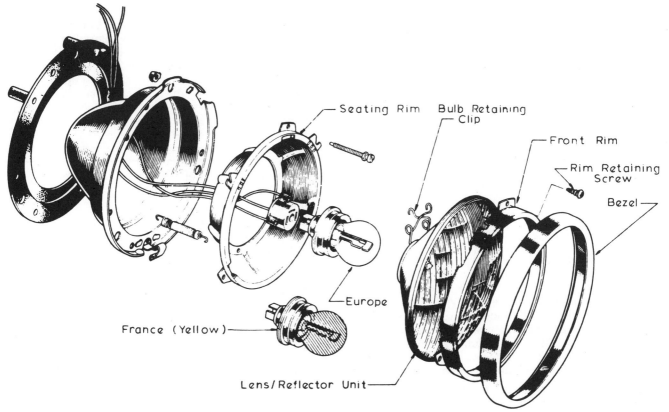

FIG 11 : 20 Headlamp (bulb type)

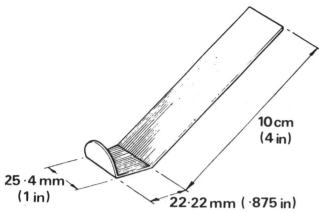

FIG 11:21 Headlamp bezel removing tool

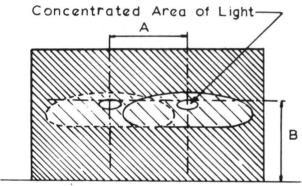

A - Distance Between Headlamps Centre
B - Height of Headlamp Above Ground

FIG 11:22 Headlamp alignment board

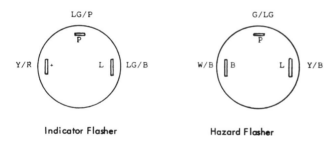

Indicator Flasher   Hazard Flasher

FIG 11:23 Flasher unit connections

Key to Fig 11:23   **B** Black   **G** Green   **LG** Light green
P Purple   **W** White   **Y** Yellow

cars respectively). Its function is to preclude fluctuation readings on relevant instruments by supplying them with constant voltage. It serves the fuel and coolant temperature gauges on all except early models and also the oil gauge in certain models. The unit must be mounted vertically to within a maximum out-of-true of 10° in any direction. Renew a defective stabiliser.

Warning and instrument illumination bulbs :

Access is from the rear of the facia panel. When renewing the bulbs in the fuel and oil gauges, it is necessary, on some models, to remove the radio.

Instrument removal and refitment :

Remove the valance from below the facia, if necessary, to give access to relevant instruments and/or remove the radio and glovebox to give access to others where necessary. Disconnect the battery before removing an instrument. Proceed then, from behind the facia, to withdraw the illumination bulb holder(s) and the knurled nuts securing the retaining strap(s). Where applicable, identify and disconnect the wiring. In the case of a speedometer, release the nut securing the drive to the instrument. In the case of the earlier (combined) temperature and oil pressure gauge, release the nut securing the oil pressure pipe to the gauge, release the union nut securing the temperature bulb to the thermostat housing and the various clips which secure the capillary tubing. Withdraw the gauges (complete with the capillary) from the front of the facia.

Refitment of an instrument is the reverse of the removal sequence in each case. Note that, where relevant, a refitted clock **must be restarted** immediately after reconnecting the battery. Failure to do so is liable to damage the mechanism.

Fuel gauge sender unit :

This is a float and arm type unit. To remove, drain the fuel tank, remove the boot backboard, identify and disconnect the wiring from the sender unit, unscrew the retaining ring and withdraw the unit. Discard the sealing ring.

To refit, use a new sealing ring and reverse the removal sequence.

11:11 Flasher units

The direction indicator flasher unit is located behind the facia panel below the window operating switch on the driver's side. Before suspecting that a flasher unit is defective, check that the bulbs are serviceable and that the fuse is intact. The correct connections for the direction indicator and the hazard warning flasher units are shown in **FIG 11:23**. A defective unit of either type should be removed and a new replacement fitted.

11:12 Fault diagnosis

(a) Battery discharged

1 Terminal connections loose or dirty
2 Shorts in lighting circuit
3 Generator or alternator not charging
4 Control or regulator defective
5 Battery internally defective

(b) Insufficient charging rate

1 Check 1 and 4 in (a)
2 Drive belt slipping

(c) Battery will not hold charge

1 Low electrolyte level
2 Battery plates and/or separators defective
3 Electrolyte leakage from cracked case

(d) Battery overcharged

1 Generator control unit out of adjustment

(e) Generator or alternator output low or nil

1 Drive belt broken or slipping
2 Control or regulator defective or out of adjustment
3 Commutator or slip rings worn, burned or shorted
4 Brushes sticking, springs weak or broken
5 Field coil or rotor windings broken, shorted or burned

(f) Starter motor lacks power or will not operate

1 Battery discharged, loose cable connections
2 Starter pinion jammed
3 Starter switch or solenoid defective
4 Brushes worn or sticking, leads detached
5 Commutator worn, burned or shorting
6 Motor shaft bent
7 Engine abnormally stiff, perhaps after rebore

(g) Starter motor runs but does not turn engine

1 Pinion sticking on screwed sleeve
2 Stripped teeth on pinion or flywheel ring gear

(h) Starter motor inoperative

1 Check 1 and 4 in (f)
2 Armature or field coils faulty

(j) Starter motor rough or noisy

1 Mounting bolts loose

2 Damaged pinion or flywheel ring gear teeth
3 Pinion spring broken

(k) Lamps inoperative or erratic

1 Battery low, bulbs burned out
2 Faulty earthing of battery or lighting circuit
3 Switch faulty, loose or broken connections

(l) Wiper motor sluggish

1 Commutator dirty or shorting
2 Brushes worn or sticking or spring broken
3 Gearbox, wheelbox or rack cable binding
4 Lack of lubrication

(m) Wiper motor runs but does not drive

1 Rack/wheelbox worn, teeth stripped
2 Motor drive shaft broken, gearbox teeth stripped

(n) Instrument(s) inoperative

1 Voltage stabiliser defective
2 Wiring discontinuity
3 Sender unit defective
4 Gauge defective
5 Speedometer drive broken or disconnected
6 Oil pressure pipe fractured (earlier models)
7 Temperature capillary fractured (earlier models)
8 Ineffective earth

NOTES

CHAPTER 12

THE BODYWORK

12 : 1 *Bodywork finish*

Large scale repairs to the fibreglass body are best left to a bodywork repair specialist. Minor damage, such as chips, scratches, abrasions and even holes which are not too large may be dealt with by an owner using appropriate proprietary fillers and fibreglass repair kits and working strictly to the manufacturer's instructions. On completion of the repairs, apply a primer surfacer and, when it is dry, rub down with medium grade 'Wet and Dry' paper and finish off with 400 grade. If necessary, apply a further coat of primer and repeat the rubbing down. Take time to achieve the best possible finish as this will control the final effect.

Touching-up of paintwork is best carried out using self-spraying cans but, since paint may change colour with age it may be better to spray a whole wing or panel rather than touch-up a small area. Before spraying, remove all traces of wax with white spirit. More drastic treatment will be required if silicone polish has been applied. After a few hours drying, use a cutting compound to remove dry spray and, when fully hardened, finish off with a liquid polish.

12 : 2 *The bonnet*

FIG 12 : 1 relates to Elan models and FIG 12 : 2 to Elan +2 models.

Elan models, removal and fitment :

Open the bonnet, detach the assisting spring from its attachment on the steering rack and, with assistance, extract the pivot bolts (as applicable) and lift off the bonnet.

To refit, reverse this sequence.

Elan +2 models, removal and fitment :

Open the bonnet, detach the assisting spring from the steering rack, release the support from the bonnet, partially unscrew the pivot bolts (work concurrently and equally at both sides) until they are clear of the body and, with assistance, lift off the bonnet.

To refit, reverse this sequence. Screw in the pivot bolts by equal amounts concurrently (there is no other bonnet side clearance adjustment). If the pivot bolts were removed completely, ensure that they are refitted by equal amounts at each side before positioning the bonnet.

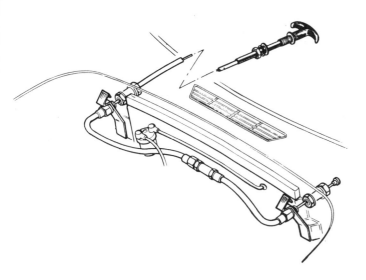

FIG 12 : 1   Bonnet locking mechanism (Elan models)

The bonnet lock :

On all models, for correct operation, the cable must be well lubricated with Shell Retinax A grease and free of kinks and tight bends. The inner and outer cable lengths must be correctly adjusted and the catch must be working freely. Additionally, on Elan +2 models, the hole in the bulkhead must line up with the centre line of the cable stop on the arm of the catch and the plunger must enter squarely into the catch.

Cable adjustment, Elan models :

The adjuster should, initially, be in the fully closed position to give the shortest outer length. On Series 1 and 3 cars, separate cables are used and no adjuster is fitted. All the spare thread of the fairlead should, initially, be towards the engine compartment. In this position there will be slack in the inner cable. Take this up by the outer cable adjuster until there is 1.6 to 3.2mm (0.062 to 0.125in) slack in the inner cable and both catches can fully close.

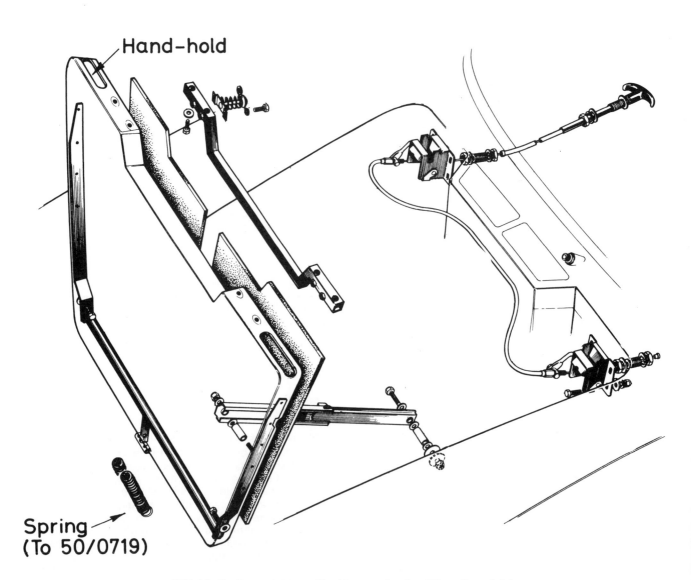

Hand-hold

Spring
(To 50/0719)

FIG 12 : 2   Bonnet stay and locking mechanism (Elan +2 models)

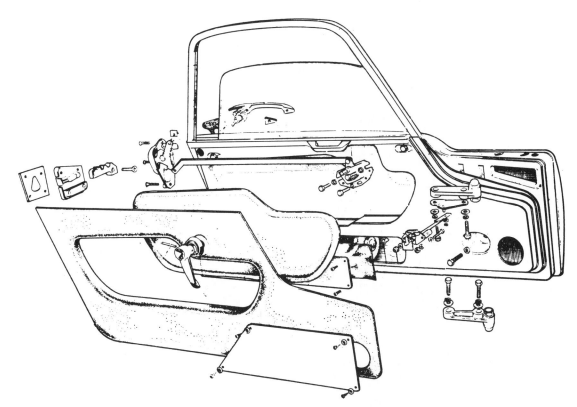

FIG 12 : 3 Door trim and fittings (Elan Series 3 models)

Catch adjustment, Elan +2 models:

The cable must run straight through the cable stop on the catch and the fairlead. If the cable is bearing on the fairlead, bend the catch arm slightly to compensate but do not impair the action of the catch. The catch may be adjusted in the vertical plane to allow correct bonnet to body alignment in the closed position. The catches must be square to the plungers on the bonnet. The plungers are not adjustable in the vertical plane. Relieve a tight catch by increasing the clearance between the moving part and the integral plate. Do not overtighten the nuts securing the outer cable. The stop must be free to swivel.

Cable adjustment, Elan +2 models:

Adjustment is as described earlier for Elan models.

12 : 3 *The luggage compartment lid*

Removal and fitment, all models:

Open the lid fully. Remove the stay by springing in its lower ends and lifting off from its bobbin. Release the nuts and washers securing the hinges to the lid and dis-mount the lid. Collect the gasket from between each hinge and the lid.

To refit, reverse the removal sequence.

Luggage compartment lock removal and fitment, Elan models:

From inside the luggage compartment, release the bolts which secure the budget lock to its mounting bracket. Remove the locking handle by releasing the securing screws.

To refit, reverse the removal sequence.

Luggage compartment lock, Elan +2 models:

The exterior locking type and the remote control type are covered separately as follows.

Exterior locking type removal, Elan +2 models:

Release the securing screws and remove the rear panel trim. Proceed, then, as described earlier for the Elan models.

Remote control type removal, Elan +2 models:

Unhook the return spring from its retaining plate. From inside the shut face of the drivers door, release the locknut of the outer cable. From inside the luggage compartment, release the locknut securing the inner cable adjuster. Turn the adjuster to give as much slack as is required to unhook the inner cable from its retaining plate. Release the bolts passing through the cable and spring retaining plates, lock mounting bracket, luggage compartment lock slide and tapping plate.

Refitting both types, Elan +2 models:

Reverse the removal sequence in each case. If adjustment of the lid is required, screw the plunger bolt in or out as necessary. If trouble is experienced with the lock keeper striking the bollard mounting plate, fit up to two plain washers to space the lock further inboard.

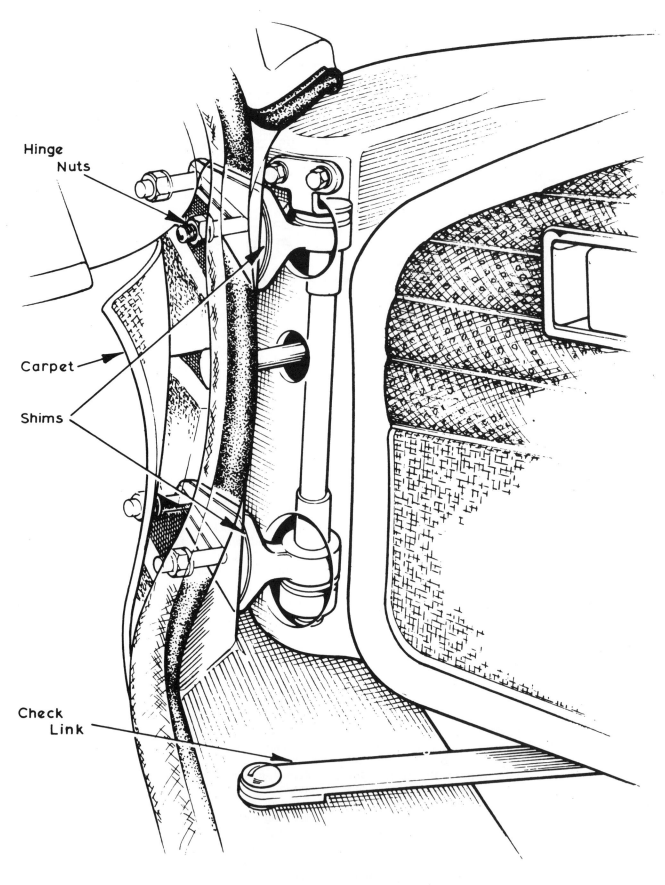

Hinge Nuts

Carpet

Shims

Check Link

FIG 12 : 4   Door hinge and check link (Elan +2 models)

Jammed remote control, Elan +2 models :

If the control jams and the lid cannot be opened by operating the control, procede as follows.

Remove the number plate. From the top edge of the luggage compartment opening, on the centre line of the car, measure down 63.5mm (2.50in) and 44.5mm (1.75in) in a horizontal line from the vertical, drill a 4.76mm (0.1875in) diameter hole on the left of the centre line on a righthand drive car and on the right of the centre line on a lefthand drive car. Insert a thin bladed screwdriver at an angle of approximately 60° through the hole until it is hard against the slide flange. Press down on the lid to relieve the load on the lock and operate the slide with the screwdriver.

Before closing the lid, ensure that the lock assembly is well lubricated with Shell Retinax A grease, the hook is towards the boot floor, the lockplate is positioned with the tag away from the cable and the slide is assembled with the slot bias towards the spring. The cable must be free from tight bends and the operating load must not exceed 9kg (20lb) pull. Ensure that the plunger locknut on the lid is secure. Insert a small grommet into the drilled hole, refit the number plate and reseal its fixing bolts with Prestik sealant.

12 : 4 *Door trim*

Removal and refitment :

Release the screws and remove the armrest (if fitted). Open the ash tray to expose the retaining screws and remove the ash tray (if fitted). On doors with a flush fitting type remote control, lift the flap and trim (earlier models only) and remove three securing screws. On earlier models fitted with doors with a handle type remote control or with a direct acting handle (Series 1 and 2 cars), press the escutcheon, push out the pin then exposed and pull off the handle or, on later models, remove the handle retaining central screw and pull off the handle. On early Series 3 cars, remove the kick-plate from the lower forward edge of the trim pad.

Insert a screwdriver under a top edge of the trim pad, slide the blade along until it encounters a clip, ease the pad away from the door working progressively round and keeping as close to the clips as possible. On Elan models, when all the clips are free, ease the pad from around the remote control or the handle shank and dis-

mount the trim or, on relevant models, pull the trim pad downwards to clear the handle. On Elan +2 models, when the clips are free, ease the trim pad from around the remote control, lift the lower edge until the top edge can be raised clear and unhook the pad from the door window aperture. Depending upon model, remove the polythene draught cover.

To refit, reverse the removal sequence as applicable to each model.

12 : 5 *Door components*

FIG 12 : 3 relates to Elan models. **FIG 12 : 4** relates to Elan +2 models. **FIG 12 : 5** relates to all relevant models. **FIG 12 : 6** relates to Elan models. **FIG 12 : 7** relates to all relevant models though the Elan +2 centre screw type of lever is shown. **FIG 12 : 8** relates to Elan +2 models.

Door lock remote control :

Remote control is not fitted to Elan Series 1 and 2 cars. On these models the lock is operated by an internal handle attached directly to the lock.

Lever-type remote control removal and fitment :

Remove the trim pad as described in **Section 12 : 4**. Remove the bolts and washers which secure the remote control to the door. Remove the splitpin and cotterpin which retain the operating link to the lock.

To refit, reverse this sequence.

Flush-type remote control removal and fitment :

Remove the three screws which secure the flush handle to the door. Note that the handle cannot be fully released until the trim pad is dismounted as described in **Section 12 : 4**. Lift out the locking (small) flat locking rod from the nylon block and the operating rod from the handle mechanism. Dismount the control handle.

To refit, reverse this sequence.

Door locks :

Three types of lock are fitted to Elan and Elan +2 models. The first is related to direct operation of the lock and the second and third to the two types of remote control mechanisms (lever and flush).

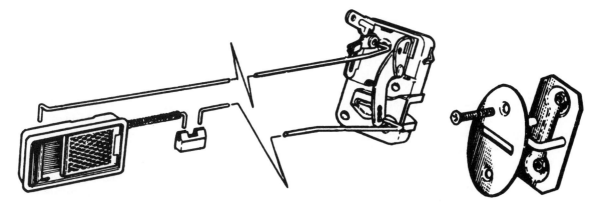

FIG 12 : 5   Flush-type remote control, door lock and striker

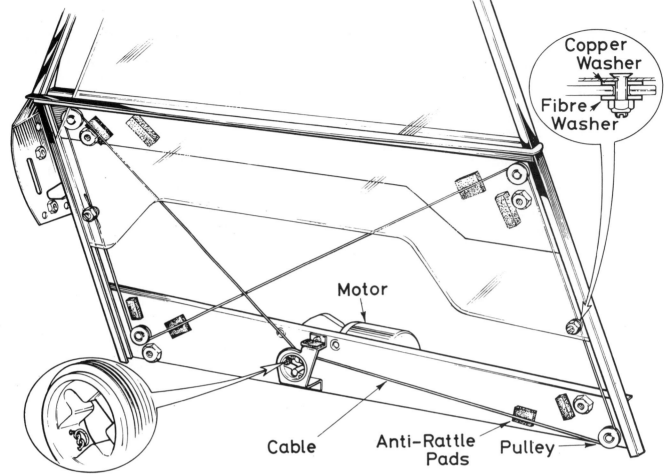

Copper Washer
Fibre Washer

Motor

Cable **Anti-Rattle Pads** **Pulley**

FIG 12:6   Door window mechanism (Elan models)

First type, Elan Series 1 and 2 cars, removal:

Remove the trim pad as described in **Section 12:4**. Remove the bolts which secure the chromed lock mounting plate to the door and dismount the assembly. Remove four cross-headed screws to separate the lock from the mounting plate.

Second type, Elan Series 3 and relevant Elan +2 cars, removal:

Remove the trim pad as described in **Section 12:4**. From the interior of the door, release the remote control link of the lock. From the door shut face, release the screws securing the lock and the lock cover to the door. Dismount the lock.

Third type, Elan Series 4 and relevant Elan +2 cars, removal:

Remove the trim pad as described in **Section 12:4**. From the interior of the door, release the rods from between the remote control locking flap to the lock, from the nylon block to the lock, from the exterior door handle to the lock and from the private lock to the door lock. From the door shut face, release the screws which secure the lock to the door. Dismount the lock.

Lock refitment:

Reverse the removal sequence in each case. Ensure that the lock mechanism and the associated parts are serviceable. Lubricate with Shell Retinax A grease before refitting the trim pad.

Lock striker:

Do not disturb this component unless adjustment or renewal is necessary. To adjust, loosen the retaining screws, move the striker as appropriate and retighten the retaining screws. Check the closure and repeat the adjustment as necessary.

If the retaining screws are inadvertently fully released, the tapped plate (behind the door shut face) will become displaced and, to gain access to retrieve it, it will be necessary in the case of Elan models to remove the rear quarter trim or, on Elan +2 models, to remove the dust shield in the wheel arch.

Door window regulator, Elan Series 1 and 2 cars:

To remove, raise the window fully. Remove the trim pad. Remove two bolts and withdraw the window and the regulator from its runners. Separate the regulator from its guide on the window lower edge.

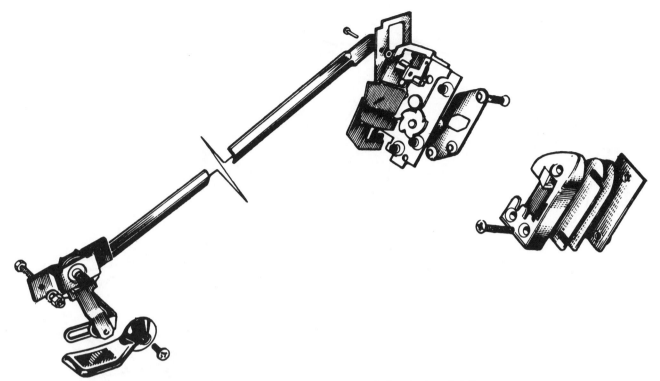

FIG 12 : 7 Lever-type remote control, door lock and striker

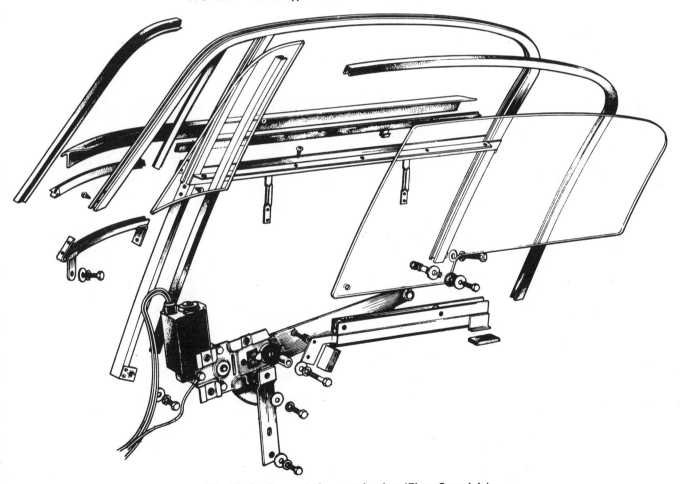

FIG 12 : 8 Door window mechanism (Elan +2 models)

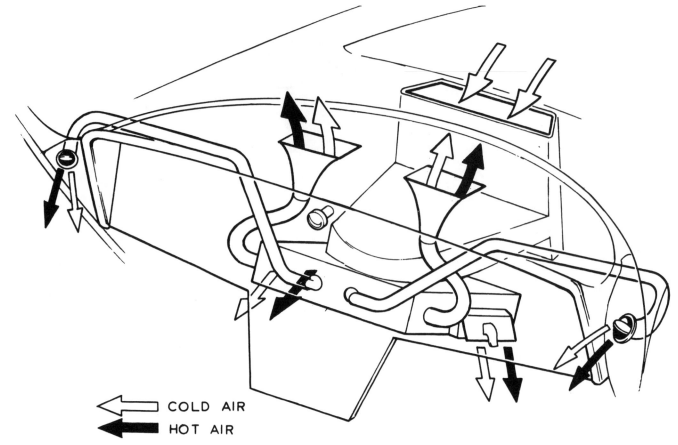

← COLD AIR

◄ HOT AIR

FIG 12 : 9   Diagram of air flow

To refit, reverse this sequence but do not fully tighten the two retaining bolts until satisfactory operation of the window is achieved. The bolt holes are elongated to allow adjustment. Runners and moving parts of the regulator should be greased with graphite based grease.

Door window motor, Elan Series 3 cars and onwards :

To remove, dismount the door trim pads as described in **Section 12 : 4**. Disconnect the battery. Remove the waterproof cover from the motor. Identify and disconnect the cables from the motor. Release the securing bolts and withdraw the motor. Have a defective motor checked and repaired by a Lotus agent.

To refit, reverse the removal sequence.

Door window motor, Elan +2 cars :

To remove, dismount the trim pad as described in **Section 12 : 4**. Set the window at about two thirds closed (with the operating arm horizontal). Disconnect the battery. Identify and disconnect the cables from the motor. Remove the securing screws, slide the operating arm from the window steady plate, lower the motor to the inner bottom of the door, support the window with a block of wood (to avoid the possibility of it becoming displaced from its channels), turn the motor through 90° and withdraw it up and out through the aperture in

the door inner panel. Have a defective motor checked and repaired by a Lotus agent.

To refit, reverse the removal sequence.

Door window glass, Elan Series 1 and 2 cars :

Removal and refitment is covered earlier and is included in the window regulator removal and refitment procedures.

Door window glass, Elan Series 3 cars and onwards :

To dismount, remove the window motor, lock and remote control as described earlier. Remove the setscrews at the lower ends of the front and rear channel uprights and the shut face of the door adjacent to the lock aperture (the upper screw is provided with a nut). Raise the rear of the frame and, guiding the lower part past the bobbins, withdraw completely.

To refit, reverse the removal sequence. Use Dunlop S758 adhesive to secure the window 'silent channel' to the frame.

Door window glass, Elan +2 cars :

To dismount, remove the window motor as described earlier. Remove the setscrews from the lower ends of the front and rear channel uprights, the forward end of the fixed quarterlight base channel and the mid centre of the door below the window aperture. Remove the self-tapping screws from the inner lower flange of the

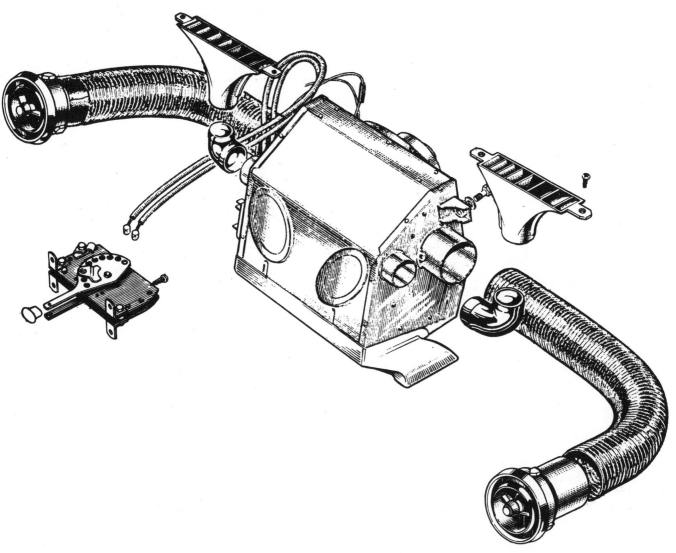

FIG 12 : 10 Heater and ventilation components

window aperture. Withdraw the window and frame from the door.

To refit, reverse the removal sequence. Remove all traces of old adhesive from the 'silent channel' and the window frames before re-attaching with Dunlop S758 adhesive.

Exterior door handle, all models :

To remove, dismount the door trim pad as described in **Section 12 : 4**. Release the setscrews from the inner side of the door panel and remove the exterior handle. Do not misplace the seating washers from between the handle and the exterior of the door. On models with flush fitting type remote control, disconnect the rod from between the exterior door handle and the door lock. On models fitted with a private lock, note that this is retained by a single nut. Note also that the private

lock is interconnected to the door lock by a small rod.

To refit, reverse the removal sequence.

12 : 6 *Facia*

Removal :

1 Disconnect the battery. Release the upper steering column clamp. On Elan Series 4 and on Elan +2 cars, remove the securing nut and release the bonnet control from its bracket below the facia.
2 Refer to **Chapter 11**, **Section 11 : 10**. Uncouple the speedometer drive and the trip reset control from the back of the speedometer. On earlier models, remove the combined coolant temperature and oil pressure gauge.
3 On Elan models, remove the tunnel top by lifting up from its rear end. On Elan +2 models, remove the rear seat backrest followed by the tunnel top.

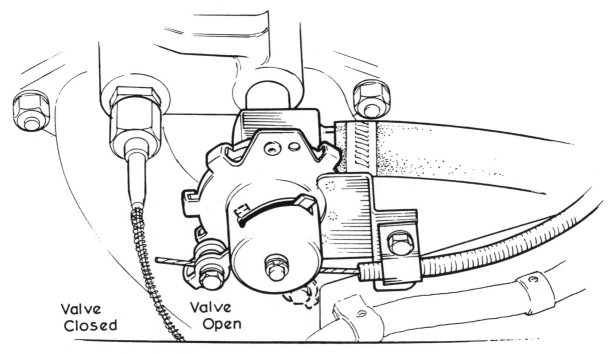

FIG 12 : 11   Temperature control valve (Elan models)

4 Remove the demister grilles from the top of the crash pad. Remove the face level ventilators (if fitted). Release the nuts securing the side brackets which carry the door courtesy light switches (if fitted).

5 On Elan +2 models, release the forward end of the transmission tunnel side valance by lifting up. Remove the facia panel securing bolts along the top and at the centre bottom and pull the panel forwards. Release the radio earth strap (if fitted).

6 Hold the facia panel at about 60° to the vertical and remove the heater control to the heater unit. On Elan Series 1 to 3 cars, remove the choke and bonnet control cables. Identify and note the dispositions of all electrical wiring before disconnecting them.

7 Lift the facia panel from its location. Confirm that no wiring, etc., remains linking the panel with the car. Withdraw the panel. Any further dismantling which may be necessary can be carried out on a felt covered bench.

Refitting :

Follow the reverse of the removal sequence applicable to each model. It is recommended that, after reconnecting all the wiring, the battery be reconnected and all electrical circuits checked. If they are satisfactory, disconnect the battery, complete the facia refitment and, finally, reconnect the battery.

12 : 7 The heater

FIG 12 : 9 shows, diagramatically, the heating and ventilating air flows. **FIG 12 : 10** shows the Elan +2 heater unit, controls and ductings.

Adjustment, Elan models :

FIG 12 : 11 shows the coolant valve control on the cylinder head. This is the only control and is adjusted as follows.

Release the inner cable from the valve and close the valve fully. Ensure that the outer cable is clamped firmly but not so tightly as to restrict movement of the inner cable. Fully close the facia panel control (heat off). Reconnect the inner cable to the coolant valve and check operation.

Adjustments, Elan +2 models :

Remove the facia panel as described in **Section 12 : 6**. The control cable adjustment points are located on the lefthand side of the heater unit and are shown in **FIG 12 : 12**. Adjustments are as follows:

Release the inner cable at the air distribution lever. Set the facia control to INTERIOR and the air distribution flap to its fully open position. Reconnect the inner cable and check the operation.

Release the inner cable at the air temperature lever. Set the facia control to HOT and the flap covering the heater matrix to fully open. Reconnect the inner cable and check that the flap is fully closed when the facia control is switched to COLD. Readjust as may be necessary before refitting the facia panel.

Heater removal :

1 Drain the cooling system as described in **Chapter 4, Section 4 : 2**. Remove the facia panel as described in **Section 12 : 6** and release the ventilation ducts from the heater unit. Release the demister ducts from the heater unit.

2 On **Elan models**, refer to **FIG 12 : 11** and release the control cable from the coolant valve on the cylinder head. On **Elan +2 models**, refer to **FIG 12 : 12** and release the control cables from their trunnions on the heater unit levers.

3 From the rear of the engine compartment, remove both the flow and the return coolant hoses from the heater unit.

4 On **Elan models**, release the two screws securing the heater to the facia support bracket. Pull the unit from its location taking care not to damage the sealing ring between the unit and the plenum chamber.

5 On **Elan +2 models**, release the four bolts (two at each side) securing the heater. Lift up and out to ensure that the heater deflector (if fitted) is not damaged. Note that, on later models, the deflector is riveted to the heater unit while, on earlier models, the deflector (if fitted) may be removed after extracting four self-tapping screws.

Heater refitment :

Check that all hoses, seals and sealing rings are undamaged and in good condition.

To refit, reverse the removal sequence but note that on Elan +2 models, the controls must be adjusted as described earlier **before the facia panel is refitted.** Note also that, on Elan +2 models, the return coolant hose (to the coolant pump) must pass **outside the fuel pump and not over it.** Refill the cooling system as described in **Chapter 4, Section 4 : 2.**

12 : 8 *Windscreen and backlight*

Renewing a broken windscreen (indirect glazed) :

Remove the wiper blades and arms (see **Chapter 11, Section 11 : 7**) and the interior rear view mirror. Protect the facia and bodywork. Start at the lower outer centre and, using a small blunt screwdriver, prise out the plastic filler strip from the windscreen rubber weatherstrip. Working round the outside, ease the weatherstrip from the glass. From inside, and with due care to avoid cutting the hands, knock out the windscreen fragments. The weatherstrip should be pushed out with the glass. If it is not, pull it off the body aperture flange.

Remove all traces of old sealing compound, glass granules and splinters from the weatherstrip. A small fragment left in the strip can initiate the fracture of the new glass. If the condition of the weatherstrip is doubtful, obtain a new replacement. Check the body aperture flange and correct any damage or file away any small bumps (which could also initiate fracture of the new glass). The procedure for fitment of the new glass is as follows (it differs between S-type and other cars).

1 **Except on S-type cars,** apply a continuous strip of Bostick 692 sealer to the flange of the body aperture. Fit the weatherstrip (use soft soap to simplify fitment) with its joint at the top centre. Push the weatherstrip well into its seating, particularly at the corners.

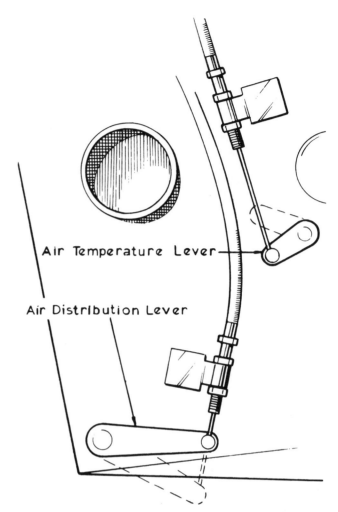

FIG 12 : 12   Cable adjustment (Elan +2 models)

2 Apply a continuous strip of Bostick 692 sealer to the face of the weatherstrip which will be in contact with the new glass. Lay the windscreen on the weatherstrip and, starting at the lower corner and using a small blunt screwdriver lift the lip of the rubber over the edge of the glass.

3 Using a windscreen strip tool, insert the filler strip into the weatherstrip starting at the lower centre.

4 Clean off excess sealer with white spirit (or an equivalent). Refit the interior rear view mirror. Refit the wiper arms and blades. Check that all glass fragments have been removed from the interior of the car and from the heater air intakes (use a vacuum for this).

On S-type cars, refer to the earlier procedure but omit operation 1. Carry out operation 2 and then proceed as follows.

Fit the moulding into the weatherstrip. Use the cord technique (cord ends inside at the top centre) to fit the windscreen to the weatherstrip but, before offering up the glass to the body aperture, apply a continuous strip of Bostick 692 to the outer channel of the weatherstrip which will be in contact with the body aperture flange. Press the windscreen into place and work the lip of the rubber over the complete aperture flange by pulling on the cord ends until the cord is gradually pulled out completely. Finally, carry out operation 4 of the earlier procedure.

Renewing a broken windscreen (direct glazed) :

Commencing with chassis No 7001010001N, all cars delivered where the USA Federal Motor Vehicle Safety Regulations are in force are fitted with a direct glazed windscreen in which the glass is retained by a strip of butyl rubber compressed between it and the body aperture flange. The aperture flange is increased in depth to accommodate this method of fixing.

The procedure for the renewal of a direct glazed broken glass is unsuitable for an owner to carry out. The ambient temperature in an enclosed working area has to be controlled within close limits; primer fumes are toxic and highly inflammable; experience of the process is essential if a watertight seal is to be achieved without repeated refits to overcome abortive initial fits.

The renewal of this type of windscreen should be entrusted to a qualified and fully equipped agent.

Backlight renewal :

Identify and disconnect the wiring (the feed and earth cables are located behind the panel which conceals the fuel tank) if the backlight is a heated type. Proceed then as described earlier for a windscreen renewal (not the S-type procedure). On completion, reconnect the wiring if relevant.

CHAPTER 13

SERVICING

13 : 1 *Routine and special servicing*

Routine servicing :

In order to maintain the vehicle in an efficient, safe and economical running condition, regular and thorough servicing is essential. It is important that all the servicing procedures are carried out in correct sequence and at the appropriate mileage intervals. If any particular service is neglected or omitted, the remaining sequence will be affected. It may not always be convenient to carry out the next sheduled service at the scheduled mileage interval but it is most undesireable that any delay should exceed 10% of the scheduled mileage interval.

An owner who entrusts the servicing of his vehicle to a distributor or dealer need not be concerned with the service schedules but need only use the relevant Service Voucher Book. An owner who carries out his own servicing should follow the servicing schedules appropriate to his vehicle as specified in **Sections 13 : 3** and **13 : 4** or **13 : 5** and, if relevant, **13 : 6**. Only approved oils, greases and fluids should be used as given in **Section 13 : 2** and, when required, only Lotus replacement parts should be fitted.

Special servicing :

The mileage and time intervals specified are as quoted in the relevant Owner's Handbook and are laid down by the Technical Staff of Lotus Cars Limited and are based on normal operational conditions. It will be prudent of an owner of a vehicle operating in exceptional conditions to shorten the intervals between certain service procedures. The air intake cleaner and the servo air filter (if applicable to the model) of a vehicle operating in very dusty terrain or in a polluted atmosphere should be cleaned or renewed more frequently than is specified in the schedules. Similarly, if fuel supplies are dirty, the pump bowl and gauze screen will require more frequent attention. Under certain fuel and operating conditions (particularly extended city driving) sparking plugs may have to be serviced or renewed at shorter intervals and, under abnormal driving conditions, greater than normal brake pad wear should be anticipated. If the car is being driven for long mileages over rough roads, bumpy dirt tracks, etc., hubs, suspensions, tyres and pipe joints should be specially inspected at frequent intervals.

Preventive servicing :

Inspect the area over which a car is garaged for drip marks which may indicate a loose drain plug, a faulty oil seal, a perished or cracked coolant hose, a leaking caliper seal or hydraulic pipeline. Trace the source of the drip and correct the fault without delay. Do not wait until the next scheduled service.

13 : 2 Approved oils, greases and fluids

Engine oil (above 0°C (32°F)) :

A selection of approved oils is Shell Super 100, Esso Uniflow, BP Super Viscomatic 20W/50, Castrol GTX, Mobiloil Super.

Engine oil (below 0°C (32°F)) :

A selection of approved oils is Shell Super 10W/30, Esso Uniflo, BP Super Viscomatic, Castrolite, Mobiloil Special 10W/30.

Gearbox oil :

A selection of oils which are approved for use in the gearbox (4-speed and 5-speed) is Shell Spirax 80EP, Esso gear oil GX 80, BP Gear oil 80EP, Castrol Hypoy Light, Mobilube GX 80.

Rear axle oil :

Any SAE 90 Hypoid oil of reputable brand may be used.

Steering swivels (vertical links) :

Any SAE 90 Hypoid oil of reputable brand may be used.

Grease points :

A selection of greases approved for greasing points is Shell Retinax A, Esso Multi-purpose Grease, BP Ener-grease L.2, Castrolgrease LM, Mobilgrease MP.

Brake and clutch hydraulic systems :

Use Castrol/Girling Brake and Clutch Fluid Crimson to specification SAE 70 R.3.

Coolant anti-freeze :

Inhibited ethylene glycol of reputable brand to British Standards Specification BS 3151. Work to the manufacturer's instructions for the solution strength for the degree of frost protection required.

Battery terminals :

To inhibit corrosion, use a Silicone Grease.

13 : 3 Servicing schedules applicable to all Elan and Elan +2 models

Daily :

1 Refer to **Chapter 1, Section 1 : 2** and check the oil level.
2 Depending upon the type of motoring anticipated, refer to **Chapter 7, Section 7 : 2** and to **Chapter 8, Section 8 : 2** and adjust the cold tyre pressures.

Weekly :

3 Refer to **Chapter 11, Section 11 : 2**. Check the level of the battery electrolyte and top up if necessary.

Every 5000km (3000 miles) :

4 To even out tyre wear interchange the wheels as described in **Chapter 8, Section 8 : 2**. At this interchange, have the wheels dynamically balanced.

Every 18 months :

5 Every 18 months, drain, flush and refill the brakes hydraulic system as described in **Chapter 10, Section 10 : 12**.

Every 65,000km (40,000 miles) or every 3 years :

6 Every 65,000km (40,000 miles) or every three years (whichever is reached first), completely overhaul the brakes hydraulic system (see **Chapter 10, Section 10 : 2**).

13 : 4 Servicing schedules for early Elan models

The schedules specified in this section apply to all Elan models up to and including Series 2 models. There are four schedules: **'A', 'B', 'C'** and **'D'**.

'A' service, every 2500km (1500 miles) :

1 Using an oil can containing engine oil, lubricate the throttle linkages, bonnet release cables (adjacent to the catches) and the handbrake compensator pivot points.
2 Using multi-purpose grease, lubricate the propeller shaft universal joints and the handbrake cable. Grease the bonnet slide rails and the bonnet release striker plates (a light smear only is required).
3 Refer to **Chapter 5, Section 5 : 2** and to **Chapter 10, Section 10 : 2**. Check the fuel level in both the clutch and brake reservoirs. If necessary, top up with approved brake fluid. Investigate any excessive drop in the fluid levels.
4 Refer to **Chapter 6, Section 6 : 2**, check and, if necessary, top up the level of the oil in the gearbox. Refer to **Chapter 7, Section 7 : 2** and **FIG 7 : 3**, check and, if necessary, top up the level of the oil in the final drive gearbox.

'B' service, every 5000km (3000 miles) :

5 Carry out the **'A'** service as specified earlier and, in addition, carry out the following.
6 Using an oil can containing engine oil, lubricate the brake, clutch and throttle pedal pivots.
7 Using multi-purpose grease, lubricate the door engagement guides and catches. A light smear only is required.
8 Refer to **Chapter 1, Section 1 : 2**. Drain the engine sump and refill with approved oil.
9 Refer to **Chapter 2, Section 2 : 3** and clean the air intake element. With the engine warm, check the idling speed and, if necessary, adjust as described in **Section 2 : 5**. Refer to **Section 2 : 6**, check the vertical movement of the carburetters on their 'O' ring joints and, if necessary, adjust the clearance between the spring washer coils.

10 Refer to **Chapter 3, Section 3 : 2** and adjust the distributor points gap. Refer to **Section 3 : 6** and clean and regap the sparking plugs.
11 Visually inspect the cooling system and heater hoses and connections. Refer to **Chapter 4, Section 4 : 2** and top up the coolant level. Top up the windscreen washer reservoir.
12 Check and, if necessary, adjust the wheel alignment as described in **Chapter 9, Section 9 : 11**.

'C' service, every 10,000km (6000 miles) :

13 Carry out the **'B'** service as specified earlier and, in addition, carry out the following.
14 Renew the oil filter element as described in **Chapter 1, Section 1 : 3**.
15 Refer to **Chapter 2, Section 2 : 4** and clean the fuel pump bowl and gauze screen.
16 Refer to **Chapter 3, Section 3 : 6** and renew the sparking plugs. Remove the distributor rotor arm and lubricate the distributor shaft bearing and counterweights sparingly with engine oil through the hole in the top of the shaft and through the clearance hole in the base plate. Similarly and sparingly, lubricate the contact breaker pivot. Smear the cam sparingly with multi-purpose grease.
17 Lightly smear multi-purpose grease on the luggage compartment stay slide pin.
18 Refer to **Chapter 6, Section 6 : 2** and, preferably when the unit is warm, drain the gearbox and refill with new gear oil.
19 Refer to **Chapter 8, Section 8 : 2** and lubricate the vertical links (steering swivels) with Hypoid 90EP oil. Refer to **Section 8 : 3** and repack with grease and adjust the front hubs.
20 Refer to **Chapter 10, Section 10 : 2** and check the thickness of the brake caliper pad friction linings. If necessary, renew the pads as described in **Section 10 : 3**.
21 Check and adjust the valve clearances as described in **Chapter 1 Section 1 : 4**. Torque tighten the cylinder head bolts as described in **Section 1 : 7**. Adjust the camshaft drive chain tension as described in **Section 1 : 5**. Refer to **Chapter 4, Section 4 : 3**. Check and adjust, if necessary, the tension of the drive belt.

'D' service, every 20,000km (12,000 miles) :

22 Carry out the **'C'** service as specified earlier and, in addition, carry out the following.
23 Refer to **Chapter 11, Section 11 : 4** and lubricate the DC generator.
24 Refer to **Chapter 7, Section 7 : 2** and, preferably when the transmission is warm, drain, flush and refill the differential unit.
25 Refer to **Chapter 2, Section 2 : 3** and renew the air cleaner element.
26 Refer to **Chapter 9, Section 9 : 2** and, using a gun filled with multi-purpose grease, lubricate the steering unit by applying five gun strokes only.
27 Check the steering and suspension linkages for condition and wear. Check the condition of the propeller shaft universal joints. Check the intermediate drive shaft couplings for condition and wear.

Every second 'D' service, every 40,000km (24,000 miles) :

28 In addition to the **'D'** service specified earlier, refer to **Chapter 2, Section 2 : 6** and remove the carburetters. Using new 'O' rings and gaskets, refit the carburetters.

13 : 5 *Servicing schedules for later Elan and all Elan +2 models*

The schedules specified in this section apply to all Elan models not covered by **Section 13 : 4** and to all Elan +2 models. There are three schedules, **'A'**, **'B'** and **'C'**. Note that on the exhaust emission control models, the servicing covered in **Section 13 : 6** must be carried out in addition.

'A' service, every 5000km (3000 miles) :

1 Using an oil can containing engine oil, lubricate the throttle linkages, bonnet release cables, handbrake and all pedal pivots.
2 Using multi-purpose grease, lubricate the propeller shaft universal joints. Apply a slight smear to the bonnet slide rails, all striker plates, door guides, etc., including the luggage compartment.
3 Refer to **Chapter 1, Section 1 : 2**. Drain the engine sump and refill with approved oil. Adjust the camshaft drive chain tension as described in **Section 1 : 5**.
4 Check and, if necessary, top up the oil level in the Zenith-Stromberg damper reservoirs (if relevant to the model) as described in **Chapter 2, Section 2 : 2**. Clean the air intake element as described in **Section 2 : 3**. With the engine warm, check the idling speed and adjust, if necessary, as described in **Section 2 : 5, 2 : 8** or **2 : 12**. If relevant to the model, refer to **Section 2 : 6** and check the vertical movement of the carburetters on their 'O' rings. Adjust if necessary.
5 Refer to **Chapter 3, Section 3 : 2** and adjust the distributor points gap. Clean and regap the sparking plugs (see **Section 3 : 6**). Lubricate the distributor shaft bearing, counterweights and cam as described in service operation 16 in **Section 13 : 4**.
6 Visually inspect the cooling system and heater hoses and their connections. Refer to **Chapter 4, Section 4 : 2** and top up the coolant level. Top up the windscreen washer reservoir.
7 Refer to **Chapter 5, Section 5 : 2** and to **Chapter 10, Section 10 : 2**. Check the fluid level in the clutch and brake master cylinder reservoirs and top up with approved fluid if necessary. Investigate any excessive drop in fluid levels.
8 Refer to **Chapter 6, Section 6 : 2**. Check and, if necessary, top up the gearbox oil level. Refer to **Chapter 7, Section 7 : 2** and check the final drive oil level. Top up if necessary.
9 Check the wheel alignment (see **Chapter 9, Section 9 : 11**) and adjust if necessary.
10 Refer to **Chapter 10, Section 10 : 2** and check the thickness of the brake caliper pad friction linings. Renew the pads as described in **Section 10 : 3** if they are at or closely approaching minimum acceptable thickness.

'B' service, every 10,000km (6,000 miles) :

11 Carry out the **'A'** service as specified earlier in this section and, in addition, carry out the following.

12 Renew the oil filter element as described in **Chapter 1, Section 1 : 3.** Check and adjust the valve clearance as described in **Section 1 : 4.** Torque tighten the cylinder head bolts as described in **Section 1 : 7.**

13 Clean the fuel pump bowl and gauze screen as described in **Chapter 2, Section 2 : 4** (but see **Section 13 : 1**).

14 Refer to **Chapter 4, Section 4 : 3.** Check the condition of the pump drive belt and adjust the tension if necessary.

15 Preferably when the unit is warm, drain and refill the gearbox with approved oil as described in **Chapter 6, Section 6 : 2.**

16 Refer to **Chapter 8, Section 8 : 2** and lubricate the vertical links (steering swivels) with Hypoid 90EP oil. Refer to **Section 8 : 3,** adjust the hubs and repack with grease.

17 If relevant, renew the vacuum servo air filter as described in **Chapter 10, Section 10 : 14** (but see **Section 13 : 1**).

'C' service, every 20,000km (12,000 miles) :

18 Carry out the **'B'** service as specified earlier in this section and, in addition, carry out the following.

19 Renew the air cleaner element as described in **Chapter 2, Section 2 : 3.** If applicable to the model, carry out the Yellow service to the Zenith-Stromberg carburetters as described in **Chapter 2, Section 2 : 10.**

20 Refer to **Chapter 3, Section 3 : 6** and renew the sparking plugs (but see **Section 13 : 1**).

21 Refer to **Chapter 7, Section 7 : 2** and, preferably when the transmission is warm, drain the differential unit. Flush and refill with approved oil.

22 Using a gun filled with multi-purpose grease, lubricate the steering unit by applying five strokes only as described in **Chapter 9, Section 9 : 2.**

23 If applicable, lubricate the DC generator as described in **Chapter 11, Section 11 : 4.**

Every second 'C' service, every 40,000km (24,000 miles :

24 In addition to the **'C'** service specified earlier in this section, refer to **Chapter 2, Section 2 : 6, 2 : 9** or **2 : 13,** remove the carburetters and refit using new 'O' rings and new gaskets. In the case of Zenith-Stromberg carburetters, carry out the Red service as described in **Section 2 : 10** before refitting the carburetters.

25 Check the steering and suspension linkages for condition and wear. Check the condition of the propeller shaft universal joints. Check the intermediate shaft couplings for condition and wear.

13 : 6 *Servicing of exhaust emission control models*

The servicing schedules in **Sections 13 : 4** and **13 : 5** apply to models provided with exhaust emission control features though some service procedures should be carried out at shorter intervals than are recommended for vehicles not fitted with those features. Amended intervals given in this section override the intervals quoted in earlier sections.

In addition to the main schedules there are a few additional service operations and these are given in this section.

Induction system :

It is particularly important that there shall be no induction system air leaks as these can affect the effectiveness of the emission control. gaskets, 'O' rings, pipes and their joints must be maintained in good order at all times irrespective of routine servicing. All vacuum pipes and their connections must be free of leaks and correctly connected.

Sparking plugs :

Renew sparking plugs at least every 10,000km (6000 miles). Depending upon the type of motoring (see **Section 13 : 1**), plugs should be cleaned and regapped more frequently than normally scheduled and their efficient operation under pressure should be particularly ensured.

Distributor and ignition timing :

Contact breaker points should be kept in peak condition and should be renewed at least every 20,000km (12,000 miles). The ignition timing is equally important and should be checked and adjusted at least at this same mileage interval. Note (see **Chapter 2, Section 2 : 11**) that the static timing for exhaust emission control engines is 5° BTDC.

Ensure that the piping to the vacuum capsule is at all times serviceable and correctly coupled. Refer to **Chapter 2, Section 2 : 11** and note that the adjusting screw on the rear carburetter (which operates the actuation valve) is factory set and that the resetting instructions given in that section do not comprise a routine procedure.

Carburetter servicing :

The Yellow and Red servicings at 20,000km (12,000 miles) and 40,000km (24,000 miles) respectively are covered in **Chapter 2, Section 2 : 10.** These are standard scheduled servicings but they should be carried out with very particular care. When the carburetters are removed for these servicings, renew the adaptor flange 'O' rings and renew all gaskets which have been disturbed. On refitment of the carburetters, ensure that there are no induction leaks.

Crankcase breather tube :

The breather tube should be clear at all times and cleaned at least every 20,000km (12,000 miles).

Bypass valve gasket (evaporative loss control system) :

Renew the valve gasket every 40,000km (24,000 miles). The procedure is described in **Chapter 2, Section 2 : 15**).

Evaporative loss control system charcoal canister :

Ensure that all pipes and their connections are maintained in good order. Every 40,000km (24,000 miles), refer to **Chapter 2, Section 2 : 15** and renew the charcoal canister as a unit.

APPENDIX

METRIC CONVERSION TABLES

TECHNICAL DATA

Engine Fuel system Ignition system Cooling system
Clutch Transmission Suspension Steering Brakes
Electrical equipment Capacities Dimensions

HINTS ON MAINTENANCE AND OVERHAUL

WIRING DIAGRAMS

GLOSSARY OF TERMS

INDEX

Inches	Decimals	Milli-metres	Inches to Millimetres Inches	Inches to Millimetres mm	Millimetres to Inches mm	Millimetres to Inches Inches
1/64	.015625	.3969	.001	.0254	.01	.00039
1/32	.03125	.7937	.002	.0508	.02	.00079
3/64	.046875	1.1906	.003	.0762	.03	.00118
1/16	.0625	1.5875	.004	.1016	.04	.00157
5/64	.078125	1.9844	.005	.1270	.05	.00197
3/32	.09375	2.3812	.006	.1524	.06	.00236
7/64	.109375	2.7781	.007	.1778	.07	.00276
1/8	.125	3.1750	.008	.2032	.08	.00315
9/64	.140625	3.5719	.009	.2286	.09	.00354
5/32	.15625	3.9687	.01	.254	.1	.00394
11/64	.171875	4.3656	.02	.508	.2	.00787
3/16	.1875	4.7625	.03	.762	.3	.01181
13/64	.203125	5.1594	.04	1.016	.4	.01575
7/32	.21875	5.5562	.05	1.270	.5	.01969
15/64	.234375	5.9531	.06	1.524	.6	.02362
1/4	.25	6.3500	.07	1.778	.7	.02756
17/64	.265625	6.7469	.08	2.032	.8	.03150
9/32	.28125	7.1437	.09	2.286	.9	.03543
19/64	.296875	7.5406	.1	2.54	1	.03937
5/16	.3125	7.9375	.2	5.08	2	.07874
21/64	.328125	8.3344	.3	7.62	3	.11811
11/32	.34375	8.7312	.4	10.16	4	.15748
23/64	.359375	9.1281	.5	12.70	5	.19685
3/8	.375	9.5250	.6	15.24	6	.23622
25/64	.390625	9.9219	.7	17.78	7	.27559
13/32	.40625	10.3187	.8	20.32	8	.31496
27/64	.421875	10.7156	.9	22.86	9	.35433
7/16	.4375	11.1125	1	25.4	10	.39370
29/64	.453125	11.5094	2	50.8	11	.43307
15/32	.46875	11.9062	3	76.2	12	.47244
31/64	.484375	12.3031	4	101.6	13	.51181
1/2	.5	12.7000	5	127.0	14	.55118
33/64	.515625	13.0969	6	152.4	15	.59055
17/32	.53125	13.4937	7	177.8	16	.62992
35/64	.546875	13.8906	8	203.2	17	.66929
9/16	.5625	14.2875	9	228.6	18	.70866
37/64	.578125	14.6844	10	254.0	19	.74803
19/32	.59375	15.0812	11	279.4	20	.78740
39/64	.609375	15.4781	12	304.8	21	.82677
5/8	.625	15.8750	13	330.2	22	.86614
41/64	.640625	16.2719	14	355.6	23	.90551
21/32	.65625	16.6687	15	381.0	24	.94488
43/64	.671875	17.0656	16	406.4	25	.98425
11/16	.6875	17.4625	17	431.8	26	1.02362
45/64	.703125	17.8594	18	457.2	27	1.06299
23/32	.71875	18.2562	19	482.6	28	1.10236
47/64	.734375	18.6531	20	508.0	29	1.14173
3/4	.75	19.0500	21	533.4	30	1.18110
49/64	.765625	19.4469	22	558.8	31	1.22047
25/32	.78125	19.8437	23	584.2	32	1.25984
51/64	.796875	20.2406	24	609.6	33	1.29921
13/16	.8125	20.6375	25	635.0	34	1.33858
53/64	.828125	21.0344	26	660.4	35	1.37795
27/32	.84375	21.4312	27	685.8	36	1.41732
55/64	.859375	21.8281	28	711.2	37	1.4567
7/8	.875	22.2250	29	736.6	38	1.4961
57/64	.890625	22.6219	30	762.0	39	1.5354
29/32	.90625	23.0187	31	787.4	40	1.5748
59/64	.921875	23.4156	32	812.8	41	1.6142
15/16	.9375	23.8125	33	838.2	42	1.6535
61/64	.953125	24.2094	34	863.6	43	1.6929
31/32	.96875	24.6062	35	889.0	44	1.7323
63/64	.984375	25.0031	36	914.4	45	1.7717

UNITS	Pints to Litres	Gallons to Litres	Litres to Pints	Litres to Gallons	Miles to Kilometres	Kilometres to Miles	lbs per in² to bars	Bars to lbs per in²
1	.57	4.55	1.76	.22	1.61	.62	.069	14.50
2	1.14	9.09	3.52	.44	3.22	1.24	.138	29.00
3	1.70	13.64	5.28	.66	4.83	1.86	.207	43.50
4	2.27	18.18	7.04	.88	6.44	2.49	.276	58.00
5	2.84	22.73	8.80	1.10	8.05	3.11	.345	72.50
6	3.41	27.28	10.56	1.32	9.66	3.73	.414	87.00
7	3.98	31.82	12.32	1.54	11.27	4.35	.483	101.50
8	4.55	36.37	14.08	1.76	12.88	4.97	.552	116.00
9		40.91	15.84	1.98	14.48	5.59	.621	130.50
10		45.46	17.60	2.20	16.09	6.21	.690	145.00
20				4.40	32.19	12.43	1.380	
30				6.60	48.28	18.64	2.070	
40				8.80	64.37	24.85	2.760	
50					80.47	31.07	3.450	
60					96.56	37.28		
70					112.65	43.50		
80					128.75	49.71		
90					144.84	55.92		
100					160.93	62.14		

UNITS	lbf ft to daNm	daNm to lbf ft	UNITS	lbf ft to daNm	daNm to lbf ft
1	.136	7.38	7	.949	51.63
2	.271	14.76	8	1.080	59.01
3	.406	22.13	9	1.220	66.38
4	.542	29.50	10	1.360	73.76
5	.678	36.88	20	2.720	147.52
6	.813	44.26	30	4.080	221.28

TECHNICAL DATA

Dimensions are in millimetres (with inch equivalents in brackets) unless otherwise stated. If necessary, refer to the Conversion Tables

ENGINE

Engine type	4 cylinder, 4-stroke, water cooled
Engine capacity	1558cm^3 (95.06in^3)
Bore and stroke	82.550 x 72.746 (3.250 x 2.864)
Compression ratio :	
Elan	9.5 : 1
Elan Sprint	10.3 : 1
Elan +2	9.5 : 1
Elan +2 S130	10.3 : 1
Compression pressure	In excess of 11.03 bars (160lb in^2) at sea level
Variation (maximum)	1.38 bar (20lb in^2) cylinder to cylinder
Cylinder block	Cast iron
Bore:	
Grade 1	82.550 to 82.558 (3.2500 to 3.2503)
Grade 2	82.558 to 82.565 (3.2503 to 3.2506)
Grade 3	82.565 to 82.573 (3.2506 to 3.2509)
Grade 4	82.573 to 82.580 (3.2509 to 3.2512)
Cylinder head	Aluminium alloy
Depth:	
Small valve	117.8 to 117.9 (4.638 to 4.643)
Big valve	116.8 to 116.9 (4.598 to 4.603)
Minimum depth:	
Small valve	−1.14 (−0.045) below standard
Big valve	−0.254 (−0.010) below standard
Camshafts	Separate inlet and exhaust

Valve timing (degrees):	Elan	Elan Sprint, S/E and Elan +2
Inlet opens BTDC	22	26
Inlet closes ABDC	62	66
Exhaust opens BBDC	62	66
Exhaust closes ATDC	22	26

End float	0.076 to 0.254 (0.003 to 0.010)
Journal diameters (5)	25.400 to 25.413 (1.0000 to 1.0005)
Running clearance	0.013 to 0.050 (0.0005 to 0.0020)
Cam followers :	
Bore in head	See **FIG 1 : 11**
Follower diameter	34.904 to 34.912 (1.3742 to 1.3745)
Clearance with bore	0.013 to 0.036 (0.0005 to 0.0014)
Camshaft drive	Chain, tensioner and sprockets
Jackshaft	Driven by camshaft drive chain
End float	0.063 to 0.190 (0.0025 to 0.0075)
Journal diameters (3)	39.624 to 39.637 (1.5600 to 1.5605)
Running clearance	0.025 to 0.050 (0.001 to 0.002)
Crankshaft	Cast iron
Main journal diameters (5)	53.987 to 54.000 (2.1255 to 2.1260)
Crankpin diameters (4)	49.201 to 49.214 (1.9370 to 1.9375)
End float	0.076 to 0.203 (0.003 to 0.008)
Controlled by	Centre bearing thrust washers

Running clearance:
Main journals	0.038 to 0.076 (0.0015 to 0.0030)
Big-ends	0.013 to 0.051 (0.0005 to 0.0022)
Undersize on regrind	−0.762 (−0.030) on diameter (maximum)

Flywheel .. .. Clutch operates on rear face
Face runout .. .. 0.101 (0.004) maximum
Ring gear runout:
Lateral	0.406 (0.016) maximum
Radial	0.152 (0.006) maximum

Connecting rods .. .. Forged steel, H-section
End float on crankpin .. .. .. 0.101 to 0.254 (0.004 to 0.010)
Running clearance .. .. 0.013 to 0.0513 (0.0005 to 0.0022)
Small-end bore .. .. Bushed
Grade A (silver) .. .. 20.635 to 20.637 (0.8124 to 0.8125)
Grade B (green) .. .. 20.637 to 20.642 (0.8125 to 0.8127)

Gudgeon pins .. .. Floating, circlip located
Diameter:
Grade A	20.627 to 20.628 (0.8121 to 0.8122)
Grade B	20.628 to 20.632 (0.8122 to 0.8123)
Class of fit	Finger push-fit

Pistons .. .. Tin plated aluminium alloy
Diameter, A type:
Grade 1	82.474 to 82.481 (3.2470 to 3.2473)
Grade 2	82.481 to 82.489 (3.2473 to 3.2476)
Grade 3	82.489 to 82.497 (3.2476 to 3.2479)
Grade 4	82.497 to 82.504 (3.2479 to 3.2482)

Diameter, C type:
Grade 1	82.466 to 82.474 (3.2467 to 3.2470)
Grade 2	82.474 to 82.481 (3.2470 to 3.2473)
Grade 3	82.481 to 82.489 (3.2473 to 3.2476)
Grade 4	82.489 to 82.497 (3.2476 to 3.2479)

Weight variation per set .. . . 4g maximum
Clearance in cylinder bore:
A type	0.068 to 0.083 (0.0027 to 0.0033)
C type	0.076 to 0.091 (0.0030 to 0.0036)
Gudgeon pin offset	1.016 (0.040) towards thrust face

Piston rings .. .. Two compression, one oil control
Gap, fitted:
Compression rings	0.229 to 0.356 (0.009 to 0.014)
Oil control ring	0.254 to 0.508 (0.010 to 0.020)

Ring to groove clearance:
Compression rings	0.041 to 0.076 (0.0016 to 0.0030)
Oil control ring	0.046 to 0.097 (0.0018 to 0.0038)

Valves .. .. Seat face angle, 45°
Clearance (cold):
Inlet	0.127 to 0.177 (0.005 to 0.007)
Exhaust (to engine No 9951)	0.152 to 0.203 (0.006 to 0.008)
Exhaust (from engine No 9952)	0.228 to 0.279 (0.009 to 0.011)

Head diameter:
Inlet (except Sprint and S 130)	38.760 to 38.862 (1.526 to 1.530)
Inlet (Sprint and S 130)	39.624 to 39.776 (1.560 to 1.566)
Exhaust	33.553 to 33.655 (1.321 to 1.325)

Stem diameter:
Inlet	7.874 to 7.899 (0.310 to 0.311)
Exhaust	7.874 to 7.899 (0.310 to 0.311)

Clearance in guide:		
Inlet	0.007 to 0.058 (0.0003 to 0.0023)	
Exhaust	0.063 to 0.076 (0.0025 to 0.0030)	

Valve springs .. .. Two per valve

Free length:
Inner 28.70 (1.130)
Outer 36.83 (1.450)

Valve guides:
Bore diameter (unreamed) .. .. .. 7.91 to 7.93 (0.3113 to 0.3123), ream to suit stem after fitting
Length .. .. 38.61 (1.520) inlet, 37.86 (1.480) exhaust
Fitted height above head 8.128 (0.320)

Lubrication .. .. Dual rotor pump, fullflow filter
Oil pressure (hot) .. .. 2.41 to 2.76 bar (35 to 40lb in^2)
Oil:
Temperate climates .. .. SAE 20W/50 of reputable brand
Cold climates .. .. SAE 10W/40 of reputable brand

FUEL SYSTEM

Pump, type .. .. Mechanical, actuated from the jackshaft

Pressure .. .. 0.086 to 0.172 bar (1.25 to 2.50lb in^2)

Air cleaner .. .. Dry paper element
Carburetters .. .. Two Weber, two Zenith-Stromberg or two Dellorto

Slow-running speed:
Weber .. .. 800 to 900r/min
Zenith-Stromberg:
Non-exhaust emission .. .. .. 800 to 900r/min
Exhaust emission 950r/min

Weber carburetters:
Elan models .. .. 40 DCOE 18

	Std	*SE*	
Choke	*30mm*	32mm	–
Main jet	*115*	115	–
Air correction jet	*200*	150	–
Slow-running jet	*45 F9*	50 F8	–
Accelerator pump jet	*40*	40	–

Elan models .. .. 40 DCOE 31

	Std	*SE*	*Sprint, S130*
Choke	30mm	32mm	33mm
Main jet	115	115	120
Air correction jet	200	150	155
Slow-running jet	50 F8	50 F8	50 F8
Accelerator pump jet	40	40	35

Elan +2 models .. .. 40 DCOE 31

Choke	30mm	32mm	33mm
Main jet	110	115	120
Air correction jet	155	150	155
Slow-running jet	45 F8	45 F8	50 F8
Accelerator pump jet	35	35	35

Elan and Elan +2 models:
Common settings .. .. 40 DCOE 18 and 40 DCOE 31
Accelerator pump stroke 10mm
Starter air jet 100
Starter petrol jet .. .. F 5/100

Emulsion tube	..	..	..	..	F 11
Needle valve	..	..	..	..	1.75

Ait trumpet length:
  40 DCOE 18 carburetters 44.4mm
  40 DCOE 31 carburetters 38.0mm

Zenith-Stromberg carburetters:

Non-exhaust emission	175 CD 2S	–
Exhaust emission	–	175 CD 2SE
Needle	B 1Y	B 1G
Spring colour	Natural	Blue/black
Damper oil	SAE 20W/50	SAE 20W/50

Identification:
  Front   ..   ..   ..   Suffix S 710
  Rear   ..   ..   ..   Suffix S 711

Type:
  E26   ..   ..   ..   Fixed needle B 1G with idle return valve
  G26   ..   ..   ..   Fixed needle B 1G, throttle edge drillings, idle return valve deleted
  I26   ..   ..   ..   Adjustable needle B 1Y with side entry balance pipe
  J26   ..   ..   ..   Adjustable needle B 2AR with overhead balance pipe
  F26   ..   ..   ..   Fixed needle B 1Y with side entry balance pipe

Dellorto carburetters   ..   ..   Colour coded RED
  Domestic   ..   ..   ..   DHLA 40
  European ECE 15   ..   ..   DHLA 40E

Identification:
  Front   ..   ..   ..   Suffix S 0710W
  Rear   ..   ..   ..   Suffix S 0711W

Type	Q026	R026
Choke	33mm	32mm
Auxiliary venturi	7848-1	7848-1
Main jet	120	120
Main air corrector	130	160
Idling jet	50.02	50L
Idling jet holder	7850-2(120)	7850-1(140)
Pump jet	45 or 35	33
Starter jet	70	70
Main emulsion tube	7772-5	7772-5
Starter emulsion tube	7482-1.28	7482-1.28
Needle valve	150.33	150.33
Float assembly	7298-01	7298-02
Air trumpet length	40mm	40mm

IGNITION SYSTEM

Type   ..   ..   Coil and distributor
Firing order 1, 3, 4, 2
Distributor:
  Make   ..   ..   Lucas
  Type   ..   ..   23D4 or 25D4 (exhaust emission)
  Points gap   ..   ..   ..   0.35 to 0.40 (0.014 to 0.016)
  Cam dwell   ..   ..   .. $60° \pm 3°$
Ignition timing:
  Static timing data   ..   ..   ..   See **Chapter 2, Sections 2 : 5, 2 : 8, 2 : 11** or **2 : 12**

Dynamic timing data	..	..	..	..	Refer to **Chapter 3, Section 3 : 5**
Sparking plug types and gaps		..	..	..	Refer to **Chapter 3, Section 3 : 6**

COOLING SYSTEM

Filler cap pressure rating :
Elan models	..	..	..	..	..	0.69 bar (10lb in²)
Elan +2 models	..	..	..	..	..	0.48 bar (7lb in²)

Antifreeze solution .. .. Refer to **Chapter 4, Section 4 : 8**

Thermostat opening temperatures :
Temperate climates	..	..	..	..	78°C (173°F), standard fitment
Tropical climates	..	..	..	..	71°C (160°F)
Cold climates	..	..	..	..	88°C (190°F)

CLUTCH

Make and type	..	..	..	..	..	Borg & Beck, diaphragm spring
Operation	..	..	..	..	..	Hydraulic
Fluid	..	..	..	..	..	As for braking system

Driven plate diameter :
With 4-speed gearbox	..	..	..	..	203 (8.0)
With 5-speed gearbox	..	..	..	..	215.9 (8.5)

TRANSMISSION

Gearbox type	..	..	..	..	..	4 or 5-speed and reverse
Gearchange	..	..	..	..	..	Manual, synchromesh on all forward ratios

Gearbox ratios (: 1) :

						Semi-close	Close	5-speed
Reverse	..	..	..	..	..	3.324	2.807	3.467
1	..	..	..	..	..	2.972	2.510	3.200
2	..	..	..	..	..	2.009	1.636	2.010
3	..	..	..	..	..	1.396	1.230	1.370
4	..	..	..	..	..	1.000	1.000	1.000
5	..	..	..	..	..	N/A	N/A	0.800

Final drive ratio :
Elan Series 1, 2 and early 3	..	..	..	3.900 : 1
Later Elan models	..	..	..	3.777 : 1
Elan +2 models	..	..	..	3.777 : 1
Optional	..	..	..	3.555 : 1

Lubrication :
Gearbox	..	..	..	..	EP80 gear oil of reputable brand
Final drive	..	..	..	..	EP90 gear oil of reputable brand

SUSPENSION

Type	..	..	..	..	..	Independent, coil springs (front and rear
Geometry	..	..	..	..	..	Refer to **FIG 8 : 1 (front), FIG 7 : 1 (rear)**

Springs :
Front :
					Elan	Elan +2
Number of coils	..	..	..	..	19.6	15.6
Wire diameter	..	..	..	..	8.7 (0.342)	8.7 (0.342)
Free length	..	..	..	..	409 (16.08)	360 (14.19)
Fitted length	..	..	..	..	234 (9.22)	218 (8.60)
High free length	..	..	..	..	425 (16.75)	370 (14.59)
High fitted length	..	..	..	..	250 (9.86)	229 (9.00)

Rear:						Elan	Elan +2
Number of coils	..	..	..	..	..	8.7	9.7
Wire diameter	..	..	..	..	..	10.2 (0.40)	10.9 (0.43)
Free length	..	..	..	..	..	373 (14.71)	406 (16.0)
Fitted length	..	..	..	..	..	203 (8.00)	218 (8.60)

Hub bearing end float (front) .. .. 0.05 to 0.10 (0.002 to 0.004)
Toe-in (rear) .. .. Zero to 4.76 (0.1875)
Wheel camber:

Rear .. .. Zero to 1° negative

Front .. .. Elan 1 and 2, 0 to 0.5°; Elan 3 and +2, 0 to 1° positive

Wheel castor .. .. Early, 7°; later, 3° ± 5° positive
Kingpin inclination .. .. 9° ± 0.5°
Tyre pressures:

Front .. .. See **Chapter 8, Section 8 : 2**

Rear .. .. See **Chapter 7, Section 7 : 2**

STEERING

Type .. .. Rack and pinion
Toe-in (front) 4.76 (0.1875)
Turning circle diameter:

Elan Series 1, 2 and 3 .. .. .. 9.0m (29.5ft)

Elan Series 4 .. .. 10.0m (33.5ft)

Elan +2 .. .. 8.5m (28ft)

BRAKES

Make and type .. .. Girling hydraulic, disc front and rear
Hydraulic fluid .. .. Castrol/Girling Brake and Clutch Universal fluid or DOT 3/4

Single/dual line .. .. Depending on model
Servo assistance .. .. Depending on model
Minimum pad thickness:

Elan 1.5 (0.06)

Elan +2 .. .. 2.5 (0.10)

Disc diameter:					Rear	Front
Elan	..	..	..	..	254 (10.0)	231.8 (9.125)
Elan +2	..	..	..	..	254 (10.0)	254 (10.0)

Disc run out .. .. 0.10 (0.004) maximum
Handbrake .. .. Mechanical, rear wheels only

ELECTRICAL EQUIPMENT

Polarity of earth .. .. Depends upon model (see text)
Fuses .. .. Two (12 on S models)
Battery .. .. 12-volt, Exide 6VTA 29L, 39amp/hr
Generator .. .. Lucas C40

Minimum brush length 6.0 (0.25)

Cuts in at .. .. 1450r/min and 13 volts

Maximum output .. .. 22amps at 2250r/min

Field resistance .. .. 6.0 ohms

Control box .. .. RB 106/2 or RB 340

Alternator: .. .. Lucas 17 ACR (12 pole, 3-phase)

Polarity .. .. Negative only

Minimum brush length .. .. .. 5.1 (0.20) free protrusion

Rectifier .. .. Integral diode

Maximum output (hot) .. .. .. 36amps at 6000r/min

Regulator .. .. Built-in

Regulator voltage .. .. 14.1 to 14.5

Rotor winding resistance .. .. .. 4.165 ± 5% ohms at 20°C

Stator winding resistance .. .. .. 0.133 ohms per phase

Starter motor . . . . Lucas M 35G or 35J
  Switching . . . . Solenoid
  Minimum brush length 8.0 (0.31)

CAPACITIES

	Litre	Imperial	USA
Engine (including oil filter)	4.25	7.5 pints	9.0 pints
Gearbox	1.00	1.75 pints	2.1 pints
Final drive	1.2	2.0 pints	2.4 pints
Coolant (with heater)	8.0	14.0 pints	16.8 pints
Fuel :			
Elan Series 1, 2 and 3	45.0	10.0 gals	12.0 gals
Elan Series 4	42.0	9.25 gals	11.0 gals
Elan +2	59.0	13.0 gals	15.6 gals

DIMENSIONS

Track :
  Front . . . . See **Chapter 8, FIG 8 : 1**
  Rear . . . . See **Chapter 7, FIG 7 : 1**

	Elan	Elan +2
Wheelbase	2134 (84)	2438 (96)
Ground clearance	152 (6)	165 (6.5)
Overall length	3683 (145)	4286 (168.75
Overall width	1422 (56)	1682 (66.25)
Overall height	1150 (45.25)	1193 (47)

HINTS ON MAINTENANCE AND OVERHAUL

There are few things more rewarding than the restoration of a vehicle's original peak of efficiency and smooth performance.

The following notes are intended to help the owner to reach that state of perfection. Providing that he possesses the basic manual skills he should have no difficulty in performing most of the operations detailed in this manual. It must be stressed, however, that where recommended in the manual, highly-skilled operations ought to be entrusted to experts, who have the necessary equipment, to carry out the work satisfactorily.

Quality of workmanship :

The hazardous driving conditions on the roads to-day demand that vehicles should be as nearly perfect, mechanically, as possible. It is therefore most important that amateur work be carried out with care, bearing in mind the often inadequate working conditions, and also the inferior tools which may have to be used. It is easy to counsel perfection in all things, and we recognise that it may be setting an impossibly high standard. We do, however, suggest that every care should be taken to ensure that a vehicle is as safe to take on the road as it is humanly possible to make it.

Safe working conditions :

Even though a vehicle may be stationary, it is still potentially dangerous if certain sensible precautions are not taken when working on it while it is supported on jacks or blocks. It is indeed preferable not to use jacks alone, but to supplement them with carefully placed blocks, so that there will be plenty of support if the car rolls off the jacks during a strenuous manoeuvre. Axle stands are an excellent way of providing a rigid base which is not readily disturbed. Piles of bricks are a dangerous substitute. Be careful not to get under heavy loads on lifting tackle, the load could fall. It is preferable not to work alone when lifting an engine, or when working underneath a vehicle which is supported well off the ground. To be trapped, particularly under the vehicle, may have unpleasant results if help is not quickly forthcoming. Make some provision, however humble, to deal with fires. Always disconnect a battery if there is a likelihood of electrical shorts. These may start a fire if there is leaking fuel about. This applies particularly to leads which can carry a heavy current, like those in the starter circuit. While on the subject of electricity, we must also stress the danger of using equipment which is run off the mains and which has no earth or has faulty wiring or connections. So many workshops have damp floors, and electrical shocks are of such a nature that it is sometimes impossible to let go of a live lead or piece of equipment due to the muscular spasms which take place.

Work demanding special care :

This involves the servicing of braking, steering and suspension systems. On the road, failure of the braking system may be disastrous. Make quite sure that there can be no possibility of failure through the bursting of rusty brake pipes or rotten hoses, nor to a sudden loss of pressure due to defective seals or valves.

Problems :

The chief problems which may face an operator are :

1. External dirt.
2. Difficulty in undoing tight fixings.
3. Dismantling unfamiliar mechanisms.
4. Deciding in what respect parts are defective.
5. Confusion about the correct order for reassembly.
6. Adjusting running clearance.
7. Road testing.
8. Final tuning.

Practical suggestions to solve the problems :

1. Preliminary cleaning of large parts – engines, transmissions, steering, suspensions, etc, – should be carried out before removal from the car. Where road dirt and mud alone are present, wash clean with a high-pressure water jet, brushing to remove stubborn adhesions, and allow to drain and dry. Where oil or grease is also present, wash down with a proprietary compound (Gunk, Teepol etc,) applying with a stiff brush – an old paint brush is suitable – into all crevices. Cover the distributor and ignition coils with a polythene bag and then apply a strong water jet to clear the loosened deposits. Allow to drain and dry. The assemblies will then be sufficiently clean to remove and transfer to the bench for the next stage.

   On the bench, further cleaning can be carried out, first wiping the parts as free as possible from grease with old newspaper. Avoid using rag or cotton waste which can leave clogging fibres behind. Any remaining grease can be removed with a brush dipped in paraffin. Avoid using paraffin or petrol in large quantities for cleaning in enclosed areas, such as garages, on account of the high fire risk.

   When all exteriors have been cleaned, and not before, dismantling can be commenced. This ensures that dirt will not enter into interiors and orifices revealed by dismantling. In the next phases, where components have to be cleaned, use a special solvent or petrol and keep the containers covered except when in use. After the components have been cleaned, plug small holes with tapered hard wood plugs cut to size and blank off larger orifices with greaseproof paper and masking tape. Do not use soft wood plugs or matchsticks as they may break.

2. It is not advisable to hammer on the end of a screw thread, but if it must be done, first screw on a nut to protect the thread, and use a lead hammer. This applies particularly to the removal of tapered cotters. Nuts and bolts seem to 'grow' together, especially in exhaust systems. If penetrating oil does not work, try the judicious application of heat, but be careful of starting a fire. Asbestos sheet or cloth is useful to isolate heat.

   Tight bushes or pieces of tail-pipe rusted into a silencer can be removed by splitting them with an open-ended hacksaw. Tight screws can sometimes be started by a tap from a hammer on the end of a suitable screwdriver. Many tight fittings will yield to the judicious use of a hammer, but it must be a soft-faced hammer, if damage is to be avoided, use a heavy block on the opposite side to absorb shock. Any parts of the steering system which have been damaged should be renewed, as attempts to repair them may lead to cracking and subsequent failure, and steering ball joints should be disconnected using a recommended tool to prevent damage.

3 It often happens that an owner is baffled when trying to dismantle an unfamiliar piece of equipment. So many modern devices are pressed together or assembled by spinning-over flanges, that they must be sawn apart. The intention is that the whole assembly must be renewed. However, parts which appear to be in one piece to the naked eye may reveal close-fitting joint lines when inspected with a magnifying glass, and this may provide the necessary clue to dismantling. Lefthanded screw threads are used where rotational forces would tend to unscrew a righthanded screw thread.

Be very careful when dismantling mechanisms which may come apart suddenly. Work in an enclosed space where the parts will be contained, and drape a piece of cloth over the device if springs are likely to fly in all directions. Mark everything which might be reassembled in the wrong position, scratched symbols may be used on unstressed parts, or a sequence of tiny dots from a centre punch can be useful. Stressed parts should never be scratched or centre-popped as this may lead to cracking under working conditions. Store parts which look alike in the correct order for reassembly. Never rely upon memory to assist in the assembly of complicated mechanisms, especially when they will be dismantled for a long time, but make notes, and drawings to supplement the diagrams in the manual, and put labels on detached wires. Rust stains may indicate unlubricated wear. This can sometimes be seen round the outside edge of a bearing cup in a universal joint. Look for bright rubbing marks on parts which normally should not make heavy contact. These might prove that something is bent or running out of truth. For example, there might be bright marks on one side of a piston, at the top near the ring grooves, and others at the bottom of the skirt on the other side. This could well be the clue to a bent connecting rod. Suspected cracks can be proved by heating the component in a light oil to approximately 100°C, removing, drying off, and dusting with french chalk. If a crack is present the oil retained in the crack will stain the french chalk.

4 In determining wear, and the degree, against the permissible limits set in the manual, accurate measurement can only be achieved by the use of a micrometer. In many cases, the wear is given to the fourth place of decimals; that is in ten-thousandths of an inch. This can be read by the vernier scale on the barrel of a good micrometer. Bore diameters are more difficult to determine. If, however, the matching shaft is accurately measured, the degree of play in the bore can be felt as a guide to its suitability. In other cases, the shank of a twist drill of known diameter is a handy check.

Many methods have been devised for determining the clearance between bearing surfaces. To-day the best and simplest is by the use of Plastigage, obtainable from most garages. A thin plastic thread is laid between the two surfaces and the bearing is tightened, flattening the thread. On removal, the width of the thread is compared with the scale supplied with the thread and the clearance is read off directly. Sometimes joint faces leak persistently, even after gasket renewal. The fault will then be traceable to distortion, dirt or burrs. Studs which are screwed into soft metal frequently raise burrs at the point of entry. A quick cure for this is to chamfer the edge of the hole in the part which fits over the stud.

5 **Always check a replacement part with the original one before it is fitted.**

If parts are not marked, and the order for reassembly is not known, a little detective work will help. Look for marks which are due to wear to see if they can be mated. Joint faces may not be identical due to manufacturing errors, and parts which overlap may be stained, giving a clue to the correct position. Most fixings leave identifying marks especially if they were painted over on assembly. It is then easier to decide whether a nut, for instance, has a plain, a spring, or a shakeproof washer under it. All running surfaces become 'bedded' together after long spells of work and tiny imperfections on one part will be found to have left corresponding marks on the other. This is particularly true of shafts and bearings and even a score on a cylinder wall will show on the piston.

6 Checking end float rocker clearances by feeler gauge may not always give accurate results because of wear. For instance, the rocker tip which bears on a valve stem may be deeply pitted, in which case the feeler will simply be bridging a depression. Thrust washers may also wear depressions in opposing faces to make accurate measurement difficult. End float is then easier to check by using a dial gauge. It is common practice to adjust end play in bearing assemblies, like front hubs with taper rollers, by doing up the axle nut until the hub becomes stiff to turn and then backing it off a little. Do not use this method with ballbearing hubs as the assembly is often preloaded by tightening the axle nut to its fullest extent. If the splitpin hole will not line up, file the base of the nut a little.

Steering assemblies often wear in the straight-ahead position. If any part is adjusted, make sure that it remains free when moved from lock to lock. Do not be surprised if an assembly like a steering gearbox, which is known to be carefully adjusted outside the car, becomes stiff when it is bolted into place. This will be due to distortion of the case by the pull of the mounting bolts, particularly if the mounting points are not all touching together. This problem may be met in other equipment and is cured by careful attention to the alignment of mounting points.

When a spanner is stamped with a size and A/F it means that the dimension is the width between the jaws and has no connection with ANF, which is the designation for the American National Fine thread. Coarse threads like Whitworth are rarely used on cars to-day except for studs which screw into soft aluminium or cast iron. For this reason it might be found that the top end of a cylinder head stud has a fine thread and the lower end a coarse thread to screw into the cylinder block. If the car has mainly UNF threads then it is likely that any coarse threads will be UNC, which are not the same as Whitworth. Small sizes have the same number of threads in Whitworth and UNC, but in the $\frac{1}{2}$ in size for example, there are twelve threads to the inch in the former and thirteen in the latter.

7 After a major overhaul, particularly if a great deal of work has been done on the braking, steering and suspension systems, it is advisable to approach the problem of testing with care. If the braking system has been overhauled, apply heavy pressure to the brake pedal and get a second operator to check every possible source of leakage. The brakes may work extremely well, but a leak could cause complete failure after a few miles.

Do not fit the hub caps until every wheel nut has been checked for tightness, and make sure that the tyre pressures are correct. Check the levels of coolant, lubricants and hydraulic fluids. Being satisfied that all is well, take the car on the road and test the brakes at once. Check the steering and the action of the handbrake. Do all this at moderate speeds on quiet roads, and make sure there is no other vehicle behind you when you try a rapid stop.

Finally, remember that many parts settle down after a time, so check for tightness of all fixings after the car has been on the road a hundred miles or so.

8 It is useless to tune an engine which has not reached its normal running temperature. In the same way, the tune of an engine which is stiff after a rebore will be different when the engine is again running free. Remember too, that rocker clearances on pushrod operated valve gear will change when the cylinder head nuts are tightened after an initial period of running with a new head gasket.

Trouble may not always be due to what seems the obvious cause. Ignition, carburation and mechanical condition are interdependent and spitting back through the carburetter, which might be attributed to a weak mixture, can be caused by a sticking inlet valve.

For one final hint on tuning, never adjust more than one thing at a time or it will be impossible to tell which adjustment produced the desired result.

WARNING

If, during any overhaul or service, it is necessary to extract any roll pins and/or circlips they MUST be discarded.

New pins and/or circlips MUST be fitted on reassembly. The refitting of used roll pins and/or circlips could result in failure of a component and possibly create a safety hazard.

WIRING
DIAGRAMS

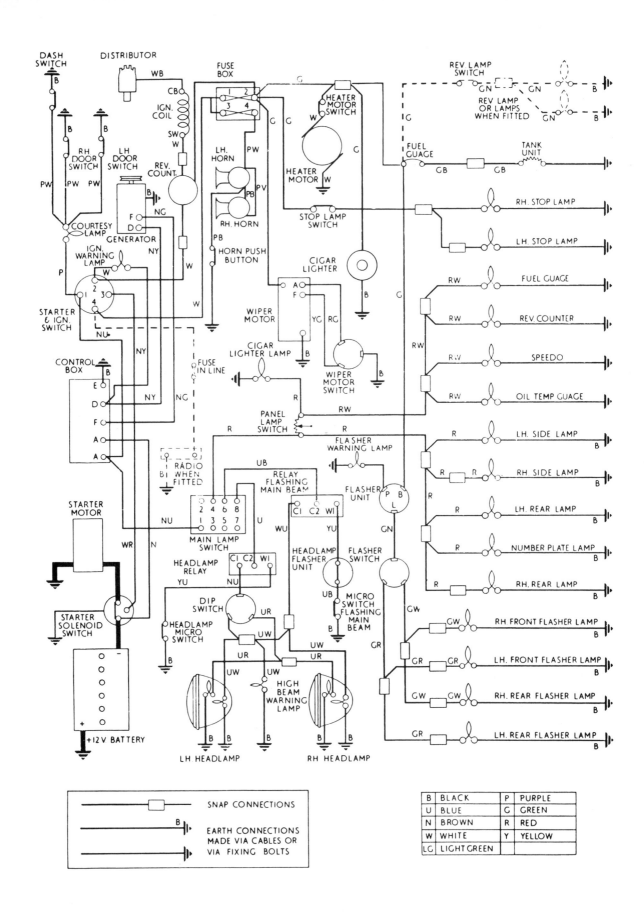

FIG (i)   Lotus Elan Series 1 and 2, positive earth

FIG (ii)   Lotus Elan Series 3, positive earth

153

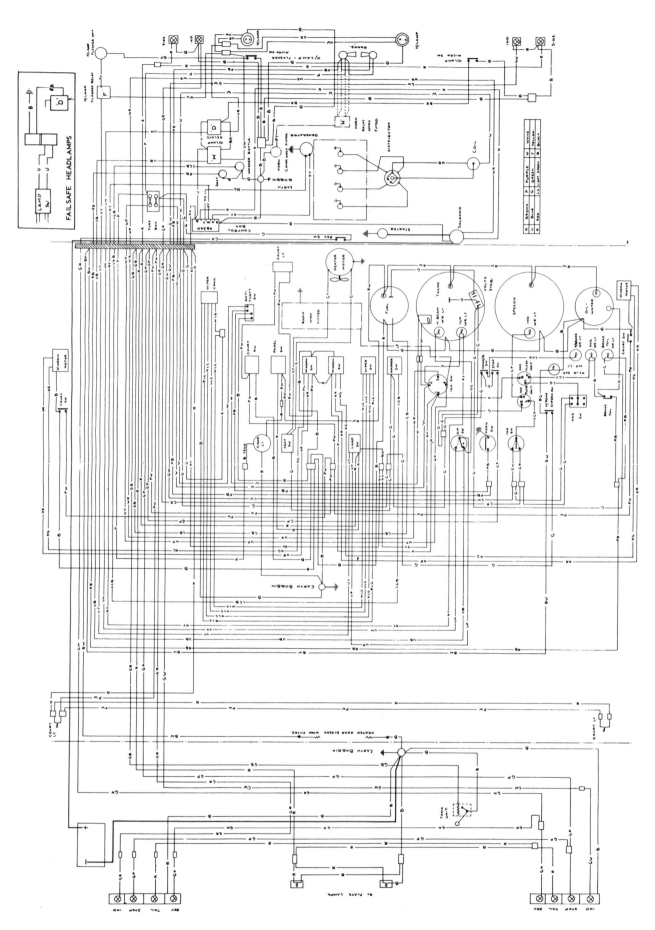

FIG (iii)   Lotus Elan Series 4, negative earth

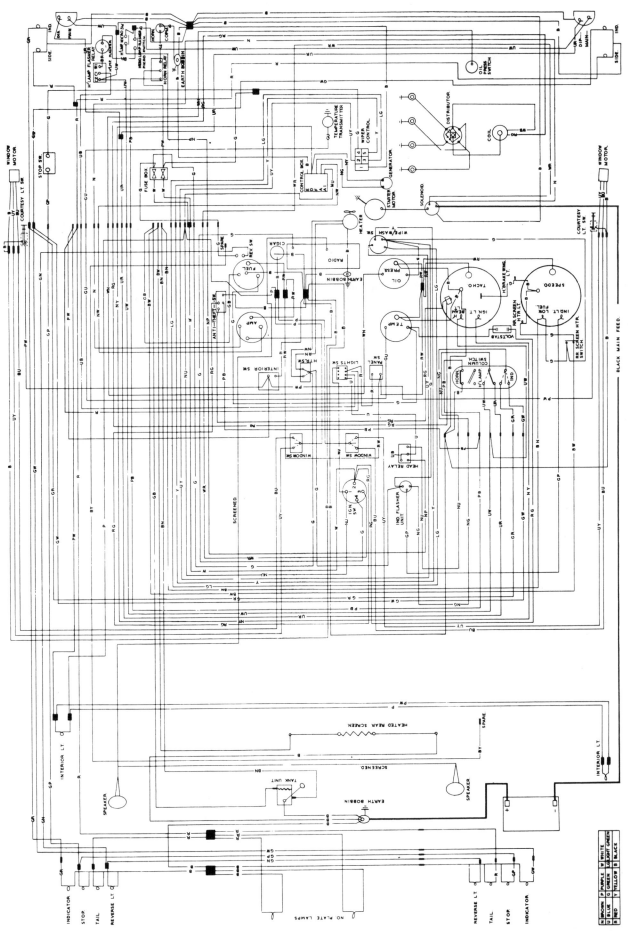

FIG (iv)   Lotus Elan +2, RB 340 control box, negative earth

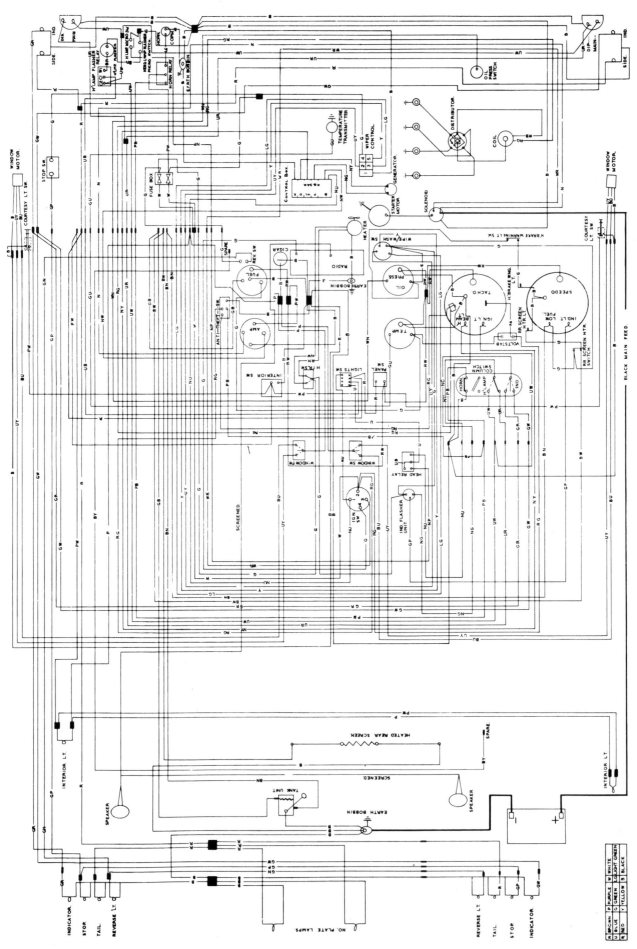

FIG (v)   Lotus Elan +2, RB 106 control box, positive earth

156

FIG (vi)   Lotus Elan +2, RB 340 control box (Federal), negative earth

LOTUS ELAN + 2 FEDERAL.
(RB 340 CONTROL BOX)

Lotus Elan +2, RB 340 control box (Federal), negative earth

LSL 135/2

EARTHING POINTS

BATTERY
NEGATIVE LEAD TO CHASSIS AT ⓫
POSITIVE LEAD TO START SOLENOID

FUEL TANK
GAUGE UNIT

BLACK/BROWN
BLACK
GREEN/BLACK

CABLE COLOUR CODING

Note new cable colour coding.

Two BLUE stripes and one RED stripe on a WHITE background denotes
BLUE/RED. Twist cable as shown to check.

BLUE background with RED stripe also denotes BLUE/RED.
These two systems may occur in one loom.
Two BLUE stripes on a WHITE background denotes BLUE/WHITE.
Twist as shown to check.

Take care not to confuse WHITE background cables (two stripes, some
colour) with the new colour coding (three stripes, two base colour).

BLUE/WHITE
BLUE/WHITE
BLUE/RED
BLUE/RED
BLUE/RED
YELLOW/RED
BLUE/RED
WHITE
GREEN
BROWN/PURPLE

BLUE/RED
BLUE/RED
BLUE
BROWN/
BLUE

RED/BLUE
RED
RED
PURPLE

BROWN/WHITE
RED/GREEN
WHITE/BLACK
BROWN

FUSES

WINDOW MOTOR
BLACK/BLUE
BLUE/YELLOW

REGULATOR
WHITE/
BROWN
WHITE/BROWN
BROWN/GREEN
WHITE/BROWN
BLACK
BROWN/
YELLOW
BROWN/
YELLOW

BLUE/PURPLE
WHITE/BROWN
BLUE/RED
PURPLE/BLUE

PURPLE/YELLOW
PURPLE
PURPLE/BLACK

ALTERNATIVE HORN RELAY

BLUE/BLACK
WHITE/BROWN
BLUE/WHITE
PURPLE/
BLUE

PURPLE/BLACK
PURPLE
PURPLE/YELLOW

RELAYS

RED/GREEN
BLACK
WHITE/BROWN
BLUE

BRAKE FLUID
LEVEL SWITCH
BLACK

STARTER SOLENOID
BROWN   WHITE/RED

PURPLE/
RED
GREEN
GREEN/
PURPLE
BRAKE SWITCH

WATER TEMP
SENDER UNIT

BLACK/RED
YELLOW
BLACK/YELLOW
PURPLE/BROWN

WIPER MOTOR

WHITE/BLACK
WHITE/YELLOW
WHITE/YELLOW
BROWN/WHITE

COIL

OIL PRESS
SENDER UNIT
BROWN/WHITE

FAN SENDER UNIT

BROWN/PURPLE
BLACK/GREEN

SIDELAMP
MICROSWITCH
BLUE
BROWN/
WHITE

FAN
BLACK   D
BLACK   D
BLACK
GREEN

NOTE Check Fan
Rotation is correct.
Reverse Black
leads if necessary

HEADLAMP
MICROSWITCH
BLUE/BROWN
BLACK

WASHER
GREEN
BLACK
BLACK

GREEN/BLUE

BROWN/YELLOW
BROWN/GREEN

GENERATOR

FIG (vii) Lotus Elan +2 S-type electrical components and connections, negative earth

158

FIG (viii) Lotus Elan +2 S with alternator, negative earth

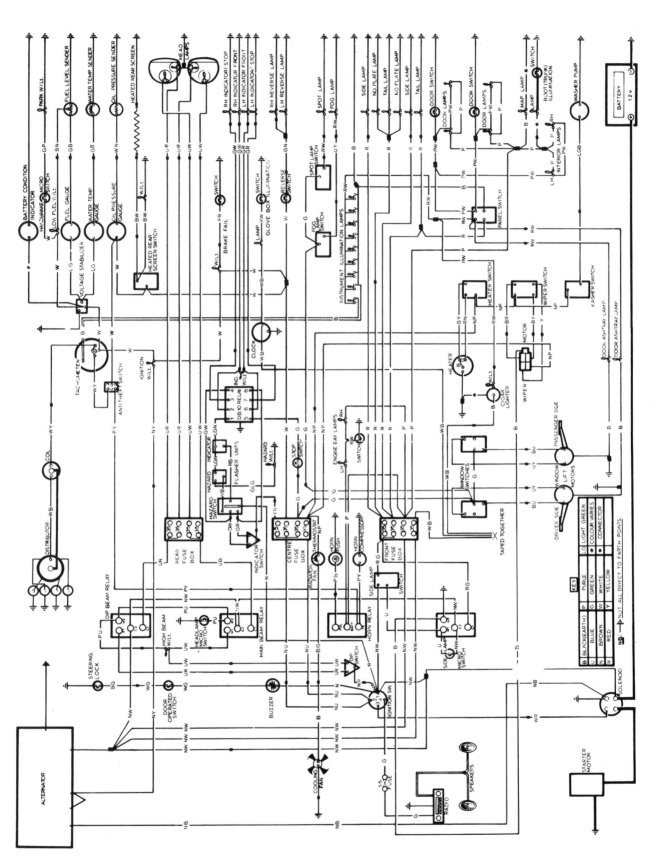

FIG (ix)   Lotus Elan + 2S with alternator (Federal), negative earth

GLOSSARY OF TERMS

Allen key   Cranked wrench of hexagonal section for use with socket head screws.

Alternator   Electrical generator producing alternating current. Rectified to direct current for battery charging.

Ambient temperature   Surrounding atmospheric temperature.

Annulus   Used in engineering to indicate the outer ring gear of an epicyclic gear train.

Armature   The shaft carrying the windings, which rotates in the magnetic field of a generator or starter motor. That part of a solenoid or relay which is activated by the magnetic field.

Axial   In line with, or pertaining to, an axis.

Backlash   Play in meshing gears.

Balance lever   A bar where force applied at the centre is equally divided between connections at the ends.

Banjo axle   Axle casing with large diameter housing for the crownwheel and differential.

Bar   Standard unit of pressure equal to 14.5lb/sq in.

Bendix pinion   A self-engaging and self-disengaging drive on a starter motor shaft.

Bevel pinion   A conical shaped gearwheel, designed to mesh with a similar gear with an axis usually at 90° to its own.

bhp   Brake horse power, superseded by kW.

bmep   Brake mean effective pressure. Average pressure on a piston during the working stroke.

Brake cylinder   Cylinder with hydraulically operated piston(s) acting on brake shoes or pads.

Brake regulator   Control valve fitted in hydraulic braking system which limits brake pressure to rear brakes during heavy braking to prevent rear wheel locking.

Camber   Angle at which a wheel is tilted from the vertical.

Capacitor   Modern term for an electrical condenser. Part of distributor assembly, connected across contact breaker points, acts as an interference suppressor.

Castellated   Top face of a nut, slotted across the flats to take a locking splitpin.

Castor   Angle at which the kingpin or swivel pin is tilted when viewed from the side.

cc or cm³   Cubic centimetres. Engine capacity is arrived at by multiplying the area of the bore in sq cm by the stroke in cm by the number of cylinders.

Clevis   U-shaped forked connector used with a clevis pin, usually at handbrake connections.

Collet   A type of collar, usually split and located in a groove in a shaft, and held in place by a retainer. The arrangement used to retain the spring(s) on a valve stem in most cases.

Commutator   Rotating segmented current distributor between armature windings and brushes..

Compression ratio   The ratio, or quantitative relation, of the total volume (piston at bottom of stroke) to the unswept volume (piston at top of stroke) in an engine cylinder.

Condenser   See 'Capacitor'.

Core plug   Plug for blanking off a manufacturing hole.

Crownwheel   Large bevel gear in rear axle, driven by a bevel pinion attached to the propeller shaft.

'C'-spanner   Like a 'C' with a handle. For use on screwed collars without flats, but with slots or holes.

Damper   Modern term for shock absorber, used in vehicle suspension systems to damp out spring oscillations.

Depression   The lowering of atmospheric pressure as in the inlet manifold and carburetter.

Dowel   Close tolerance pin, peg, tube or bolt, which accurately locates mating parts.

Drag link   Rod connecting steering box drop arm (pitman arm) to nearest front wheel steering arm in certain types of steering systems.

Dry liner   Thinwall tube pressed into cylinder bore.

Dry sump   Lubrication system where all oil is scavenged from the sump, and returned to a separate tank.

Dynamo   Electrical generator producing direct current.

Electrode   Terminal part of an electrical component, such as the points or 'Electrodes' of a sparking plug.

Electrolyte   In lead-acid car batteries a solution of sulphuric acid and distilled water.

End float — The axial movement between associated parts, end play.

EP — Extreme pressure. In lubricants, special grades for heavily loaded bearing surfaces, such as gear teeth in a gearbox, or crownwheel and pinion in a rear axle.

Fade — Of brakes. Reduced efficiency due to overheating.

Field coils — Windings on the polepieces of motors and generators.

Fillets — Narrow finishing strips usually applied to interior bodywork.

First motion shaft — Input shaft from clutch to gearbox.

Fullflow filter — Filters in which all the oil is pumped to the engine. If the element becomes clogged, a bypass valve operates to pass unfiltered oil to the engine.

FWD — Front wheel drive.

Gear pump — Two meshing gears in a close fitting casing. Oil is carried from the inlet round the outside of both gears in the spaces between the gear teeth and casing to the outlet, the meshing gear teeth prevent oil passing back to the inlet, and the oil is forced through the outlet port.

Generator — An alternator or a dynamo.

Grommet — A ring of protective or sealing material. Can be used to protect pipes or leads passing through bulkheads.

Grubscrew — Fully threaded headless screw with screwdriver slot. Used for locking or alignment purposes.

Gudgeon pin — Shaft which connects a piston to its connecting rod. Sometimes called 'wrist pin' or 'piston pin'.

Halfshaft — One of a pair transmitting drive from the differential.

Helical — In spiral form. The teeth of helical gears are cut at a spiral angle to the side faces of the gearwheel.

Hot spot — Hot area that assists vaporisation of fuel on its way to cylinders. Often provided by close contact between inlet and exhaust manifolds.

HT — High Tension. Applied to electrical current produced by the ignition coil for the sparking plugs.

Hydrometer — A device for checking specific gravity of liquids. Used to check specific gravity of electrolyte.

Hypoid bevel gears — A form of bevel gear used in the rear axle drive gears. The bevel pinion meshes below the centre line of the crownwheel, giving a lower propeller shaft line.

Idler — A device for passing on movement. A free running gear between driving and driven gears. A lever transmitting track rod movement to a side rod in steering gear.

Impeller — A centrifugal pumping element. Used in water pumps to stimulate flow.

Journals — Those parts of a shaft that are in contact with the bearings.

kW — Standard unit of power, equal to 1.34102hp

Kingpin — The main vertical pin which carries the front wheel spindle, and permits steering movement. May be called 'steering pin' or 'swivel pin'.

Layshaft — The shaft which carries the laygear in the gearbox. The laygear is driven by the first motion shaft and drives the third motion shaft according to the gear selected. Sometimes called the 'countershaft' or 'second motion shaft'. '

lbf ft — A measure of twist or torque. A pull of 10lb at a radius of 1ft is a torque of 10lbf ft.

lb/sq in — Pounds per square inch.

Little-end — The small, or piston end of a connecting rod. Sometimes called the 'small-end'.

LT — Low Tension. The current output from the battery.

Mandrel — Accurately manufactured bar or rod used for test or centring purposes.

Manifold — A pipe, duct or chamber, with several branches

Nm — Standard unit of torque equal to 0.738lbf ft.

Needle rollers — Bearing rollers with a length many times their diameter.

Oil bath — Reservoir which lubricates parts by immersion. In air filters, a separate oil supply for wetting a wire mesh element to hold the dust.

Oil wetted — In air filters, a wire mesh element lightly oiled to trap and hold airborne dust.

Overlap — Period during which inlet and exhaust valves are open together.

Panhard rod — Bar connected between fixed point on chassis and another on axle to control sideways movement.

Pawl — Pivoted catch which engages in the teeth of a ratchet to permit movement in one direction only.

Peg spanner — Tool with pegs, or pins, to engage in holes or slots in the part to be turned.

Pendant pedals — Pedals with levers pivoted at the top.

Phillips screwdriver A cross-point screwdriver for use with the cross-slotted heads of Phillips screws.

Pinion A small gear, usually in relation to another gear.

Piston-type damper Shock absorber in which damping is controlled by a piston working in a closed oil-filled cylinder.

Preloading Preset static pressure on ball or roller bearings not due to working loads.

Radial Radiating from a centre, like the spokes of a wheel.

Radius rod Pivoted arm confining movement of a part to an arc of fixed radius.

Ratchet Toothed wheel or rack which can move in one direction only, movement in the other being prevented by a pawl.

Ring gear A gear tooth ring attached to outer periphery of flywheel. Starter pinion engages with it during starting.

Runout Amount by which rotating part is out of true.

Semi-floating axle Outer end of rear axle halfshaft is carried on bearing inside axle casing. Wheel hub is secured to end of shaft.

Servo A hydraulic or pneumatic system for assisting, or, augmenting a physical effort. See 'Vacuum Servo'.

Setscrew Fastener threaded the full length of the shank.

Shackle A coupling link, used in the form of two parallel pins connected by side plates to secure the end of the master suspension spring and absorb the effects of deflection.

Shell bearing Thinwalled steel shell lined with anti-friction metal. Usually semi-circular and used in pairs for main and big-end bearings.

Shock absorber See 'Damper'.

Silentbloc Rubber bush bonded to inner and outer metal sleeves.

Socket-head screw Screw with hexagonal socket for an Allen key.

Solenoid A coil of wire creating a magnetic field when electric current passes through it. Used with a soft iron core to operate contacts or a mechanical device.

Spur gear A gear with teeth cut axially.

Stub axle Short axle fixed at one end only.

Tachometer An instrument for accurate measurement of rotating speed. Usually indicates in revolutions per minute.

TDC Top Dead Centre. The highest point reached by a piston in a cylinder, with the crank and connecting rod in line.

Thermostat Automatic device for regulating temperature. Used in vehicle coolant systems to open a valve which restricts circulation at low temperature.

Third motion shaft Output shaft of gearbox.

Threequarter floating axle Outer end of rear axle halfshaft flanged and bolted to wheel hub, which runs on bearing mounted on outside of axle casing. Vehicle weight is not carried by the axle shaft.

Thrust bearing or washer Used to reduce friction in rotating parts subject to axial loads.

Torque Turning or twisting effort. See 'lbf ft'.

Track rod The bar(s) across the vehicle which connect the steering arms and maintain the front wheel alignment.

UJ Universal joint. A coupling between shafts which permits angular movement.

UNF Unified National Fine screw thread.

Vacuum servo Device used in brake system, using difference between atmospheric pressure and inlet manifold depression to operate a piston which acts to augment brake pressure as required. See 'Servo'.

Venturi A restriction or 'choke' in a tube, as in a carburetter, used to increase velocity to obtain a reduction in pressure.

Vernier A sliding scale for obtaining fractional readings of the graduations of an adjacent scale.

Welch plug A domed thin metal disc which is partially flattened to lock in a recess. Used to plug core holes in castings.

Wet liner Removable cylinder barrel, sealed against coolant leakage, where the coolant is in direct contact with the outer surface.

Wet sump A reservoir attached to the crankcase to hold the lubricating oil.

Essential reading for Elan owners

LOTUS ELAN - A RESTORATION GUIDE.

By Gordon Lund

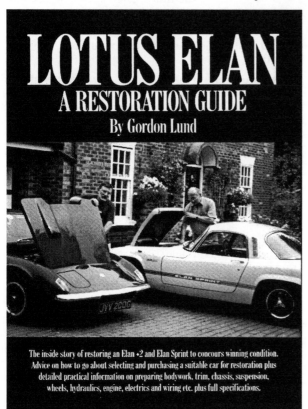

A practical guide written with the home restorer in mind. Well illustrated and with clear instructions this book guides the amateur through dismantling, repair and rebuilding. Included are a series and body type guide - advice on buying an Elan to restore - detailed information on chassis changing - body restoration, including Elan +2 sills - rebuilding the Lotus/Ford Twin Cam engine - electrics including fitting a new loom, plus tips on tuning, running-in and preparing the car for concours presentation.

Over 200 illustrations and diagrams with many in colour. 128 pages, Soft Bound.

Ref. A-LTENR   (ISBN 185520 5963)

What Club Lotus said about this book......

Gordon's Good Guide

Gordon Lund has been a keen and active member of Club Lotus North West area for at least twenty years. His Elan Plus Two and Elan Sprint have made regular welcome appearance at the Lakes and other social events nationwide. Gordon spent years, with his son, meticulously restoring their sprint coupe. The Lotus Elan Restoration Guide not only contains the why, the where and the how of restoration but includes a mass of hints, tips and experiences that he has chronicled for us all to read. Gordon writes as if he is talking to you over a pint so the book is much more readable than some we have seen on similar subjects. The author's dry sense of humour also comes through very clearly, I really enjoyed every page.

An Essential Publication

This is an essential publication for all Elan owners. Published in card back by Brooklands it has 128 pages, profuse colour plus many B&W pictures, plus drawings to explain and illustrate every stage in the restoration.

Brooklands Books Ltd., P.O. Box 146, Cobham, Surrey, KT11 1LG, England Phone: 01932 865051
E-mail us at info@brooklands-books.com or visit our website www.brooklands-books.com

INDEX

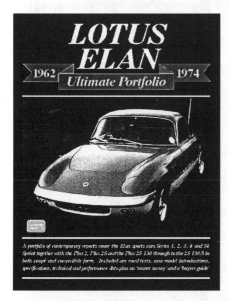

LOTUS

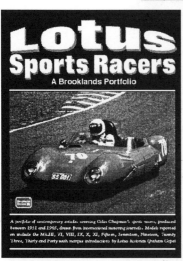
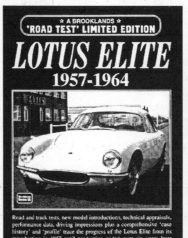
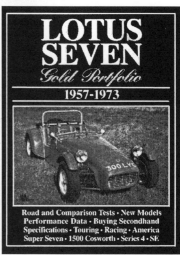

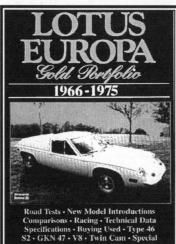

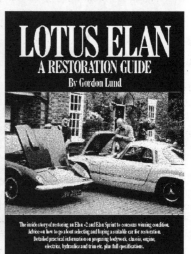